# Decision Support System and Automated Negotiations

Decision support systems are developed for integrated pest and disease management and nutrition management using open-source technologies as Java, Android and low-cost hardware devices like Arduino micro controller. This text discusses the techniques to convert agricultural knowledge in the context of ontology and assist grape growers by providing this knowledge through decision support system.

The key features of the book are as follows:

- It presents the design and development of an ontology-based decision support system for integrated crop management.
- It discusses the techniques to convert agricultural knowledge in text to ontology.
- It focuses on an extensive study of various e-Negotiation protocols for automated negotiations.
- It provides an architecture for predicting the opponent's behavior and various factors which affect the process of negotiation.

The text is primarily written for graduate students, professionals and academic researchers working in the fields of computer science and engineering, agricultural science and information technology.

# Decision Support System and Automated Negotiations

Prof Debajyoti Mukhopadhyay
Director, Web Intelligence & Distributed Computing Research Lab, India
Former Dean, School of Engineering & Applied Sciences, Bennett University, India
Former Scientist, Bell Communications Research, New Jersey, USA

Dr Archana Chougule
Professor of Computer Engineering
AD College of Engineering and Technology, Kolhapur, Maharashtra, India

Dr Sheetal Vij
Assistant Professor of Computer Science, MIT World Peace University, India

CRC Press
Taylor & Francis Group
Boca Raton London New York

CRC Press is an imprint of the Taylor & Francis Group, an **informa** business
A CHAPMAN & HALL BOOK

First edition published 2023

by CRC Press
6000 Broken Sound Parkway NW, Suite 300, Boca Raton, FL 33487-2742

and by CRC Press
4 Park Square, Milton Park, Abingdon, Oxon, OX14 4RN

*CRC Press is an imprint of Taylor & Francis Group, LLC*



ISBN: 978-1-032-52363-7 (hbk)
ISBN: 978-1-032-52759-8 (pbk)
ISBN: 978-1-003-40825-3 (ebk)

DOI: 10.1201/9781003408253

Typeset in Palatino
by SPi Technologies India Pvt Ltd (Straive)

# Contents

## Part 2 Automated Negotiation

# Preface

Recently, I was leading research in search engine design, page-ranking algorithms development, ontology-based searching design and developing E-Negotiation protocols. One of my research scholars, Archana Chougule worked with me in designing and developing an ontology-based decision support system for integrated crop management. Agricultural researchers and experts generate useful knowledge every year and develop expert systems and decision support systems. It will be of great use if all knowledge can be represented in the format which can be easily understood and shared among research centers also. This situation motivated this project to work on techniques to convert agricultural knowledge in text to ontology and assist grape growers by providing this knowledge through decision support system. Context of knowledge can be represented effectively and can be shared by automated devices using ontology. Decision support systems are developed for integrated pest and disease management and nutrition management using open source technologies as Java, Android and low-cost hardware devices like Arduino micro controller. Another of my research scholars, Sheetal Vij did extensive study on various E-Negotiation protocols for automated negotiations. With the advancements and proliferation of web technologies, it is becoming more important to make the traditional negotiation pricing mechanism automated, intelligent and efficient. The behavior of software agents which negotiate on behalf of humans can be determined by their tactics in the form of decision functions. Prediction of partner's behavior in negotiation has been an active research direction in recent years as it will improve the utility gain for the adaptive negotiation agent and also achieve the agreement much quicker or look after much higher benefits. Although negotiation is practically a very complex activity to automate without human intervention, this is an attempt to propose an architecture for predicting the opponent's behavior and various factors which affect the process of negotiation. The concept is such that the information about negotiators, their individual actions and dynamics can be used by software agents which are equipped with adaptive capabilities to learn from past negotiations and assist in selecting appropriate negotiation tactics. So, ultimately, this is an era where we have to have computer programs/software agents/agents to negotiate on our behalf. These research outcomes have created the materials for this book.

I take this opportunity to extend my sincere thanks to CRC Press and Isha Singh of Taylor and Francis group for their constant support while preparing the manuscript.

Mumbai, India

**Prof. Debajyoti Mukhopadhyay**
Web Intelligence and Distributed
Computing Research Lab

# Author Bio

Professor **Debajyoti Mukhopadhyay** (Senior Member, IEEE) received the B.E. degree in electronics from the Indian Institute of Engineering Science and Technology (IIEST) Shibpur, Shibpur, India, in 1977; the D.C.S. degree in computer science and applications from Queen's University Belfast, Belfast, U.K., in 1979; the M.S. degree in computer science from the Stevens Institute of Technology, Hoboken, NJ, USA, in 1984; and the Ph.D. degree in Computer Science and Engineering from Jadavpur University, Kolkata, India, in 1994. He has been the Founding Director of the Web Intelligence & Distributed Computing Research Laboratory, Kolkata, since 2002. In the last few years, he has been the Dean of the School of Engineering and Applied Sciences, Bennett University, Greater Noida, India; the Director and Dean (R&D) of the New Horizon Institute of Technology and Management, Mumbai University, Thane, India; the Dean and Distinguished Professor with Adamas University, Kolkata; the Dean (R&D) and Head of Information Technology with the Maharashtra Institute of Technology, Pune, India; the Director of the Balaji Institute of Telecom and Management, Pune; and the Founding Head and Professor of Information Technology and Management Information Systems with the Calcutta Business School, Kolkata. He was a Visiting Scholar with George Mason University, Fairfax, VA, USA, during June–July 2014. He was a Distinguished Adjunct Professor with Curtin University, Perth, WA, Australia. He has held Adjunct Professorship with the Monarch Business School, Switzerland, and Thapar University, Patiala, India. He was a full Professor of Computer Science and Engineering with the West Bengal University of Technology affiliated Engineering Colleges from 2001 to 2008. He was a Visiting Professor with Chonbuk National University, Jeonju, South Korea, from 2006 to 2007. He also taught at the Stevens Institute of Technology from 1982 to 1984 and at IIEST Shibpur from 1980 to 1981. He was a Research Fellow with the Indian Statistical Institute, Kolkata, from 1979 to 1980. He was with the Computing Systems and Architecture Laboratory, Bell Communications Research, Piscataway, NJ, USA, from 1987 to 1994. He has authored or coauthored over 240 research articles in international journals, conference proceedings, and research reports. He holds three patents. He has guided six Ph.D. research scholars. Prof. Mukhopadhyay received the National Scholarship by the Government of India; the G. P. Ghosh Scholarship by the University of Calcutta; the

Graduate Assistantship by the Stevens Institute of Technology; and the Peer Award by Bell Communications Research. For his outstanding performance in Higher Secondary Examinations, Sodepur High School offered him K.N. Memorial Award. The Maharashtra Institute of Technology, Pune, bestowed upon him the Ideal Teacher Award. Stars of the Industry Group and Dainik Bhaskar conferred National Education Leadership Award for Best Professor in Information Technology. Cognizant Technology Solutions bestowed upon him the Cognizant Best Faculty Award for Outstanding Performance. He is cited in the Who's Who in the World. He is a Distinguished Speaker of the Computer Society of India. He is a Senior Member of the Association for Computing Machinery, a Fellow of the Institution of Engineers (India), a Fellow of the Institution of Electronics and Telecommunication Engineers (India), a Chartered Engineer, a Senior Member of the Computer Society of India, a Member of the All India Management Association, and an Elected Member of Eta Kappa Nu.

**Dr. Archana Chougule** has worked as an Associate Professor and Head of Computer Science & Engineering Department at Sanjay Ghodawat University, Kolhapur. Earlier she was an Assistant Professor of Information Technology at Maharashtra Institute of Technology, Pune. She has earned BE and ME in Computer Science from Shivaji University. She carried out her PhD research under the direct guidance of Prof. Debajyoti Mukhopadhyay and obtained her PhD Degree from BIT Mesra.

**Dr. Sheetal Vij** has been working as an Assistant Professor of Computer Science & Engineering at MIT World Peace University, Pune. She has earned BE and ME in Computer Science from Pune University. She did her PhD research under the direct guidance of Prof. Debajyoti Mukhopadhyay and has earned her degree from Nagpur University.

# Part 1

# Decision Support System

# 1

# *Decision Support System for Agriculture*

## 1.1 Problem Statement

Agriculture is the main source of income for most of the Indian population, especially from rural areas. Hence, Indian economy depends on agricultural production. Considerable percentage of GDP comes from agriculture sector. Use of Information Technology in Indian farms to increase crop production and minimize yield loss is the need of the hour. Information Technology can be used on farms for automation of irrigation, soil monitoring, aerial imagery, crop nutrient content monitoring, fertilizer recommendation, crop pest and disease management and integrated communications between electronic devices on farms.

Farming community is facing problems to improve crop productivity and to raise annual income. Due to various constraints, even though much research is centered on new agricultural practices regarding crop cultivation, most of the farmers are not getting expected maximum yield and losing profit margin. One of the constraints is that expert's knowledge and advice regarding crop cultivation is not reaching to farmers on time. Even though much research is done in crop cultivation, it is observed that a wide knowledge gap exists between research and practice by farmers. Farmers need timely expert advice to make farming more productive and competitive. With the help of information and communication technology advances, fast and accurate information can be sent from source to the destination, i.e. from experts to farmers. Powerful end-user devices and multimedia technology can be very well utilized for bridging the gap between crop cultivation research and farmers.

## 1.2 Motivation

Many standard precision agriculture products exist in market like Raven precision, Trimble Ag Software, TopCon, AGCO, John Deere Precision Ag and Accenture Digital Agriculture Solutions. But almost all precision agriculture

DOI: 10.1201/9781003408253-2

products are either costly or applicable on large fields. Most of Indian farmers own farm fields on very small scale. Precision agriculture solutions must be affordable and applicable on small fields. The solutions should be developed using open source software and low-cost hardware.

A number of research centers of various crops are run by Indian government. Agricultural researchers and experts generate useful knowledge every year and also develop expert systems and decision support systems. It will be of great use if all knowledge can be represented in the format which can be easily understood and shared among research centers too.

This situation motivated us to work on techniques to convert agricultural knowledge from text to ontology and assist grape growers by providing this knowledge through decision support systems. Context of knowledge can be represented very well, and it can be shared by automated devices using ontology. Decision support systems are developed for integrated pest and disease management and nutrition management using open source technologies as Java, Android and low-cost hardware devices like Arduino micro controller.

## 1.3 Grape Production in India

In India, grape is grown in hot tropical, mild tropical and sub-tropical regions (S.D. Shikhamany 2001). Grape is harvested once in a year in hot tropical region of India. Hot tropical region includes Sangli, Solapur, Nashik, Pune, Satara, Osmanabad and Latur districts of Maharashtra; Hyderabad, Medak, Anantpur, Ranga Reddy and Mahbubnagar districts of Andhra Pradesh; and Gulbarga, Belgaum, Bagalkot and Bijapur districts of Karnataka. Out of total grape production in India, more than 75% production is from these regions. For current research, grape production in the above-mentioned regions is considered. Numerous varieties of grapes are produced in India like anab-e-shahi, blue Syn, bhokri, flame seedless, perlette, sharad seedless and thomson seedless.

Grape growers in these areas often face loss in total yield due to pests and diseases. Major pests on grapes are Berry moth, Flea beetle, Caterpillar, Mealy bug and Stem borer (Vikaspedia.in, Grapes: Insect Pests Management).

Downy mildew, powdery mildew and anthracnose are the major diseases on grape plant (https://nrcgrapes.icar.gov.in). Downy mildew form yellow and brown patches on veins of leaves. They affect stems, leaves and berries of grapes. Color of leaf changes to white or brown, berries become grey; spores come on berry, dry down, sometime drop off. These pests and diseases occur during different growth stages of grapes like delay dormant, bud-break period, rapid shoot growth period, bloom to veraison period, veraison period, harvest period, post-harvest period and dormant period (http://ipm.ucanr.edu/). The current research considers these growth stages for pest forecasting.

**FIGURE 1.1**
Grape growing areas in hot tropical region of India.

**FIGURE 1.2**
Insect pests on grapes.

## 1.4 Decision Support Systems

Grape growers need to take decisions every day on various aspects of farming like how to do pest and disease management, when to apply which fertilizers, when to irrigate the yard, etc. Decision support system is a system which helps human beings to take such decisions based on available knowledge. It is basically a computer-based system that implements decision-making algorithms based on available knowledge. Algorithms available under machine learning like artificial neural networks, genetic algorithms, decision trees, naïve Bayes algorithms and regression techniques can be used. Using decision support systems in agriculture helps farmers to take better decisions on all aspects of crop growth. The aspects can be planning, managing and operating various tasks in farms. It helps improve quality and quantity of production and reduce side effects on farm and surroundings. Decision can be taken in measurable terms using DSS. For example, it can be determined how many liters of water should be supplied at specific time and at specific region of farm.

## 1.5 Integrated Pest Management

It is observed that excessive use of pests has adverse effect on human health and also on environment. Many diseases are caused because of toxic pesticides used to control pests on crops. As pesticides are sprayed evenly on complete crop field; it can affect soil, running water and air at and across the crop field. It also affects other species which are not targeted by the pesticide.

Excessive use of pesticides and fungicides for controlling pests and diseases is harmful to human health. Fungicides applied in the grape farms tend to dissipate in the grapes. They are present in finished wine at varying levels. Overspraying of chemicals also affects environment. It adds to water and soil pollution and becomes toxic to other organisms in the surrounding. These side effects are rarely considered when pesticide spray decision is taken only based on farmer's experience. More than 22000t of grapes are exported from India to Middle East and European countries (S. D. Shikhamany 2001). To improve export quality of grapes and to minimize side effects, integrated pest management (IPM) of grape farms is must. A rational IPM program for grape pests and diseases needs to be developed to increase competitiveness and reduce expenses on pesticides.

To reduce these risks, Integrate Pest Management (IPM) technique is used. Use of computerized systems to implement IPM techniques is obvious.

As these systems are of varying kinds, there must be a way to represent knowledge which can be easily shared among heterogeneous systems. One of the best approaches to represent domain knowledge is through ontologies. Formal representation of concepts, relationships, assumptions and constraints in specific domain can be done using ontology. The ontology can be used as a classification tool in specific domain as it defines structure and hierarchy of concepts in the domain. This work contributes in elaborating how one can have integrated pest management and diagnosis of diseases on grapes in hot tropical region of India.

IPM involves use of multiple techniques in coordination with each other which will minimize undesirable side effects on ecology and increase safety of human health. Coordination of cultural, chemical, biological and mechanical practices is employed under IPM. The decision to spray is made after evaluating the consequences of this decision on production and the environment. There are advantages of IPM like reduction in total management cost and environmental pollution; maintenance of ecological balance by minimum disturbance to ecosystem. As one IPM technique is not enough to control pests, combination of suitable IPM techniques is used. For integrated pest management of grapes, a decision support system for pest occurrence forecasting is developed in the current work.

## 1.6 Integrated Nutrient Management and Smart Irrigation

For quality production of grapes, precise nutrition management of vineyards is must. Not just insufficient supply but also excess supply of nutrients has adverse effect on grapes. With insufficient nutrition provision, berry growth reduces and grape quality deteriorates. When grapes are exported outside India, presence of excess amount of certain chemicals in grapes turns into rejection for sale. Hence, proper management of nutrients supply is must. This can be achieved through integrated nutrient management, i.e. using information and communication technology for knowledge management and decision making on nutrients supply to grapes throughout year. Chapter 6 describes how it is achieved in this research.

As water is most important resource on earth for vineyards and agriculture in general, proper management of water supply must be done. Detailed knowledge about water requirement by vines at different growth stages and at different weather situations helps in wise decision making. It will help reducing water wastage and improving quality of grapes.

## 1.7 Government of India Initiatives for Decision Support to Farmers

Department of Agriculture, Cooperation and Farmers Welfare under Ministry of Agriculture and Farmer's Welfare, Government of India runs many activities and schemes to help and support farmers across nation. Research centers are established across India to promote research on various crops. Experts from research centers publish their research on department websites, but farmers merely visit websites to look into this research. Information about crop management and risk management is given on a portal for farmers on farmer.gov.in. Quarterly newsletters are published about agriculture. 'Kissan Call Centre' facility is also available where farmers can call and ask any queries related to farms and get answers from experts. But all these facilities are not location specific and farmers have to explicitly go to information resources. Having the information access through smart phone application is a more convenient option for farmers.

# 2

# *Ontology Development*

## 2.1 Building Ontology from Text

Ontology can be developed from scratch by defining all terms explicitly, or it can be generated by extracting text from relevant documents. The general steps followed for building ontology from text are as follows: concepts, individuals, attributes and relationships are extracted from documents and glossary of important terms is prepared. Classification of terms from glossary is done based on similarity between terms in the second step. In the third step, relationships between similar terms are found out. Then the terms are identified as class, attribute or individual. Relationships between attributes, classes and individuals are found out in the last step (Chris Biemann, 2005).

Various approaches used by researchers to prepare ontology from textual resources are as follows:

Clustering-based or classification-based approaches are used for ontology building. Clustering-based approaches use semantic distance between terms and merge similar terms to create clusters. Semantic distance can be measured based on co-occurrence between verbs and nouns. For extracting noun hierarchies from text, dictionaries and vocabularies are used. Along with first-order co-occurrence, second-order co-occurrence can also be used. Probabilistic latent semantic analysis can be used to decide weights of terms and define concept hierarchies. Noun candidates can be extracted by considering conjunction and appositive data using cosine similarity between concept vectors and use of Hearst patterns and WordNet.

Decision trees and other machine learning techniques are used in classification-based approach. Training sets are provided for machine learning. Classification algorithms like Bayesian networks and support vector machines use training sets and classify the input words from text descriptions. In decision tree, new concept is added to the node which has maximum similarity (Alfonseca and Manandhar, 2002). Top-down or bottom-up traversal approach can be used for adding new concept. Adjective of nouns can also be considered for concept similarity matching. Sentence-based concurrence statistics and named entity recognizers are also used by some of the researchers.

DOI: 10.1201/9781003408253-3

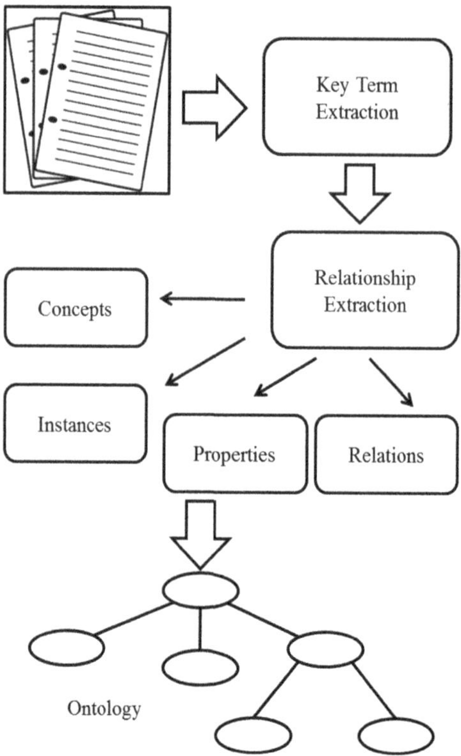


**FIGURE 2.1**
Ontology extraction from text.

A plug-in called OntoLT (Paul Buitelaar et al., 2004) is available in protégé for extracting ontology from text. The plug-in contains mapping rules for extracting classes and attributes of ontology from text. User-defined rules can also be used. Rules are defined using XPATH expressions derived from linguistic annotations. Linguistic annotations are done using SCHUG. It provides German and English analysis by annotation of part-of-speech, morphological and dependency structure and grammatical function analysis. Mapping rules contain constants, functions and predicates. Predicates can be one of the containsPath, hasValue, hasConcept, AND, OR, NOT and EQUAL. For adding terms extracted from text to ontology after applying rules, operators are provided namely CreateCls, AddSlot, CreateInstanc and FillSlot. Chi-square function is used under statistical preprocessing. It helps in determining domain relevance. Operators are required to be entered manually.

Approach for managing changes in the ontology by creating new versions based on types of changes is proposed (Wassim Jaziri, 2009). To ensure coherence of ontology, coherence changes kit was prepared. For versioning control, protégé plug-in called Changes was developed which used a trace file containing sequence of changes to ontology. A user-centric web portal for generating domain ontology is created (Qi Yu-Dong, 2010). It contains ontology visual editor, knowledge search engine, workflow engine, ontology mapping tools, ontology merging tools, tagging and checking tools and ontology analyzing tools.

Python script is used to generate ontology from weather observations based on SSN ontology (Ghislain Atemezing et al., 2011). Modular development of ontology is done using OWLD consisting measurement ontology, location ontology and time ontology.

Pointers, synsets and word tables from WordNet database are used for automated construction of wine ontology (Hyunjang Kong et al., 2005).

Ontology building from domain-related web pages is done (Wu Yuhuang and Li Yusheng, 2009). Candidate words are extracted from web pages using TF-IDF technique. Term extraction is done by anchoring sentence and noun extraction. Domain relativity and domain consistency of extracted terms is calculated using method given by Roberto Navigli. The wrong words are removed using probabilistic model, concepts are chosen and classified using K-nearest neighbor algorithm.

Decision trees can be used for adding new concepts to ontology after extracting concept from text using text mining techniques (Hans Friedrich Witschel, 2005).

RelExt is a tool proposed for extracting relation from text while extending ontology (Alexander Schutz and Paul Buitelaar, 2005) as a part of SmartWeb project. They considered role of verb in a sentence to find out relations between concepts. Tool works on linguistic and statistical processes. SCHUG system is used for linguistic analysis. This system provides part-of-speech and phrase structure for given text in XML format. SCHUG divides noun phrases in three parts as nominal head, pre-modifier and post-modifier. RelExt uses gazetteer lists for named entity recognition. Gazetter lists are documents about football. Using NER concepts from football corpus are mapped to ontology classes. Concept tagging was done after NER. Synonyms of terms are mapped to ontology concepts in concept tagging. For building triples, co-occurrence measures are calculated statistically. The list of head nouns and the list of predicates from linguistic analysis are used in statistical analysis. Chi-square test is used for computing relevance ranking of head nouns. Highly ranked head nouns and predicates are considered in last step of relation extraction. The subject is taken as domain and objects and adjuncts as range of the relation.

Formal concept analysis can be used for deriving concept hierarchy from domain corpus (Rokia Bendaoud et al., 2007). The relationships between individuals in text are modeled using relational concept analysis. Here celestial objects are classified from astronomy text. In RCA, links between individuals are used to rank relations between concepts. Before using FCA, NLP steps

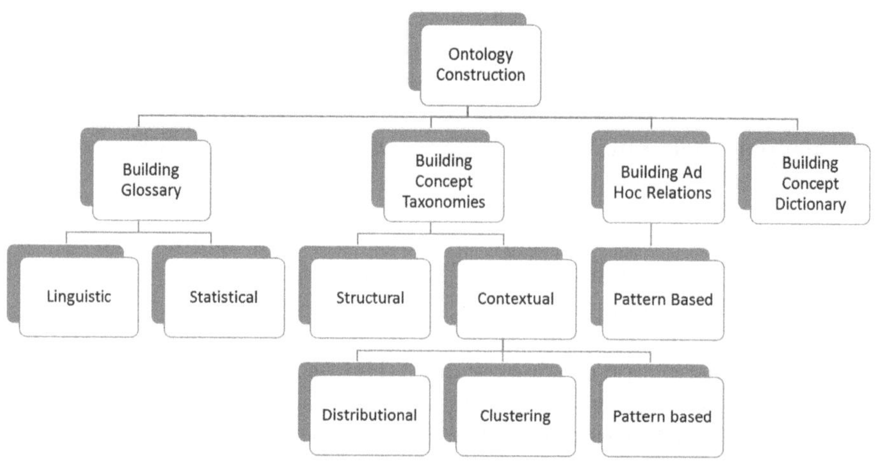


**FIGURE 2.2**
Ontology construction approaches.

are carried out to process text. Object-property and object-relation-object tuples are extracted.

FCA is also used by Suqin Tang and Zixing Cai (2010) for constructing tourism ontology. Here concepts from text are analyzed, formal contexts are defined and then concept lattice is generated. A system named OntoUSP was developed for generating probabilistic ontology from text. Here, Lambda form clusters are prepared from text. IS-A & IS-PART hierarchies are formed and unsupervised semantic parser is prepared. Higher-order Markov model is used to extend USP for hierarchical clustering.

Automatic Content Extraction (ACE) and General Architecture for Text Extraction (GATE) can be used for extraction of relations and features from text for ontology construction (Ting Wang et al., 2006). The paper mentions use of following features for relation extraction: word features, POS tag features, entity features, mention features, overlap features, chunk features, dependency features, parse tree features, semantic features from SQLF and semantic features from WordNet.

Comparison of four ontology building tools, namely OntoLearn, Alvis, Text2Onto and SPART, is done based on tasks performed as building glossary of terms, building concept taxonomies, building diagrams for ad hoc binary relations and building the concept dictionary (Toader Gherasim et al., 2013). Tools are compared based on approach used for performing tasks, technical features and experimental analysis. Linguistic and statistical techniques can be used for building glossary of terms. Techniques for building concept taxonomies are structural and contextual. Contextual techniques are again divided into sub-types as distributional, clustering and pattern based. Pattern-based techniques are used for identifying ad hoc relations. The framework used for comparison was called methontology. Rene Witte et al. (2010) proposed constructing NLP ontology using GATE and populating it with domain ontology. The tool was called OWL exporter.

### 2.1.1 Building Agricultural Ontology

Use of ontology for agricultural knowledge management is discussed by many researchers. Following is the review of some research papers in this regard.

Xiong Jinhui et al. (2010): In this paper, a semantic search engine based on SKOS model for agricultural ontology is proposed. The knowledge base is ranked using theme-relevance algorithm. It is based on distance between terms in ontologies. Under SKOS model, the Chinese Agricultural Thesaurus is mapped to a light ontology system.

Yong Yang et al. (2010): In this paper, two types of ontologies, namely domain ontology and task ontology, are developed for grapes. Domain ontology contains static information during whole life period of grapes such as soil, seed and agriculture machinery information. For each stage of plant growth, task ontology is built. It contains knowledge about soil selection, seed selection, fertilization and irrigation. Knowledge base is built based on grape cultivation standards (GCS) and good agricultural practices (GAP). V-model theory of systems engineering is used for analyzing user's need, and task ontologies are built accordingly.

Nishu Bansal and Sanjay Kumar Malik (2011): In this paper, ontology of grape production cycle is developed. It is called GRAPEont. Developed ontology is based on AGROVOC vocabulary. Semantic graphical search interface is provided for farmers. It provides information by executing SPARQL queries on expert knowledge base. They have used JESS inference engine for reasoning of GRAPEont and for converting it into expert knowledge base.

Anita C. Liang et al. (2006): In this paper, conversion of AGROVOC thesaurus to agricultural ontology service is done. Agriculture ontology service contains OWL ontologies which are built on three concepts: category, classification scheme and lexicalization.

Wei Yuanyuan et al. (2010): In this paper, declarative and procedural representation of agricultural knowledge is done. Frame knowledge unit (FKU) contains declarative knowledge, and solving knowledge unit (SKU) contains procedural knowledge. Ontology-based representation of this knowledge is done using OWL language. The relationship between FKU and SKU is established so that farmers can be provided with related procedural knowledge along with declarative knowledge for agricultural concepts.

Xiuqin Qiu and Jun Yue (2010): In this paper, a seven-step model is used for agricultural ontology construction. The ontology for vegetable supply chain model is constructed in Protégé editor. The semantic server is built. It is used to parse, reason or transform ontology.

Hang Xiao et al. (2013): In this paper, the integration process of heterogeneous agricultural information systems is analyzed. Authors have analyzed the problem of system heterogeneity, mode heterogeneity and semantic heterogeneity. Mode heterogeneity refers to data modes as structured, semi-structured and unstructured. Agricultural information bus is developed with four layers as service layer, protocol layer, data layer and router layer to address system heterogeneity. For mode heterogeneity, ontologies are built. Ontologies are divided into two parts as local domain ontology and global domain ontology. To overcome semantic heterogeneity, semantic interoperability between agricultural ontologies is checked. Semantic similarity is calculated by finding out concept similarity, relation similarity and attributes similarity.

Xuguang Liu et al. (2012a): In this paper, an ontology model for classification of agricultural products information is introduced. The ontology model is defined by setting reasonable hierarchy structure of class and subclass. Before construction of ontology, agricultural information is preprocessed by text segmentation and tagging of words. Ontology model is built using space vector model and relationship learning.

Shyamaladevi K et al. (2012): In this paper, a farmer helping system is developed. They demonstrated process for development of ontology for soil information, pesticide information, plant information and weather information. Rules in agricultural knowledge are also developed in OWL. The system is provided as a web service.

Fang Wang et al. (2008): In this paper, an ontology-based agricultural FAQ retrieval system is presented. Different categories of agricultural information are defined. The concept similarity matching algorithm is used to match farmer's question with category. To match question in FAQ base, the farmer's question is converted into three parts as keyword segment, focus segment and question word segment. They also used spitted vector space model for question matching calculation in FAQ base.

## 2.2 Ontology Merging

Several approaches for ontology merging are proposed by various authors worldwide. This chapter discusses some of those approaches. An approach to ontology merging using concept lattice technique under formal concept analysis is provided by Shixiang Li et al. (2009). They defined matrix for ontology matching. Matrix mentions similarity between instances, definition and structure of ontologies, respectively. They proposed assigning of weights to all these parameters for measuring similarity. They took threshold value from user for deciding similarity. Decision on similarity between two ontologies is taken based on threshold value and calculated similarity. The next step was to build concept lattice using concept lattice construction algorithm. Global ontology was generated using generated concept lattice. The relationships in ontologies were constructed as the last step.

Special notations for ontology merging called Ontology Merging (OM) notations are presented by Alma Delia Cuevas Rasgado and Arenas (2006). They also presented ontology merging algorithm where merging takes place automatically without user intervention. They provided list of labels to be used in ontology which identify the description of the concepts and relations among them. In OM algorithm, similarity of concepts from two ontologies is measured. Similar concepts are added once to a new third ontology, and all differing concepts from both ontologies are added as new concept in third ontology. They also considered relation similarity. For concepts which are synonyms of each other, they used COM algorithm of OM. They also mentioned about removing nested relations.

An ontology merging method based on WordNet is proposed by Hyunjang Kong et al. (2005). It is specifically developed for merging heterogeneous domain ontologies. In this work, sets of concepts are prepared. Equality of concepts is measured after that. WordNet Synset number is used for this purpose. They also measured values of sets of concepts using Jaccord coefficient and subclass relationships using most-specific-parent method. Hypernym and hyponym relations are checked for using PTR field in WordNet. Hierarchy is reconstructed based on the measurements.

Target-driven merging of ontologies is proposed by Salvatore Raunich and Rahm (2011). An attempt is made to save the structure of target taxonomy. The approach is based on equivalence matching between a source taxonomy and target taxonomy for merging. They used integrated concept graph to adapt and extend properties of merged taxonomy. Multiple inheritance is supported with is-a relationship. The integrated concept graph of two participating ontologies is created, cycles are removed if any and then source and target edges are translated to remove redundancy.

Use of machine learning techniques for ontology merging is discussed by Richardson and Mazlack (2005). Use of hierarchical clustering algorithm for ontology learning and use of Bayesian theorem, cosine and KL divergence functions is discussed in the paper. Threshold value for cosine similarity computation is taken from user. Existence of thesaurus is assumed for each ontology. Thesaurus is used to understand relations between terms. Decision to merge ontologies is based on probability computed by Bayesian theorem. Only similar concepts are merged and different terms are preserved separately in newly created ontology.

An algorithm for merging domain ontologies using description logic and augmented description graph is proposed by Gupta and Chaudhary (2009). Ontology concepts are divided in TBOX and ABOX constructs. Named instances and values of attributes are used to resolve mismatches. Mapping rules are defined to map TBOX and ABOX constructs to graphs. For merging description graphs, they are mapped to three relational tables containing concepts, instances, attribute names, values and types.

Combination of lexical, semantic and rule-based methods can be used for ontology merging (Julia M. Taylor et al., 2005). Name similarity and syntactic string similarity is calculated for lexical matching. For semantic matching, OpenCyc and WordNet are used for finding synonyms. Simple Hearst patterns and propositional formulae are used for rule-based matching. The concepts are merged only if the similarity value is above a user-defined threshold.

Similar approach is mentioned by Guanyu Li (2010). Detail algorithms for ontology merging, attribute merging, relation merging and superclass merging are explained in the paper. Rules are also defined for handling conflicts. Sigmoid function is used for smoothing weighted similarity calculations.

Prompt plug-in available with protégé can be used for ontology merging (Sanjay Kumar Malik et al., 2010). Semi-automatic approach of ontology merging is used under Prompt. Detail process used under Prompt is described in the paper. Inconsistencies are identified and reported to user by prompt plug-in. Merging of ontologies is done at the level of classes, slots, facets and instances. Information about types, approaches, tools, techniques and co-ordination of ontology merging is detailed in the paper.

Clustering technique for merging multiple ontologies is proposed by Fabiana Freire de Araujo et al., 2010. Unsupervised and hierarchical approach of clustering is used here. They generate similarity matrix by matching classes and properties. From similarity matrix, two ontologies with highest degree of similarity are considered. After carrying out merging process, the newly constructed ontology is added under similarity matrix and the similarity calculation is repeated.

Ontology merging system based on semantics named DKP-O is developed by Muhammad Fahad and Muhammad Abdul Qadir, 2009. Concept name, datatype properties, object properties, parent concepts, child concepts and axioms are considered for syntactic similarity computation. Data and object properties, linguistic matching and synonym matching strategies are used for finding similarity between concepts. Consistency checking of ontology mappings by using ontology evaluation knowledge within the semantic knowledge of merging system is proposed here.

Fully automated ontology matching using upper ontologies is proposed by Viviana Mascardi et al. (2010). Three algorithms, namely uo-match, structural-uo-match and mixed-match are implemented for ontology matching. They used SUMO-OWL as upper ontology for running experiments. The implementation is done using the Alignment API. Detailed evaluation of proposed algorithms along with experimental results is provided in the paper.

Computing similarity between ontologies using change weights semantic graph is put forward by Feng Yang et al. (2009). They combined name-based and structure-based approach. They calculated name similarity matrix and used it as initial values for edges in change weights semantic graphs.

Petr Kremen et al. (2011) introduced OWL 2 ontology merging tool named OWLDiff. It is open source and can be used as plug-in with Protégé and NeOn toolkit. Compatibility of mappings should be checked to reduce error in merged ontology. OWLDiff helps for syntactic, explanation-based and semantic comparison, merging and versioning of ontologies. Three scenarios for change in ontology are defined as refactoring, defining new terms and redefining existing terms. Merging of axioms is possible using OWLDiff.

Galois connection for deciding compatible and incompatible ontology mappings while merging them is described by Muhamad Aun Abbes et al. (2015).

Approach for analysis and preservation of disjoint knowledge before actually merging two ontologies is provided by Muhammad Fahad et al. (2010). It helps to remove inconsistencies and conflicts among relations.

Alignment between ontologies to be merged can be done by using multiple knowledge bases (Mohammed Maree and Mohammed Belkhatir, 2015). Majority voting from multiple knowledge bases is considered for relations of type equivalence, specialization, generalization, disjointness and unknown. Both one-to-one and one-to-many relations are considered for merged concepts, relations, individuals and axioms. Jaro-Winkler distance function is used for finding equivalence relationship. Knowledge bases are enriched by adding missing concepts from merged ontologies that come from other knowledge bases.

Web service ontology merging is done by using concept lattice (Hong Xia et al., 2007). Capability matching algorithm is used for this purpose. Venn diagrams can be used for visualization of ontology merging process (Martin Eller, 2008). Parameter-based technique can also be used for ontology merging (Sabino Pariente Juarez et al., 2011). Classification of concepts can be done using classification tree and the tree can be used for ontology merging (Kai Yang and Robert Steele, 2009). Concept dimensions like named concepts, intersections, unions, complements and restrictions are used for mapping ontologies before merging (Jingxian Zhang et al., 2009).

## 2.3 Use of Image Processing for Pests and Diseases Detection

Many approaches are proposed by researchers to detect diseases on crops using image processing techniques namely original data-based query, use of perceptual hash algorithm or hamming distance, color-based retrieval, color histogram, shape-based retrieval, texture-based retrieval and content-based multi-feature retrieval. Techniques used by researchers are reviewed in this chapter.

Detection of six types of wheat diseases is done using support vector machine (SVM) (Punnarari Siricharoen et al., 2016). It is a mobile system developed using Android and openCV. System first rotates captured image using 2-D Discrete Fourier transform. It also allows for manual rotation of image. Background is removed using crop interface and then interested features are extracted. Three types of features namely texture, color and shape are used. Under texture features, local homogeneity and local linear-dependency measures, contrast and entropy are considered. These features are derived from co-occurrence matrix. Cr component from YCbCr is used for color feature extraction. Mean, standard deviation and skew-ness is measured from histogram of intensity values. Otsu thresholding is applied to Cb and Cr components to extract disease areas from main leaf. Contours of disease patches are extracted using two shape features as elongatedness and hydraulic radius. After extracting all nine features, support vector machine is used initially to remove non-disease leaves and then to predict disease on leaf.

Disease detection by segmenting image using histogram analysis can also be done (J. G. A. Barbedo, 2016). The rules are formed based on H channel from HSV transformation and A channel from L*a*b* transformation to distinguish healthy pixels from disease pixels. Detection of borer in tomato image is done by defining threshold values for Y, Cb and Cr (Prathibha G. P. et al., 2014). Leaf image is converted from RGB to HIS. Then spatial gray-level dependence matrix is used and masking of green pixels is done for detection of disease on grape leaf (Pradnya Narvekar et al., 2014).

Use of deep learning technique for counting moths from trap images is done (Weiguang and Graham, 2016). Convolution neural network is used as classifier under sliding window approach. Detection of powdery mildew, downy mildew, black rot and leaf roll is done using back propagation neural network.

Energy, entropy, cluster shade, cluster prominence and correlation are the features extracted from image and stored as gray-level co-occurrence matrix (Nivedita Kakade and Dnyaneshwar Ahire, 2015).

Efforts are taken by various researchers to detect pests and diseases by processing crop images for various crops like maize (Ding and Taylor, 2016). Techniques based on data, color, shape, texture or context features of images are used for pest and disease diagnosis. Hamming distance is considered in data-based technique whereas color space histograms are matched in color-based retrieval (Wang et al., 2014). In shape-based methods, edges and region are considered. For edge extraction, Canny, Robert, Prewitt, Sobel or Wavelet operators can be used. One of the statistical, structural, model-based method, space method or frequency domain analysis method can be used for texture-based image analysis. Combination of multiple features is mostly used for pest and disease detection from image. After feature extraction, one of the classification or clustering techniques can be used for disease detection, e.g. artificial neural networks (Weiguang Ding et al., 2014, P. Boniecki et al., 2015, Karlos Espinoza et al., 2016, Sachin D. Khirade et al., 2015), spatial gray-level dependence matrices (Wang Zhi-jun et al., 2014), fuzzy logic (S. S. Sannakki et al., 2011, Archana Chougule et al., 2016), Bayesian decision theory (Jing-Lei Tang Jing-Lei et al., 2016) and SGDM matrix (Pradnya Ravindra Narvekar et al., 2014).

## 2.4 Decision Support Systems and Expert Systems

Computer Centre for Agricultural Pest Forecasting (CIPRA) is a popular software that can predict the development of pests and some post-harvest disorders based on hourly weather data. CIPRA includes forecast models which include 35 insect pest models, 14 disease models, 24 crop phenology models and 2 post-harvest physiological disorder models. All these models are available for 23 different crops.

Clima-rice (www.climarice.com) is a system for pest and disease forecasts on rice. It is based on weather forecasts specifically for paddy blast disease and paddy leaf mite pest.

DemiAg (www.demiag.com), expert system for agricultural pest management, is an open source system for providing forecasts for plant diseases. It is being developed by DeMilia Research LLC.

Research papers have been published proposing decision support systems and expert systems for various crops by researchers all over the world. Some of such systems are discussed here.

An online portal for agricultural ontology access is presented by Xiong Jinhui et al. (2010). They have collected agricultural information from Web using distributed crawler. Collected information is used for generating OWL classes. The paper explains mapping for ontologies for multiple languages. The OWL classes extracted from information are mapped with OWL classes provided by AGROVOC, and new merged OWL classes are used as Knowledge base. It is named AOS. Jena APIs and Pellet inference engine is used for answering questions from farmers.

Weather-based expert system for forecasting diseases on corn crop is proposed by Vidita Tilva, Jignesh Patel, and Chetan Bhatt (2012). They used fuzzy logic technique for developing inference engine of expert system. They used temperature, humidity and leaf wetness duration as weather parameters for defining fuzzy rules to estimate plant disease. They defined five classes for input and output member functions as very high, high, medium, low and very low.

A decision support system for management of Powdery Mildew in grapes is developed by K. Y. Mundankar et al. (2007). They estimate disease risk by considering plant growth stage and weather conditions. All the details about weather conditions, field condition and plant growth stage are taken from the end user through software interface. Expert system provides information regarding fungicide spray name and its dose for various fields and weather conditions.

An agent-oriented method for developing decision support system is adopted by Ann Perini and Angelo Susi (2003). They describe software-development phases as early requirement analysis, late requirement analysis, architectural design and implementation for integrated production in agriculture. They list various actors in agriculture production and show their relationship in architectural design.

An expert system for the diagnosis of pests, diseases and disorders in Indian mango is proposed by Rajkishore Prasad et al. (2005). They describe development of a rule-based expert system using ESTA; Expert System Shell for Text Animation. The system is based on answers to questions taken from farmers regarding disease symptoms.

An expert system for pest and disease management of Jamaican coffee named CPEST is developed by Gunjan Mansingh et al. (2007). It is built in wxCLIPS. Forward chaining is used as reasoning mechanism. They developed rule base containing 150 production rules. CPEST has three stages for solving problem as general data-gathering phase, diagnosis and possible treatments and integration of treatments.

A rule-based expert system to diagnose honeybee pests is described by B. D. Mahaman et al. (2002) which can be used by beekeepers. It is implemented using EXSYS for Microsoft windows environment with backward chaining method. A decision support system for pest management in Australian cotton systems is described by M. P. Bange et al. (2008). It can be used on handheld devices to collect data required for pest management from different locations.

An expert system for identification of pests, diseases and weeds in olive crops is provided by J. L. Gonzalez-Andujar (2009). The knowledge base is created using interviewing technique and represented using IF-THEN rules. The knowledge base contains information for identification of 9 weed species, 14 insect species and 14 diseases.

An agent-based model for integrated pest management by coupling a pest model with farmer behavior model is developed by (Francois Rebaudo and Olivier Dangles (2013). It is convinced in paper that passive IPM information diffusion is better than active diffusion.

Effectiveness of location aware system of pest management for olive fruit fly was investigated by Costas m Pontikakos et al. (2012). The described system uses information regarding olive fruit fly, meteorological conditions and spatiotemporal details of spraying areas. Location aware system has client-server architecture and it utilizes web services, geographic information system, expert system and multimedia technology.

An intelligent system, named JAPIEST, for disease and pest diagnosis and control of tomatoes in greenhouses is proposed by V. Lopez-Morales et al. (2008). The system computes vapor pressure deficit to detect probable development of diseases on tomatoes. Graphical support is also provided with disease detection results.

An integrated Web geographical information system for control of pests on olive-fruit fly is presented by Ioannis Karydis et al. (2013). They describe how webGIS can be extended to provide temporal and/or spatial prediction on pests' life cycle and to suggest proposals on pests' life-cycle suppression. Pest life cycle is simulated and predictions are done on measurements provided as input. Temperatures, humidity, altitude, number of male and female pests are the measurements taken periodically and provided as input.

## 2.5 Nutrition Management

The brief about articles published and tools developed on nutrition management of grapes are published worldwide. Researchers from National research center for grapes, India, also publish research documents and information on websites about application of fertilizers on grapes. Farmers need to read these documents for decision support on fertilizers application. Author of the thesis did not find a decision support system for nutrient management of grapes in India.

Spectrum analytics Inc., Washington, provides soil, plant tissue and fertilizers analysis services (www.spectrumanalytic.com). They provide information about nutrition requirements and application of fertilizers on grape farms at different growth stages.

SMART (www.smart-fertilizer.com) is a fertilizer management platform which provides optimized fertilizer application program to their customers based on analysis of on-field data. It works for 250 types of crops. It contains crop database and fertilizers database. Different kinds of reports, including fertilizers' schedule is provided by SMART. Names of fertilizers to be used along with its amount are recommended for each growth stage of crop.

Precision Fertilization Management Information System (PFMIS) (Zhimin Liu et al., 2012) uses GIS and GPS technologies for fertilization recommendation. Artificial neural network technique is used for data processing. Three-dimensional co-ordinates system on GPS is used for getting soil attributes of nutrients. Web-based expert system is connected to ArcGIS server containing spatial data grid maps about soil resources.

Representation of production knowledge for citrus in hilly areas is explained (Ying Wang et al., 2015). Conversion of production knowledge from text and reports to fertilization and irrigation ontology is elaborated in the paper. They have developed and evaluated support system which uses developed ontology. They have represented nutrition deficiency symptoms and soil moisture observations as triples and relations between triples.

## 2.6 Ontology Management

For building and maintaining meaningful and accurate ontologies, help should be taken from ontology engineering frameworks. For ontology editing KAON (Gabel and Sure, 2004), Protege (protege.stanford.edu) and OntoEdit (Y. Sure et al., 2002) are the tools used. PROMPTDIFF (Natalya and Mark, 2002) is a tool used to record structural changes done after updating ontology. It compares ontology versions using a fixed-point algorithm. Synonym or subsume relation is used by EMTREE to specify conceptual changes in different versions.

IAIF (R. Alfred et al., 2014), ONTAgri (S. Z. Aqeel-ur Rehman, 2011), AGROVOC (C. Caracciolo et al., 2013), AOS (B. Lauser et al., 2006) and WAICET (A. Mangstl and Judy, 1997) are examples of existing ontologies in agriculture domain. AGROVOC is developed and maintained by food and agricultural organization. The ontology covers almost all areas related to agriculture and is available in multiple languages. AGRIS is an application ontology used as metadata for searching research papers in journal on agriculture (FAO).

Yong Yang et al. (2010) have developed two types of ontologies for grapes management as domain ontology and task ontology. While constructing domain ontology, information about stages in whole life period of grape is considered. It contains details on soil, seed and agriculture machine information. Task ontology is built for each stage of plant growth. It contains knowledge base about soil selection, seed selection, fertilization and irrigation for the specific growth stage of grapes. For building knowledge base, grape cultivation standards (GCS) and good agricultural practices (GAP) are used. Before building task ontology, user's needs are analyzed using V-model theory of systems engineering. But the built ontology does not give details of nutrition management. AGROVOC and DBPedia ontologies have 'Grape' class but contain very short information. No ontology is available online to the best of our knowledge which details nutrition management of grapes.

Ontology learning is creating ontology automatically or semi-automatically by extracting related terms and relations from domain knowledge. Ontology learning techniques help in building and maintaining ontologies. Various approaches are proposed for ontology leaning. Data mining techniques like frequent item sets can be used for building ontology from text (J. I. Toledo-Alvarado et al., 2012). Linguistic and statistical techniques are used for extracting terms from unstructured text. Some researchers have developed ontology development tools as protégé plug-ins. OntoLT (Paul Buitelaar et al., 2004), TextToOnto (P. Cimiano et al., 2005) and Ontolearn (Paola Velardi et al., 2013) are examples of such plug-ins. OntoLT uses linguistic analysis technique for building ontology. Operators to create classes, slots and instances are provided by OntoLT. TextToOnto is an open source tool built in Java. It uses text mining techniques for building ontology, and it builds on KAON. Ontolearn uses graph-based technique for finding taxonomies from text. It first extracts relevant terms using domain corpus. Hypernym graph is then built from these terms and directed acyclic graph is developed then. OwlExporter (René Witte et al., 2010) is a tool developed using general architecture for text engineering for populating ontology from text. Relational concept analysis (Rokia Bendaoud et al., 2007) and formal concept analysis (Suqin Tang and Zixing Cai, 2010) techniques are also used widely for text-based ontology construction. OntoComp (B. Sertkaya, 2009) is a protégé plug-in used for completing ontology using formal concept analysis. RelExt (A. Schutz and P. Buitelaar, 2005) is a tool for finding out relationships between terms which can be used for extending ontology. Machine learning techniques in combination with natural language processing techniques are used by many people for automation of ontology building (P. Cimiano and S. Staab, 2005, P. Buitelaar et al., 2005). OntoUSP is an ontology learning system based on unsupervised semantic parsing (Hoifung Poon and Pedro Domingos, 2010). It builds a probabilistic ontology from dependency-parsed text. Built ontology comprises concepts, relations and sub concepts.

Various approaches are proposed for managing ontology evolution (G. Flouris et al., 2008). A model for ontology evolution is developed using Pi-Calculus (Rui Zhang et al., 2016). They consider ontology entities as agents and any changes to be done in ontology as information exchange among agents. They have used hyper graphs for formalizing Pi-Calculus processes. Pieter De Leenheer and Tom Mens (2008) give an overview of models and mechanisms used for ontology evolution. PromptDiff (F. N. Natalya and A. M. Mark, 2002) is a protégé plug-in used for detecting changes in different ontology versions. It integrates various matchers in fixed-point manner. OntoAMAS (S. Benomrane, Z. Sellami and M. B. Ayed, 2016) is a tool based on an adaptive multi-agent system used for ontology evolution using feedback from ontologists. The tool organizes the changes in ontology based on feedback and returns updated ontology. With adaptive algorithm, tool can rename a concept, add a sub concept and merge or split concepts. Evolva (Z. Fouad et al., 2009) is an automatic ontology evolution system in which ontologies are evolved from texts. It uses available online ontologies as background knowledge. Efforts have been taken to use ontology for generating decision trees using Ontology Decision Tree (ODT) (A. Bouza et al., 2007) and SemTree (P. Klinov and Maxlack, 2006) algorithms. The approach implemented in current work being described in subsequent chapters is reverse of ODT, i.e. extending ontology from decision tree. Supervised learning approach is used for decision tree based ontology granulation (B. Gajderowicz and Alireza, 2009). Here categories of objects stored in database are used for decision tree. Ontologies are matched by matching granules of ontology using ontology hierarchy, attribute relevance, information gain and concept granulation measures. For deciding hierarchies in ontology, use of text mining techniques and decision trees is proposed by F.W. Hans (2005). Tracing of decision tree in bottom-up direction for replacing low-level concepts with higher-level concepts is proposed here. Use of decision trees for learning relationships between two ontologies belonging to same domain is described (R. Mirambicka et al., 2013). They build training matrices from both ontologies and use it for constructing decision trees. Conclusions about equivalence of classes are drawn by parsing decision tree. Ontology can be built from texts by applying natural language processing techniques (A. Chougule et al., 2016). A completely integrated system for fully automated evolution of ontology does not exist till date.

## 2.7 Irrigation Management Systems

Ontology is developed for irrigation systems (J. I. Toledo-Alvarado et al., 2012). It is generic ontology and does not consider any crop-specific details for irrigation. As it was built long back, it does not consider IoT-related concepts for automated irrigation system.

Smartvineyards (www.smartvineyards.net) is an irrigation management system that uses soil water tension to monitor vine and water stress in each vineyard block. Readings of sensors are displayed on web browser in graphical form. It uses soil tension sensors for the same purpose. Irrisoft (www.irrisoft.net) provides software for irrigation scheduling named InSite Irrigation Scheduling. It provides summary of evapotranspiration (ET) values and station-wise irrigation schedules based on various parameters like weather details, plant type and soil type. Basic Irrigation Scheduling (BIS) is an excel application for irrigation scheduling. It is developed for crops in California. It estimates annual trends of ET. C. Cornejo et al. have developed irrigation ontology which is used for educational purpose. Cropx is one of the leading IoT-based irrigation automation system (cropx.com). Netafim (www.netafim.com) is a smart drip irrigation system that can be controlled by application on smartphone. It requires the irrigation schedule to be defined explicitly by farmers.

# 3

# *Building Vineyards Knowledge Base*

## 3.1 Introduction

Success of any decision support system depends on accuracy and richness of knowledge base used by decision support system. The knowledge to be used is generally available in different formats. To make it useful for DSS, it needs to be represented in a structured and consistent way. The knowledge base can be in the form of relational database, XML or any other format. This chapter describes how the knowledge base is generated in the form of ontology to be used by decision support systems described in subsequent chapters.

### 3.1.1 Ontology

Use of computers and electronics for integrated pest management is unavoidable. Information available in brochures, magazines and journals is not interactive and doesn't reach much to farmers. Information required for finding out relationships between different parameters required to predict pests and diseases occurrence must be stored in a knowledge base on computer.

Definition: Ontology is formal specification of knowledge. Important entities and relationships from knowledge base can be represented meaningfully using Ontology. Any assumptions related to concepts can be made explicit using ontology. Ontology is the key concept in Semantic Web.

Analysis of knowledge to be used becomes easier when it is in the form of ontology. All agricultural knowledge represented as ontology can be shared by agricultural experts working at various agricultural research centers across India. Ontology developed for one agricultural software system can be used by another without much hassle.

World Wide Web consortium (W3C) plays main role in developing ontology standards. Various formats for representing ontology are available like SKOS, Turtle, RDF, RDF-S, OWL and OWL-S.

There are two main types of ontologies based on the level of abstraction as follows:

DOI: 10.1201/9781003408253-4

#### 3.1.1.1 Upper Ontology

Description of very general and abstract concepts like time, matter and space is mentioned in upper ontology. It is meant to be derived by other domain ontologies as common knowledge base for many other domain ontologies is stored in upper ontology. Examples of upper ontologies are WordNet, SUMO, GFO, OpenCYC, DOLCE and BFO. SUMO ontology contains concepts like entity, object, number and attribute.

#### 3.1.1.2 Domain Ontology

Domain ontology contains terms and descriptions of a specific domain only. Relationships mentioned between concepts are specific to domain under consideration. Same concepts are represented differently in different domain ontologies based on context. Upper ontologies are helpful for building domain ontologies. Domain ontologies can extend concepts from upper ontologies. Domain ontology can be checked against upper ontology for missing of any important foundation concept by mapping concepts from upper ontology to domain ontology. Examples of ontologies available on internet are Dublin core ontology, the friend of a friend ontology, music ontology and marineTLO ontology.

Ontology can be developed manually by using any editor. It can be constructed using semi-automated or automated approach by converting text to ontology. Editors like protégé, chimaera, NeOn, open semantic frameworks; TODE and HOZO are available for ontology development. Ontology contains concepts named classes, properties of concepts named slots or properties or roles, restrictions on properties and instances named individuals.

Conditions for integrated pest management can be mentioned as rules. In Web Ontology Language, the rules can be specified using Semantic Web Rule Language (SWRL) (Martin Joseph O'Connor, 2016). With the advancement of IoT tools and techniques, capturing and processing real-time environmental data is easier than early days. Use of classes from standard SSN ontology (M. Compton et al., 2012) can be done for this purpose.

Before developing ontology, scope and use of ontology should be very clear. Figure 3.1 is an example of ontology.

### 3.1.2 AGROVOC

AGROVOC is the famous ontology available online related to food and agriculture. It is published by Food and Agriculture Organization (FAO) of United Nations. It is multilingual thesaurus supporting 27 languages. AGROVOC is freely available for use. It can be downloaded or accessed in programs through web service. It can be used for indexing and organizing agricultural documents. One can search for specific terms or go through hierarchies of

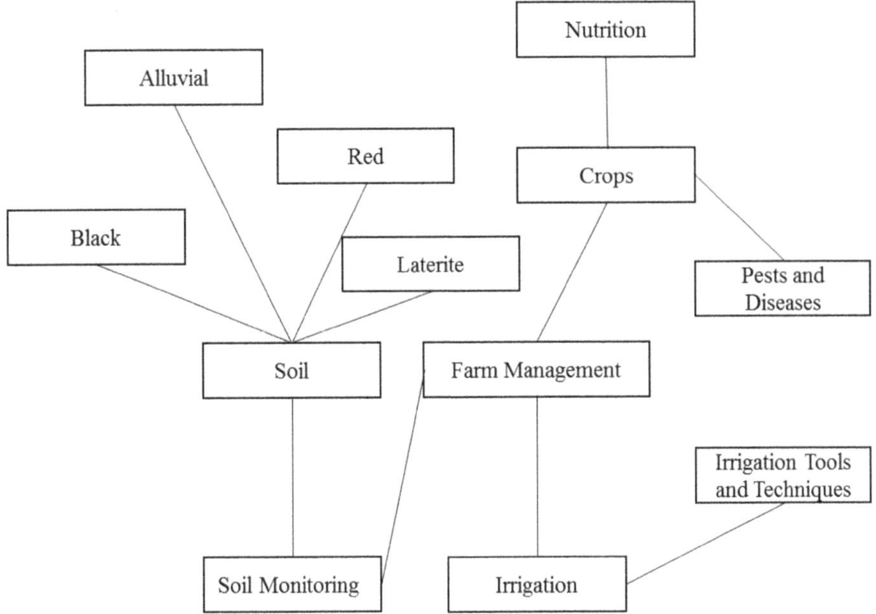


**FIGURE 3.1**
Example of agriculture ontology.

concepts in agriculture. AGROVOC contains terms, relationships between terms and between concepts. It provides semantic information in terms of definitions, pictures and notes wherever required. Twenty-five top-level concepts from AGROVOC are namely organism, substances, entities, phenomena, activities, products, methods, properties, features, objects, resources, subjects, systems, locations, groups, measures, state, stages, technology, processes, factors, time, events, site and strategies. Under organism concept, all plant-related concepts are involved. It is extendible, i.e. new concepts or new language support can be provided with AGROVOC. Community of experts edits the AGROVOC vocabulary.

### 3.1.3 Web Ontology Language

One of the ontology representation languages developed by W3C is Web Ontology Language (OWL). OWL is based on Resource Description Framework. Representation of knowledge in terms of triples, i.e. subject–predicate–object is possible using OWL. OWL is used to show semantic relationships between concepts in respective domain. Using OWL, more information about properties and classes can be represented than with RDFS. Similarity between concepts can be shown in OWL. More complex knowledge can be represented using OWL than with RDF. It is possible to represent hierarchies of properties and classes in OWL. Three types of properties exist in OWL as data property, object property and annotation property. Data property is used to mention values of attributes of individuals. Object properties are used when value of the property is an individual of any other existing concept. Annotation properties are used to mention extra information in ontology.

There are three types of OWL as OWL-Lite, OWL-DL and OWL-Full. OWL-Lite is used for very simple ontologies with no complex relationships and where expressivity requirement is not major. Properties can be stated in OWL-Lite as inverseOf, transitive property, symmetric property, functional property and non-functional property. For more expressiveness and complex ontologies, OWL-DL can be used. With some computational restrictions, better ontology building is possible in OWL-DL. DL stands for description logic. For most complex relationships between concepts and more hierarchies and expressiveness, one should go for OWL-Full. There are no syntactic restrictions in OWL-Full. So it should not be used under fully automated systems.

### 3.1.4 Protégé

Open source and user friendly editor and framework for building and modifying ontologies is protégé ontology editor. It contains tabs to create hierarchy

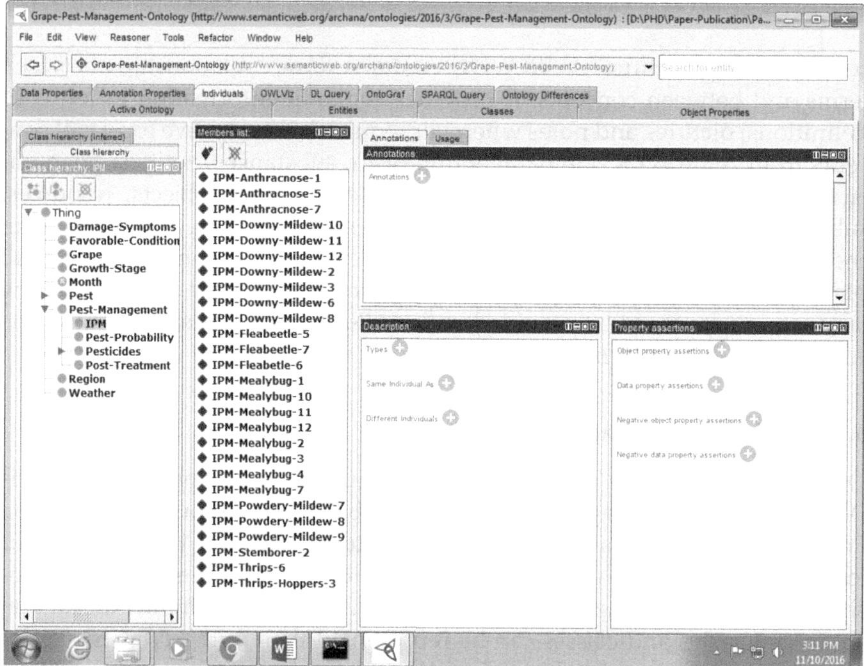


**FIGURE 3.2**
Protégé ontology editor.

of classes, add individuals, data properties and object properties to classes. Graphical representation of class hierarchy of open ontology in protégé is also possible. Protégé 5.2 is adopted in this work. Protégé APIs are also available which can be used in Java programs to access and manipulate ontologies.

### 3.1.5 Jena API

Apache Jena is a free and open source library available to work with semantic data. It is available in Java language. For this research, APIs available for manipulation of ontologies are used. With Jena API, one can create, read and modify RDF documents. Querying to RDF is also possible using ARQ engine which supports execution of SPARQL queries on RDF. Inference API is also available to reason over RDF document. Pellet reasoner can also be used with Jena.

## 3.2 Ontology Construction from Text

Agricultural experts have many description documents related to crop pests and disease management. These documents are generally in text format. These text descriptions cannot be used directly by automated systems.

For directly using this kind of text descriptions, it must be represented in well-structured format. With ontologies, one can represent hierarchy of crop pests. Once pest ontology is prepared, it can be easily converted in any language, which farmers can understand. It is difficult for agricultural experts to represent knowledge in terms of ontologies.

An effort is made here for semi-automated construction of crop pests and disease management ontology from text documents. The developed system is named CropPestOntoGenerator.

The system is developed in Java language which provides easy-to-use interface for agricultural experts. The system provides simple interface where grapes expert can add information like types of pests and diseases occurring on grapes and details like symptoms, reasons and remedy for grape pests/diseases. Protégé APIs (Protégé, http://protege.stanford.edu/) have been used to store this information in terms of ontology.

The overall workflow of CropPestOntoGenerator is shown in Figure 3.3.

The result of workflow is an integrated ontology denoted as $\mathbf{U_o = \langle F_o, K_c, M_o \rangle}$, where

$U_o$ – Integrated ontology

$F_o$ – Foundation Ontology element

$K_c$- Retrieved knowledge from Corpus

$M_o$ – Mapping rules for ontology

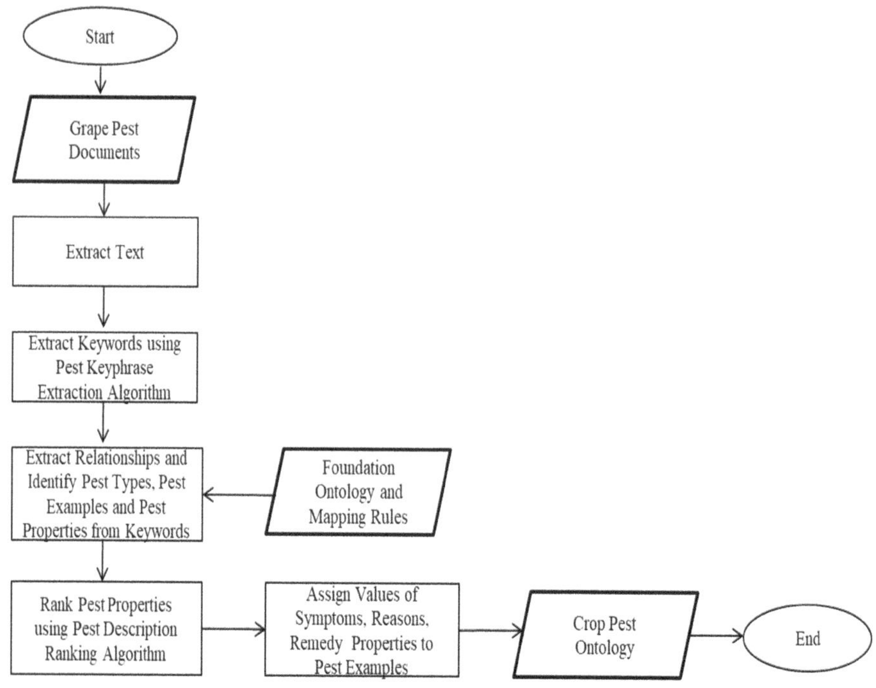


**FIGURE 3.3**
Workflow of the CropPestOntoGenerator.

The developed system provides the foundation ontology to agricultural experts as shown in Figure 3.4. $K_c$ is a set of extracted keywords that is framed by applying rules given by experts for adding keywords to ontologies. OWL is chosen as the language for constructing ontology.

OWL is meant to represent information on internet; once complete crop pest knowledge is stored as OWL document, it can be accessed using internet or can be used by any other agricultural expert systems with ease. The foundation ontology mentions basic categories of crop pests as insect pests, non-insect pests and diseases. Diseases are again divided into three subcategories as fungal diseases, bacterial diseases and viruses.

To add more categories of pests, pest examples and pest details; agricultural expert is assisted with extracted keywords from text descriptions. Agricultural expert needs to provide text corpus containing details of pests for particular crop. The user friendly interface is provided where agricultural expert can add or remove text descriptions in corpus.

For extracting keywords, steps mentioned in machine learning algorithm KEA (keyphrase extraction algorithm) (Witten I. H. et al., 1999) are followed. It has a two-step process; first step is training, i.e. creating a model

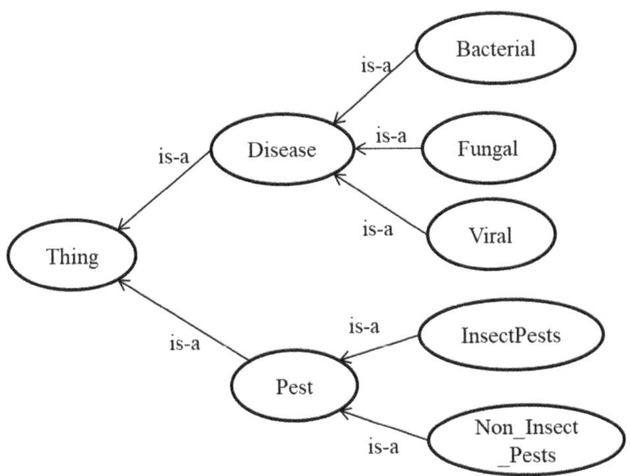


**FIGURE 3.4**
Foundation ontology for crop pest management used by CropPestOntoGenerator.

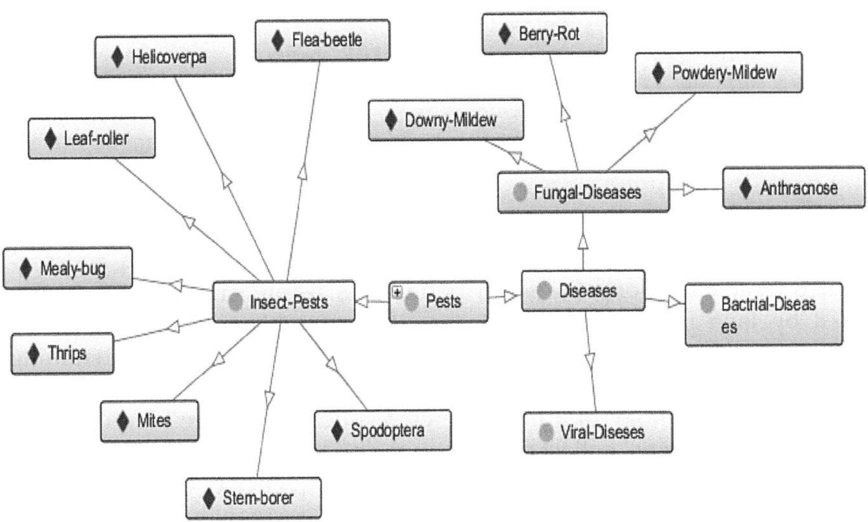


**FIGURE 3.5**
Knowledge base of grape pests and diseases.

for identifying key phrases, and the second step is choosing keywords from a new document, using the model developed in step one. The input text is cleaned by removing punctuation marks, brackets and numbers. In the next step of phrase identification, stop-words are removed. Stemming and case-folding is applied in the next step. It converts variations on a phrase to one phrase.

Text description documents are taken one by one and keyword extraction steps are applied. At the end, all keywords are collected together, duplicate keywords are removed and final keyword list is provided for updating pest ontology. Step by step details, input and output are mentioned in the pest keywords extraction algorithm.

**Algorithm: PEST KEYWORDS EXTRACTION ALGORITHM**

```
Input: Pest/Disease Description Corpus
Output: Related Keywords
 1: Begin
 2: Extract text from document
 3: Tokenize text
 4: Remove stop-words
 5: Apply stemming to phrases
 6: Extract nouns and proper nouns by applying openNLP
    POS tagger and retain POS tags
 7: Compare keywords with AGROVOC vocabulary and remove
    unrelated keywords
 8: Rank all keywords using TFxIDF vectorizer
 9: Repeat from step 2 until all documents are extracted
10: Remove duplicate keywords
11: Divide the list into two lists one containing nouns
    and another containing proper nouns.
12: End
```

The text from each document related to crop pest is extracted and segmented in tokens along the word boundaries using StringTokenizer provided by Java programming language. Important keywords from string tokens are retrieved by applying tokenization, stopping and stemming (Olena Medelyan and Ian H. Witten, 2005). Stop-words in document are not useful for ontology building. Therefore, such words are identified and removed from tokens' collection by comparing tokens with the list of stop-words in English. After removing stop-words, frequency of each keyword is counted and those keywords whose frequency is less than three are removed from the list. After stop-words removal, keywords in the list are stemmed by using Porter Stemmer Algorithm (Porter, 1980). It transforms a word to its root form.

The pest type is stored as Owl:Class in pest ontology and pest example as Owl:Individual. The classes and individuals from ontology are generally nouns and proper nouns in English sentences. Advantage of this fact is taken and only nouns and proper nouns from stemmer output are extracted using openNLP POS tagger (OpenNLP, https://opennlp.apache.org/). Keywords with tags NN, NNP and NNPS are passed to the next step of the algorithm.

To find relevance of these keywords to agricultural field, existence of that keyword is searched for in agricultural vocabulary AGROVOC (AGROVOC Thesaurus, http://aims.fao.org/agrovoc#.VF29AvmUc2U) provided by FAO. AGROVOC is a large vocabulary of almost all areas of agriculture. It also provides support for multiple languages. AGROVOC contains over 32,000 concepts in agricultural field. Those keywords which do not exist in AGROVOC vocabulary are removed from keyword list. All these steps are repeated for all documents uploaded by agricultural experts, and keywords from each document are collected together.

The next step in the pest keywords extraction algorithm is ranking of keywords and retaining only top ranking keywords. This is achieved by using TF-IDF algorithm (TFIDF Algorithm, http://en.wikipedia.org/wiki/Tf-idf). Here, frequency of each keyword in specific pest description document is calculated. Then inverse document frequency is calculated by dividing the total number of pest description documents by the number of pest descriptions containing the keyword. TF-IDF value for keyword is the product of keyword frequency and inverse document frequency. The list is then sorted according to TF-IDF value. Open source data mining library in Java: WEKA is used here to apply TF-IDF algorithm. TFxIDF for each keyword is calculated as

$$TFxIDF = \frac{\text{freq}(\text{k},\text{t})}{\text{size}(\text{t})} \text{X} \log_2 \frac{\text{docfreq}(\text{k})}{n}$$

where k is keyword in text file t, and n is size of all text files, freq(k,t) is frequency of keyword k in text file t and docfreq(k) is number of text files containing keyword k. For CropPestOntoGenerator, top hundred keywords are extracted for each document.

The next step is to prepare two lists of keywords: one of nouns and one of proper nouns. These lists are used as suggestions to add new pest types and pest examples, respectively, in pest ontology.

After identifying keywords, the next step is to extract relationships. To add keywords as concepts and maintain relationships between concepts in ontology, relationships between words in sentences need to be found. Only sentences containing these keywords are considered as candidates for relationship extraction.

### 3.2.1 Relationship Extraction

Relationships between extracted keywords are considered to add keywords to appropriate classes and instances in domain ontology. Following types of relations between keywords are considered:

- Description relationships – describes, is-described-by; keywords can be probable candidate as property of instances in domain ontology.

- Taxonomical relationships – is-kind-of, is-a; keywords can be instances of some class. For example, caterpillar is a kind of insect pest.
- Causal relationships – is-caused-by, causes; can be a reason for some pest, which will be stored as property value in domain ontology.

The Stanford Parser is used for relation extraction (D. Klein and Manning, 2003). It processes the sentences collected in the last step and outputs typed as dependency representations. The links between different words are described by a set of grammatical relationships. Semantic relationships are extracted from grammatical concept map generated from grammatical relationships. Grammatical concept maps are collection of terms that are linked by typed dependencies. Predefined patterns are retrieved from grammatical concept map. Patterns are used for semantic relationship extraction. A set of input links and a set of output links make a pattern. Various grammatical relationships represent these links. After identifying pattern, semantic structure associated with pattern is retrieved. Adjectives and noun parsers are used by terminological patterns.

For relationship extraction, verbs and their auxiliaries are considered. Using linguistic editor, rules are defined for relations mentioned above and relationships are extracted. These extracted relationships are shown

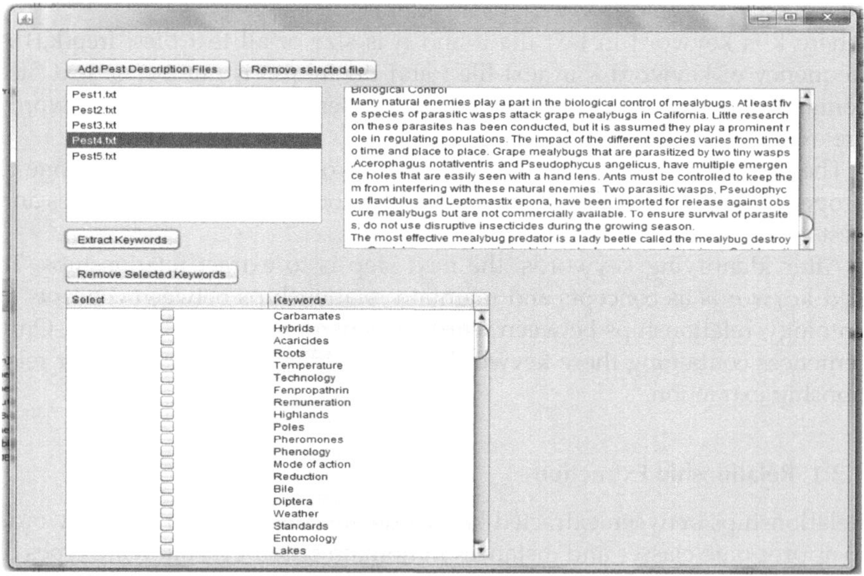


**FIGURE 3.6**
Keywords extraction from crop pests/diseases corpus.

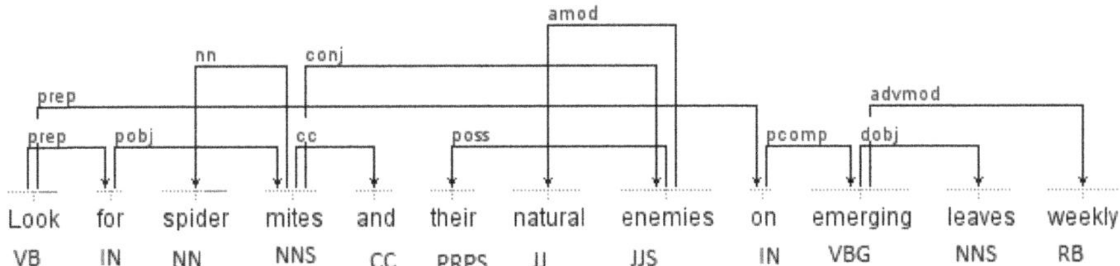


**FIGURE 3.7**
Grammatical relationships extraction from text.

**TABLE 3.1**
OWL Representation of Pest Descriptions

| Pest Description | OWL Representation |
|---|---|
| Type of Pest | Class |
| Subtypes of pest | Object property |
| Example of pest | Individual |
| Symptoms | Data property |
| Reason | Data property |
| Remedy | Data property |
| Causal relationship in description | Data property value |
| Taxonomical relationship in description | Relationship between class and individual |

as a graph. Agricultural expert will use this graph to define hierarchies of pest classes and pest properties in OWL document. Representation of pest description elements in OWL document is done as shown in Table 3.1.

Once keywords are found, agricultural expert has to remove unnecessary keywords. Two clusters of remaining keywords as pest Type cluster or pest Example cluster are available to agricultural expert. These clusters are then used to update Foundation pest Ontology. New pest Types, pest Examples and pest Properties are added to Foundation Ontology by agricultural expert. The user interface for updating foundation pest ontology is shown in Figure 3.8.

Not only keywords extracted by the system can be added to crop pest ontology, but also new keywords from experts' own knowledge can be added. Such keywords are maintained in a separate keywords ontology named EXPERTVOC. EXPERTVOC is dynamically updated whenever crop pest ontology is constructed or updated. EXPERTVOC is used along with AGROVOC, every time after first use of system. So our system is adaptive and becomes more and more robust periodically. It helps in improving accuracy of developed ontology.

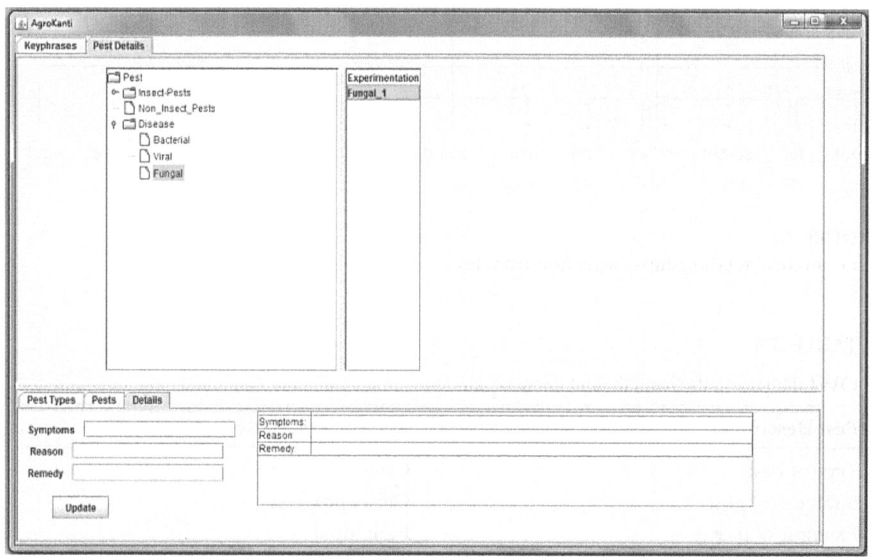


**FIGURE 3.8**
Updating foundation pest ontology.

This work uses Protégé 3.48 APIs for storing the information as OWL document. Protégé APIs provide rich collection of classes and methods for adding and removing OWL classes, individuals, data properties, annotation properties and object properties. Pest types are stored as OWL classes and pest examples as OWL individuals. Symptoms, reasons and remedy for pest example are stored as data properties of individuals in string format.

### 3.2.2 Pest Description Ranking

Agricultural expert can add or update symptoms, reasons and remedy for each pest example. The system provides assistance to add these details by Pest Description Ranking. Here user can provide more than one text description document for specific crop pest, and the system ranks these documents by applying vector space model to documents. In vector space model, a document is represented conceptually as a vector of keywords extracted from the document. Along with keywords, its associated weights are also considered. Weights represent importance of the keywords in a document and within the whole document collection. The weights of keywords in a document vector can be determined in many ways. A common approach uses the TF-IDF method. So the weights already determined in earlier phases of implementation by applying TF-IDF technique are used.

TF-IDF technique assigns high weights to terms that appear frequently in a small number of documents in the corpus. A query vector is generated as a vector of keywords which are already added to crop ontology by an agricultural expert. Cosine measure is used to measure similarity between query vector and document keywords vectors. Cosine measure determines angle between keywords document vector and the query vector. The document with maximum similarity value is suggested as the best document to be used for adding symptoms, reasons and remedy for each pest example.

## 3.3 IPM Ontology Construction

The core techniques in IPM are biological, chemical, cultural and mechanical and physical IPM. For developing IPM ontology for a specific crop, one or more of these techniques should be mentioned as IPM Type for specific crop pest or disease.

IPM ontology can be developed from text descriptions of ontologies as mentioned above. CropPestOntoGenerator is a tool developed using Java language. For developing IPM ontology for any crop pest, the upper IPM ontology mentioned in Figure 3.9 is used. Ontology shown in Figure 3.10 is used as foundation ontology for any crop pest. Agricultural experts can derive various ontologies from foundation ontology of crop-specific IPM.

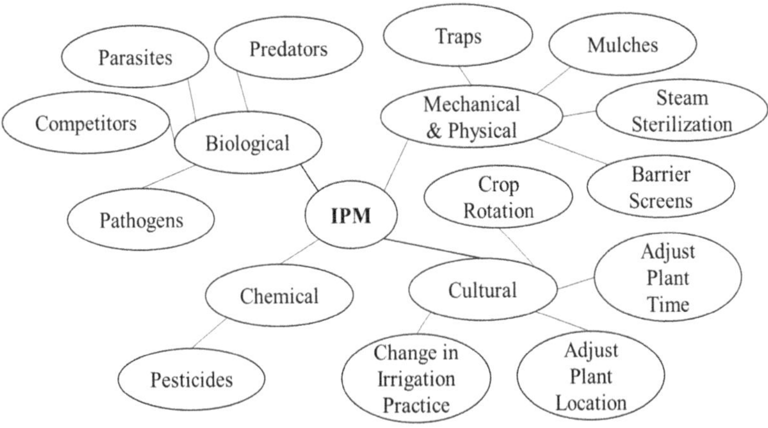


**FIGURE 3.9**
Foundation ontology for integrated pest management.

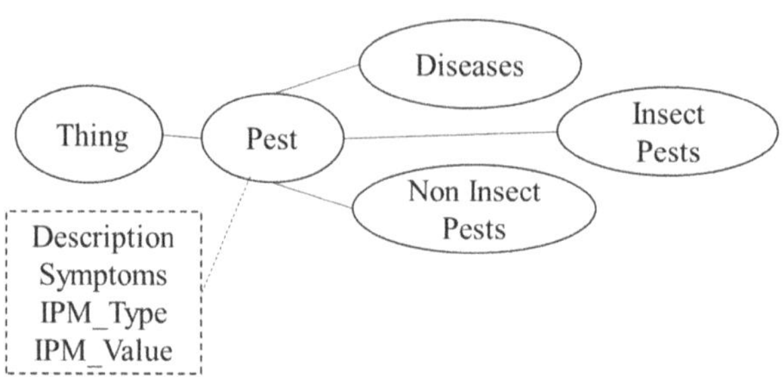


**FIGURE 3.10**
Foundation ontology for building IPM ontology.

These ontologies are then passed as input to IPMOntoShare for generating merged IPM ontology. The IPM ontology developed for grapes is named Grape-Pest-Management ontology.

For storing knowledge about management of pests and diseases on vineyards, Grape-Pest-Management ontology is used. The formal specification of concepts in any domain and the relationships between concepts can be accurately specified using ontology (T R Gruber et al., 1993). The Grape-Pest-Management ontology is developed using OWL (https://www.w3.org/OWL/). The concepts, attributes of concepts, hierarchies of concepts and attributes and individuals of concepts can be specified using OWL.

The protégé ontology editor is used for generating this ontology. Grape IPM ontology contains 20 classes, 208 individuals, 9 object properties and 41 data properties. The detailed information of each pest is mentioned in ontology. Information about each stage of pest development, i.e. egg, nymph and adult, is also described in detail. Figure 3.11 shows top-level concepts in Grape-Pest-Management ontology (http://www.ipm.ucdavis.edu/PMG/selectnewpest.grapes.html).

Pests and disease management of grapes is divided in two parts: first part is forecasting and precaution and the second part is disease identification and post treatment. Pest management knowledge like techniques, reasons, periods and in-detail methods of pest management are mentioned for all pests and diseases in Grape IPM ontology. The list of pesticides is specified as individuals of pesticide class and use of each pesticide for specific pest or disease is mentioned as object property assertion for pest management techniques under Pest-Management class.

Favorable conditions and damage symptoms for each pest and disease are also mentioned in the same ontology. It helps in forecasting and early diagnosis of pests or diseases. Based on forecasted pests, suitable IPM technique can be applied. Figure 3.12 shows relationships between concepts and properties. Characteristics of pests need to be mentioned for detection of pests.

**FIGURE 3.11**
Top-level concepts in Grape-Pest-Management ontology.

Properties of pests on grapes like features of nymphs, eggs and adults are mentioned as data properties in Grape IPM ontology. Table 3.2 lists these properties (Odile Carisse et al., 2009).

Occurrence of pests can be discovered by finding the damage symptoms of a particular pest. Table 3.6 lists the damage symptoms for pests on grapes. These symptoms are mentioned as values of symptoms data property of each pest individual in ontology.

The expert knowledge on precise techniques for pest management helps farmers to control pests with minimum use of pesticides. The detailed description of techniques for integrated pest management and post treatment of disease on grapes is mentioned in IPM ontology with the help of protégé editor. Table 3.7 contains examples of such IPM techniques.

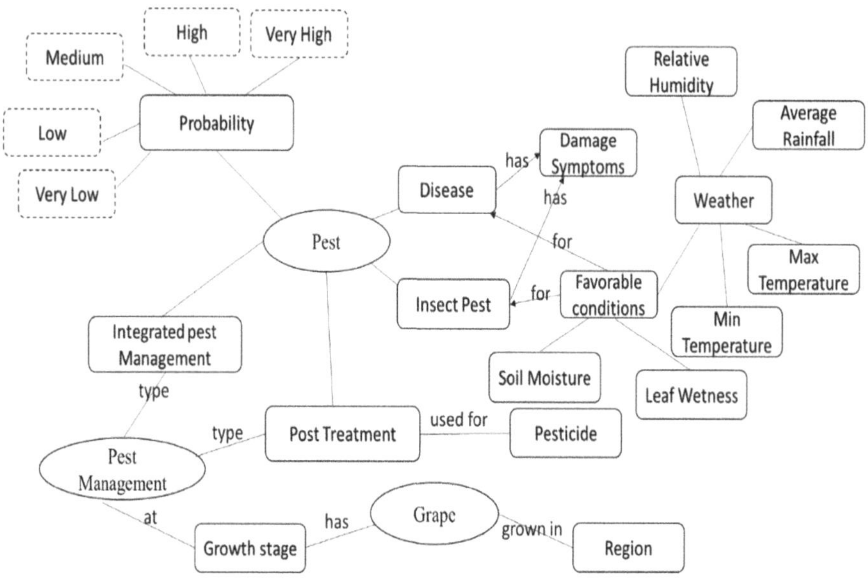


**FIGURE 3.12**
Pest and disease forecasting concepts and properties in Grape-Pest-Management ontology.

**TABLE 3.2**
Data Properties of Pests from Grape-Pest-Management Ontology

| Adult breed period | Egg hatch period |
|---|---|
| Adult color | Egg shape |
| Adult features | Larva color |
| Adult life period | Larva features |
| Egg color | Larva length |
| Egg count | Larva period |
| Egg features | Nymph features |
| Nymph period | Pupa color |
| Identity | Pupa location |
| Sex | Pupa period |
| Description | |

These descriptions are mentioned as property assertions in IPM ontology. Figure 3.13 is the snapshot of example property assertion entry in protégé editor.

The generated ontology contains content knowledge about all pests and diseases on grapes.

**TABLE 3.3**
Object Properties of Pests from Grape-Pest-Management Ontology

| hasDamageSymptoms | isGrownInRegion |
|---|---|
| hasGrowthStage | isPMTechniquesForGrowthStage |
| hasProbability | isPMTecniqueForPestType |
| isControlledBy | occursInPeriod |
| isFourableCiondiitonForPestType | usedChemicalsIn |

**TABLE 3.4**
Some Classes from Grape-Pest-Management Ontology

| Damage-Symptoms | Pupal-Parasitoids |
|---|---|
| Favorable-Conditions-For-Pests | Pest-Pathogens |
| Grape | Pest-Predators |
| Growth-Stage | Pest-Management |
| Month | IPM |
| Pest | Pest-Probability |
| Disease | Pesticides |
| Insect-Pest | Pesticide-Checklist |
| Pest-Parasites | PostTreatment |
| Pest-Parasitoids | Region |
| Egg-Parasitoids | Weather |
| Larval-Parasitoids | |

**TABLE 3.5**
Some Individuals from Grape-Pest-Management Ontology

| Anthracnose | Anab-E-Shahi | Beared-Root |
|---|---|---|
| Berry-Rot | Bangalore-Blue | Brown-Burnt-Patches |
| Powdery-Mildew | Flame-Seedless | Curling-Of-Leaves |
| Downy-Mildew | Gulabi | Defoliation |
| Fleabeetle | Manik-Chaman | Leaf-Bunches |
| Leafhopper | Manjiri-Naveen | Leaf-Folding |
| Mealybug | Sharad-Seedless | Ripening-Of-Bunches |
| Mites | Sonaka | Shoot-Tips |
| Stem-borer | Tas-A-Ganesh | Suck-The-Sap |
| Thrips | Thompson-Seedless | Scrap-Spouting-Buds |
| Budbreak | Dormant | Harvest |

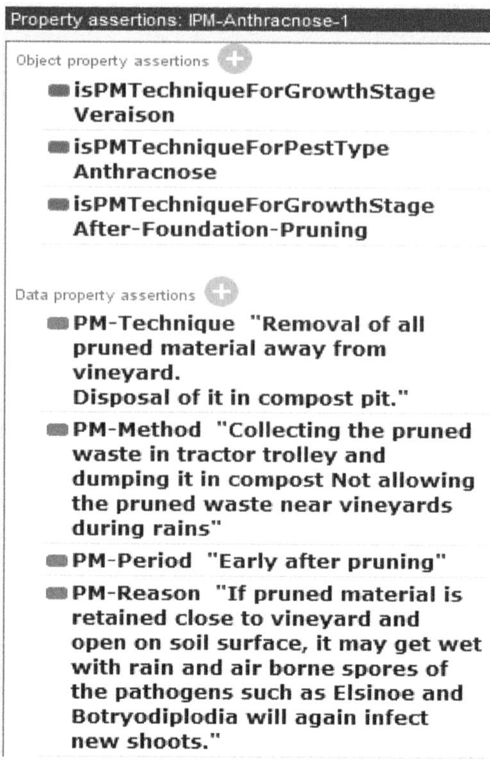


**FIGURE 3.13**
Example properties from Grape-Pest-Management ontology.

## 3.4 Evaluation of Grape-Pest-Management Ontology

Accuracy of Grape-Pest-Management ontology is checked by using it under decision support systems developed.

Pest keyword extraction algorithm is applied on around 100 documents, and precision and recall for the PKEA algorithm is calculated. Results of pest keywords extraction algorithm applied on six sample documents describing crop pests are given in Table 3.8.

Precision for PKEA is calculated as

$$\frac{\text{Precision} = \text{Retried keywords} * \text{Useful keywords}}{\text{Retried keywords}}$$

**TABLE 3.6**

Damage Symptoms of Pests from Grape-Pest-Management Ontology

| Name of Disease/ Pest | Symptoms |
|---|---|
| Downy mildew | Yellowish and oily or angular lesions<br>Yellow to reddish and brown limited by the veins |
| Flea beetle | Damaging of buds<br>Weathering of tender shoots<br>Scrap sprouting buds |
| Mealybug | Sucking of the sap<br>Shoot tips<br>Discoloration of leaves<br>Sooty mold on leaves, shoots and bunches<br>Leaf malformation |
| Mites | Brown burnt patches<br>Sucking of the sap<br>Ripening of bunches<br>Discoloration of leaves |
| Thrips | Sucking of the sap<br>Scab formation on berry surface<br>Corky layer on berries<br>Speckled silvery effect |

**TABLE 3.7**

IPM Techniques for Pests and Diseases from Grape-Pest-Management Ontology

| Name of Disease/ Pest | Technique |
|---|---|
| Anthracnose | Disposal of pruned material, Spray of Copper hydroxide 2.0 g/l, Ziram 27 SL, 4 l/ha |
| Downy Mildew | Use of Mancozeb 2 g/l, COC 3g/l, Copper hydroxide 2g/l, Captan 2g/l, Spray of Fosetyl Al 3g/l after 25 days of pruning, mixing of fungicide in GA solution, removal of dead wood, removal of shoots emerging from the crown near ground, spray of 1% Bordeaux mixture |
| Fleabeetle | Removing the loose bark, rubbing the stems with jute cloth, use of Chloropyriphos dust 10kg/ac, use of dry sheds of banana |
| Mealybug | Removal and destruction of loose bark and swabbing of stem and arms with 2 ml of Dichlorvos 76 E, use of sticky bands on main stem, removal of weeds and alternative host plants, management of ants using insecticides, use of Cryptolaemus montrouzieri 10000/ha/year during August–January |
| Powdery Mildew | Use of systemic fungicides like potassium bicarbonate 5g/l, Myclobutanil 0.4g/l, Hexaconazole 1ml/l, Tridemefon 1g/l, Use of non-systemic fungicides Dinocap 30ml/100l, Sprays of potassium sources |
| Stem Borer | Removal of grub, use of dichlorvos 2ml/vine, aluminum phosphide tablet 1/2 per vine |
| Thrips, Hoppers | Use of Endosulfan 35EC 2ml/ltr, Dimethoate 30EC 1ml/ltr, Thiamethoxam 25WG-0.25g/l, removal of weeds and host plants |

Recall for PKEA is calculated as

$$\text{Recall} = \frac{\text{Retried keywords} * \text{Useful keywords}}{\text{Useful Keywords}}$$

Average precision of CropPestOntoGenerator is 1.4 and average recall is 3.7. The algorithm is used for generating ontologies from 100 documents. Top hundred keywords from each document are retrieved. The number of useful keywords from each document is recorded. Improvement in the number of useful keywords as a result of adaptive algorithm is found. Improvement in results is shown in Figure 3.14.

**TABLE 3.8**

Results of PKEA Algorithm

| Doc Id | Retrieved keywords | Useful keywords | Keywords classified as pest examples | Keywords classified as pest types |
|---|---|---|---|---|
| 1 | 250 | 88 | 34 | 54 |
| 2 | 300 | 101 | 45 | 56 |
| 3 | 159 | 75 | 28 | 47 |
| 4 | 88 | 40 | 19 | 21 |
| 5 | 274 | 79 | 27 | 52 |
| 6 | 311 | 121 | 56 | 65 |

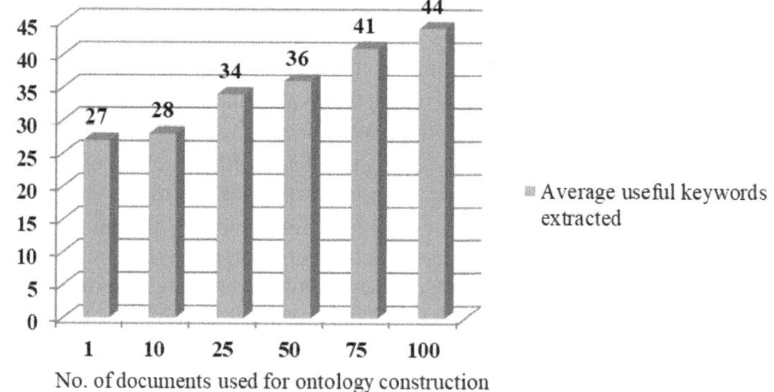


**FIGURE 3.14**
Improvement in the number of useful keywords extracted.

## 3.5 Conclusions

Ontologies play a major role in Semantic Web. It is an easy way to represent knowledge in various languages. Hence, representing agricultural knowledge in terms of ontologies is important. The system described in this chapter called CropPestOntoGenerator serves this purpose. Using natural language processing techniques, the system assists an agricultural expert to generate hierarchy of pests for a particular crop and also to identify pest examples of a specific crop type. With CropPestOntoGenerator, the agricultural expert does not need to know anything about ontologies. Using GUI provided by CropPestOntoGenerator, the agriculture expert just has to fill in details about pest types, pest examples and reasons, symptoms and remedy for pest examples. Assistance for filing this information is provided by extracting knowledge from text descriptions of pests provided by the agricultural expert. With CropPestOntoGenerator, it is demonstrated that using NLP techniques and specific representation capability of OWL, knowledge with experts can be converted into structured format and provided to farmers in various ways.

# 4

# *Knowledge Bases: Making It All Together*

## 4.1 Introduction

While building ontology, viewpoints of developers can be different. To support sharing of IPM ontologies developed by various agricultural experts, ontology merging is required. Creating a new ontology from two source ontologies is known as ontology merging. IPM ontologies developed by distinct agricultural experts can be integrated together to enrich knowledge base of IPM practices for a specific crop. The research work introduces here IPMOntoShare, a system for mapping and merging two IPM ontologies. Comparison of similarity of concepts at each level of ontology is discussed in detail.

### 4.1.1 Literature Survey

Several approaches for ontology merging are proposed by various authors worldwide. This chapter discusses some of those approaches. An approach to ontology merging, using concept lattice technique under formal concept analysis, is provided by Shixiang Li et al. (2009). A matrix for ontology matching is defined. Matrix mentions similarity between instances, definition and structure of ontologies respectively. Assigning of weights to all these parameters for measuring similarity is proposed. Threshold value from user is taken for deciding similarity. Decision on similarity between two ontologies is taken based on threshold value and calculated similarity. The next step is to build concept lattice using concept lattice construction algorithm. Global ontology is generated using generated concept lattice. The relationships in ontologies are constructed as the last step.

Special notations for ontology merging, called Ontology Merging (OM) notations, are presented by Alma Delia Cuevas Rasgado and Arenas (2006). Ontology merging algorithm, where merging takes place automatically without user's intervention, is also presented. A list of labels to be used in ontology, which identifies the description of the concepts and relations among

DOI: 10.1201/9781003408253-5

them, is provided. In OM algorithm, similarity of concepts from two ontologies is measured. Similar concepts are added once to a new third ontology, and all differing concepts from both ontologies are added as new concept in third ontology. Relation similarity is also considered. For concepts which are synonyms of each other, COM algorithm of OM is used. Removal of nested relations is also discussed.

An ontology merging method based on WordNet is proposed by Hyunjang Kong et al. (2005). It is specifically developed for merging heterogeneous domain ontologies. In this work, sets of concepts are prepared. Equality of concepts is measured after that. WordNet Synset number is used for this purpose. They also measured values of sets of concepts using Jaccord coefficient and subclass relationships using most-specific-parent method. Hypernym and hyponym relations are checked for using PTR field in WordNet. Hierarchy is reconstructed based on the measurements.

Target-driven merging of ontologies is proposed by Salvatore Raunich and Rahm (2011). An attempt is made to save the structure of target taxonomy. The approach is based on equivalence matching between a source taxonomy and target taxonomy for merging. An integrated concept graph is used to adapt and extend properties of merged taxonomy. Multiple inheritance is supported with is-a relationship. The integrated concept graph of two participating ontologies is created, cycles are removed if any and then source and target edges are translated to remove redundancy.

Use of machine learning techniques for ontology merging is discussed by Bartley Richardson and Mazlack (2005). Use of hierarchical clustering algorithm for ontology learning and use of Bayesian theorem, cosine and KL divergence functions is discussed in the paper. Threshold value for cosine similarity computation is taken from user. Existence of thesaurus is assumed for each ontology. Thesaurus is used to understand relations between terms. Decision to merge ontologies is based on probability computed by Bayesian theorem. Only similar concepts are merged and different terms are preserved separately in newly created ontology.

An algorithm for merging domain ontologies using description logic and augmented description graph is proposed by Rajesh Kumar Gupta and Chaudhary (2009). Ontology concepts are divided in TBOX and ABOX constructs. Named instances and values of attributes are used to resolve mismatches. Mapping rules are defined to map TBOX and ABOX constructs to graphs. For merging description graphs, they are mapped to three relational tables containing concepts, instances, attribute names, values and types.

Julia M. Taylor et al. (2005) mention a combination of lexical, semantic and rule-based methods that can be used for ontology merging. Name similarity and syntactic string similarity is calculated for lexical matching. For semantic matching, OpenCyc and WordNet are used for finding synonyms.

Simple Hearst patterns and propositional formulae are used for rule-based matching. The concepts are merged only if the similarity value is above a user-defined threshold.

Similar approach is mentioned by Guanyu Li (2010). Detailed algorithms for ontology merging, attribute merging, relation merging and superclass merging are explained in the paper. Rules are also defined for handling conflicts. Sigmoid function is used for smoothing weighted similarity calculations.

According to Sanjay Kumar Malik et al. (2010) Prompt plug-in available with protégé can be used for ontology merging. Semi-automatic approach of ontology merging is used under Prompt. Detailed process used under Prompt is described in the paper. Inconsistencies are identified and reported to user by prompt plug-in. Merging of ontologies is done at the level of classes, slots, facets and instances. Information about types, approaches, tools, techniques and co-ordination of ontology merging is detailed in the paper.

Clustering technique for merging multiple ontologies is proposed by Fabiana Freire de Araujo et al. (2010). Unsupervised and hierarchical approach of clustering is used here. Similarity matrix by matching classes and properties is generated. From similarity matrix two ontologies with highest degree of similarity are considered. After carrying out merging process, the newly constructed ontology is added under similarity matrix and the similarity calculation is repeated.

Ontology merging system based on semantics named DKP-O is developed by Muhammad Fahad and Muhammad Abdul Qadir (2009). Concept name, data-type properties, object properties, parent concepts, child concepts and axioms are considered for syntactic similarity computation. Data and object properties, linguistic matching and synonym matching strategies are used for finding similarity between concepts. Consistency checking of ontology mappings by using ontology evaluation knowledge within the semantic knowledge of merging system is proposed here.

Fully automated ontology matching using upper ontologies is proposed by Viviana Mascardi et al. (2010). Three algorithms namely uo-match, structural-uo-match and mixed-match are implemented for ontology matching. SUMO-OWL as upper ontology is used for running experiments. The implementation is done using the Alignment API. Detailed evaluation of proposed algorithms along with experimental results is provided in the paper.

Computing similarity between ontologies using change weights semantic graph is put forward by Feng Yang and Steele (2009). They combined name-based and structure-based approach. They calculated name similarity matrix and used it as initial values for edges in change weights semantic graphs.

Petr Kremen et al. (2011) introduced OWL 2 ontology merging tool named OWLDiff. It is an open source and can be used as plug in with Protégé and

NeOn toolkit. Compatibility of mappings should be checked to reduce error in merged ontology. OWLDiff helps for syntactic, explanation-based and semantic comparison, merging and versioning of ontologies. Three scenarios for change in ontology are defined as refactoring, defining new terms and redefining existing terms. Merging of axioms is possible using OWLDiff.

Galois connection for deciding compatible and incompatible ontology mappings while merging them is described by Muhamad Aun Abbas and Berio (2014).

Approach for analysis and preservation of disjoint knowledge before actually merging two ontologies is provided by Muhammad Fahad et al. (2010). It helps to remove inconsistencies and conflicts among relations.

According to Alignment between ontologies to be merged can be done by using multiple knowledge bases (Mohammed Maree and Mohammed Belkhatir, 2015). Majority voting from multiple knowledge bases is considered for relations of type equivalence, specialization, generalization, disjointness and unknown. Both one-to-one and one-to-many relations are considered for merged concepts, relations, individuals and axioms. Jaro-Winkler distance function is used for finding equivalence relationship. Knowledge bases are enriched by adding missing concepts from merged ontologies that come from other knowledge bases.

Web service ontology merging is done by using concept lattice (Hong Xia et al., 2007). Capability matching algorithm is used for this purpose. Venn diagrams can be used for visualization of ontology merging process (Martin Eller, 2008). Parameter-based technique can also be used for ontology merging (Sabino Pariente Juarez et al., 2011). Classification of concepts can be done using classification tree and the tree can be used for ontology merging (Kai Yang and Robert Steele, 2009). Concept dimensions like named concepts, intersections, unions, complements and restrictions are used for mapping ontologies before merging.

## 4.2 IPM Ontology Merging with IPMOntoShare

This chapter describes stages of merging two candidate IPM ontologies developed by CropPestOntoGenerator. It is named IPMOntoShare. Here it is assumed that the two IPM ontologies developed by agricultural experts are for the same crop. In ontology merging process, upper IPM ontology shown in Figure 4.1 is considered as the basis of merging. The type of IPM for each crop pest is mentioned by agricultural expert.

As pest is the basic concept in ontologies generated by CropPestOnto Generator, ontology matching is performed at level of pest individuals. A top-down approach for ontology merging is adopted. So at stage 1, similarity

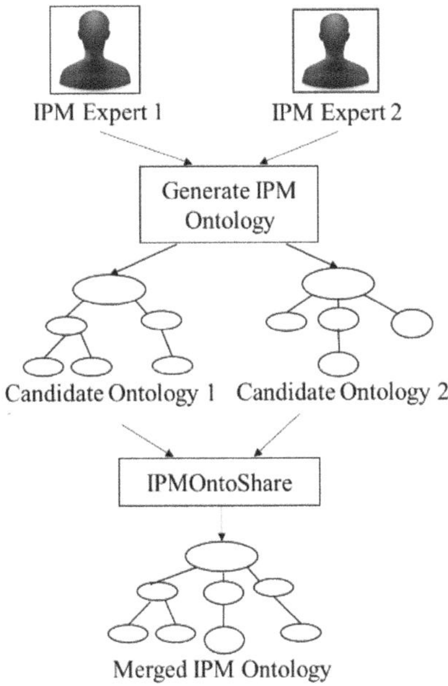


**FIGURE 4.1**
System flow of implemented approach.

matching is done by comparing at class level, i.e. comparing basic types of crop pests. At stage 2, comparison is done at individual level and at last stage 3, data properties and their values are compared. Details of each stage are as follows:

**Stage 1:** For comparison at class level, Semantic comparison of pest types is done by IPMOntoShare. Before checking for name similarity, each word in ontology is converted to its base form by using stemming algorithm. Porter's Stemmer is used for this purpose. If pest types have similar names, then it is represented as one node in merged IPM ontology. If names are different, then it is checked whether the two terms are synonyms with the help of AGROVOC and WordNet dictionary. Pest-type similarity computation is also done at structural level by using 'is-a' and 'is-part-of' relationships mentioned in candidate IPM ontologies.

**Stage 2:** At this stage of similarity computation, pest individuals of each pest type are compared using same technique mentioned above. If pest individuals are matching, then a single pest individual is added as leaf node under same pest type in IPM merged ontology, otherwise they are added as separate pest individual to common parent pest type. In formula 1, pest individual is represented as PI and P_Merge is crop pest type in merged ontology.

$$\text{If Sim}\left(PI_{1,} PI_2\right) == 1 \text{ then Add}\left(PI1, P\_Merge\right)$$

$$\text{Else Add}\left(PI1, P\_Merge\right) \text{AND Add} \left(PI2, P\_Merge\right) \tag{4.1}$$

**Stage 3:** Last stage is matching crop pest properties and their values. Properties of crop pests like IPM type, symptoms, growth stage are stored at leaf nodes of candidate ontologies. IPM type is compared for each candidate ontology generated by IPMOntoDeveloper. The IPM type is one of the IPM techniques mentioned in Upper IPM ontology. If type of IPM is matching then only IPMOntoShare proceeds to the next stage of matching, i.e. matching of symptoms. Pests have tendency to occur at specific development stages of crop. Matching of development stage of crop in which that pest occurs is also done. If all property values are matching then it is concluded that those pest individuals are similar as given in formula 2. To compare similarity at structural level, relationships like isCausedBy, hasSymptom, isAppliedRemedy are considered. In formula 2, 'S' represents pest symptoms, 'IT' represents IPM type for crop pest, 'D' is crop-development stage of crop in which that particular pest occurs and 'PI' is pest individual in candidate pest ontology.

$$\text{Sim}\left(PI_1, PI_2\right) = \text{Sim}\left(S_1, S_2\right) + \text{Sim}\left(IT_1, IT_2\right) + \text{Sim}\left(D_1, D_2\right) \tag{4.2}$$

All three stages mentioned above are followed iteratively to get final merged ontology. It is assured that all types and individuals of pests in candidate ontologies are preserved. Last step in IPM ontology merging process is checking and removing of any cycles present and removing of any repetition of pest individuals in resultant IPM ontology. This task is done manually by agricultural expert. Interface for verification and editing of merged IPM ontology is provided by IPMOntoShare.

## 4.3 Implementation and Evaluation

IPMOntoShare is developed using Java language. User friendly interfaces are provided to agricultural experts for easy development and merging of IPM ontologies.

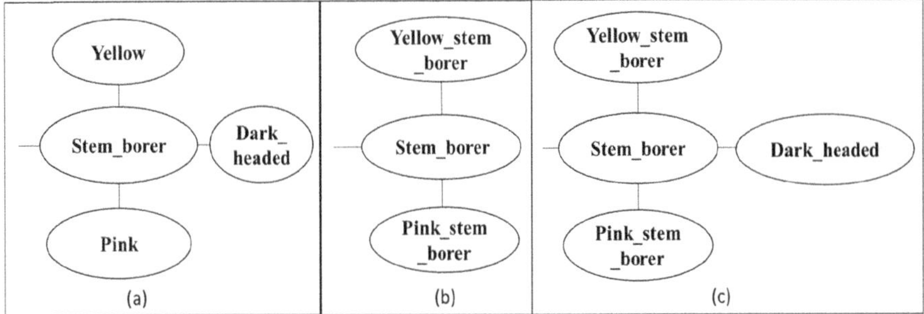


**FIGURE 4.2**
Merging at pest individual level (a) Rice IPM ontology by expert-1 (b) Rice IPM ontology by expert-2 (c) Merged rice IPM ontology generated by IPMOntoShare.

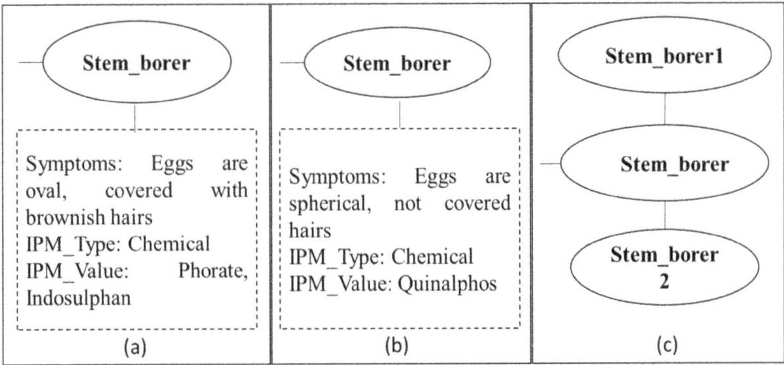


**FIGURE 4.3**
Merging at pest properties level (a) Rice IPM ontology by expert-1 (b) Rice IPM ontology by expert-2 (c) Merged rice IPM ontology by IPMOntoShare.

To analyze results of IPMOntoShare, two agricultural experts were asked to develop IPM ontology for pests on rice using IPMOntoDeveloper and then merge using IPMOntoShare. Parts of developed and merged ontologies are shown in Figures 4.2 and 4.3 to demonstrate stages of ontology merging by IPMOntoShare.

In Figure 4.2(a) Pest type Stem-borer has Dark_headed as pest individual in ontology by expert-1 and the same is not present in ontology by expert-2 as shown in Figure 4.2(b). Hence, it is added as separate pest individual in merged ontology as shown in Figure 4.2(c).

In Figure 4.3, Symptom and IPM_Value are different for pest individual Stem-borer. Hence, it is added as Stem-borer1 and Stem-borer2 in merged ontology as shown in Figure 4.3(c).

Performance of IPMOntoShare system illustrated more clearly with example of developing and merging IPM ontology for rice crop. The discussed approach helps agricultural experts to work with IPM ontologies effortlessly and saves their time to great extent.

## 4.4 Conclusions

As types of tools and techniques used for IPM are varying, representing IPM knowledge as ontology makes it possible to share IPM knowledge. This chapter described in detail how such ontology can be constructed. To integrate such various ontologies in a combined ontology for each crop, ontology merging process is discussed. This chapter demonstrates how ontology merging techniques can be utilized. Performance of IPMOntoShare system illustrated more clearly with example of developing and merging IPM ontology for rice crop. The discussed approach helps agricultural experts to play with IPM ontologies effortlessly and saves their time to a great extent.

# 5

# *PDMGrapes: Forecasting Occurrence of Pests on Grapes*

## 5.1 Introduction

To reduce loss of grape growers due to reduction in total production; production loss of grapes due to pests on grapes also should be controlled. As the proverb says, 'prevention is better than cure', in-advance forecasting of pest occurrence on vineyards can be a great help to grape growers. This chapter describes how pest occurrence can be forecasted using computerized system having knowledge base on pests and running machine learning algorithms.

### 5.1.1 Literature Survey

Computer Centre for Agricultural Pest Forecasting (CIPRA) is a popular software that can predict the development of pests and some post-harvest disorders based on hourly weather data. CIPRA includes forecast models which include 35 insect pest models, 14 disease models, 24 crop phenology models and 2 post-harvest physiological disorder models. All these models are available for 23 different crops.

Clima-rice (www.climarice.com) is a system for pest and disease forecasts on rice. It is based on weather forecasts specifically for paddy blast disease and paddy leaf mite pest.

DemiAg (www.demiag.com), expert system for agricultural pest management, is an open source system for providing forecasts for plant diseases. It is being developed by DeMilia Research LLC.

Research papers have been published proposing decision support systems and expert systems for various crops by researchers all over the world. Some of such systems are discussed here.

An online portal for agricultural ontology access was presented by Xiong Jinhui et al. (2010). They collected agricultural information from Web using distributed crawler. Collected information was used for generating OWL

DOI: 10.1201/9781003408253-6

classes. The paper explains mapping for ontologies for multiple languages. The OWL classes extracted from information were mapped with OWL classes provided by AGROVOC and new merged OWL classes were used as knowledge base. It was named AOS. Jena APIs and Pellet inference engine were used for answering questions from farmers.

Weather-based expert system for forecasting diseases on corn crop was proposed by Vidita Tilva, Jignesh Patel and Chetan Bhatt (2012). They used fuzzy logic technique for developing inference engine of expert system. They used temperature, humidity and leaf wetness duration as weather parameters for defining fuzzy rules to estimate plant disease. They defined five classes for input and output member functions as very high, high, medium, low and very low.

A decision support system for management of Powdery Mildew in grapes was developed by K Y Mundankar et al. (2007). They estimated disease risk by considering plant growth stage and weather conditions. All the details about weather conditions, field condition and plant growth stage were taken from end user through software interface. Expert system provides information regarding fungicide spray name and its dose for various fields and weather conditions.

An agent-oriented method for developing decision support system was adopted by Ann Perini and Angelo Susi (2003). They described software development phases as early requirement analysis, late requirement analysis, architectural design and implementation for integrated production in agriculture. They listed various actors in agriculture production and showed their relationship in architectural design.

An expert system for the diagnosis of pests, diseases and disorders in Indian mango was proposed by Rajkishore Prasad et al. (2005). They described development of a rule-based expert system using ESTA (Expert System Shell for Text Animation. The system is based on answers to questions taken from farmers regarding disease symptoms.

An expert system for pest and disease management of Jamaican coffee, known as CPEST, was developed by Gunjan Mansingh et al. (2007). It was built in wxCLIPS. Forward chaining was used as reasoning mechanism. They developed a rule base containing 150 production rules. CPEST has three stages for solving problem as general data-gathering phase, diagnosis and possible treatments and integration of treatments.

A rule-based expert system to diagnose honeybee pests was described by B D Mahaman et al. (2002) which can be used by beekeepers. It was implemented using EXSYS for Microsoft windows environment with backward chaining method.

A decision support system for pest management in Australian cotton systems was described by M P Bange et al. (2008). It can be used on handheld devices to collect data required for pest management from different locations.

An expert system for identification of pests, diseases and weeds in olive crops was provided by J L Gonzalez-Andujar (2009). The knowledge base was created using interviewing technique and represented using IF-THEN rules. The knowledge base contains information for the identification of 9 weed species, 14 insect species and 14 diseases.

An agent-based model for integrated pest management, by coupling a pest model with farmer behavior model, was developed by Francois Rebaudo and Olivier Dangles (2013). It is convinced in paper that passive IPM information diffusion is better than active diffusion.

Effectiveness of location aware system of pest management for olive fruit fly was investigated by (Costas m Potnikakos et al., 2012). The described system uses information regarding olive fruit fly, meteorological conditions and spatiotemporal details of spraying areas. Location aware system has client-server architecture and it utilizes web services, geographic information system, expert system and multimedia technology.

An intelligent system for disease and pest diagnosis and control of tomatoes in greenhouses, known as JAPIEST, was proposed by V Lopez-Morales et al. (2008). The system computes vapor pressure deficit to detect probable development of diseases on tomatoes. Graphical support is also provided with disease-detection results.

An integrated Web geographical information system for control of pests on olive-fruit fly was presented by Ioannis Karydis et al. (2013). They described how webGIS can be extended to provide temporal and/or spatial prediction on pests' life cycle and to suggest proposals on pests' life-cycle suppression. Pest life cycle was simulated and predictions were done on measurements provided as input. Temperatures, humidity, altitude, number of male and female pests were the measurements taken periodically and provided as input.

### 5.1.2 Using Fuzzy Logic Based Inference Engine

Out of two types of inference engines developed for pest forecasting, fuzzy logic based inference engine is described here. The probability of a particular pest is categorized as very low, low, moderate, high and very high. Probability of occurrence of some pests is more at specific growth stage of grapes.

Grape growth is divided in eight stages as delay dormant, bud-break period, rapid-shoot-growth period, and bloom-to-veraison period, veraison period, harvest period, post-harvest period and dormant period. For weather conditions, three membership functions of temperature are defined, namely 'Hot', 'Warm' and 'Cold'; membership functions for rainfall are defined as 'Heavy', 'Moderate' and 'Light'; and membership functions for humidity are defined as high, medium and low. Rules for forecasting probability of occurrence as well as spread of grape pests and diseases are defined (Figure 5.1).

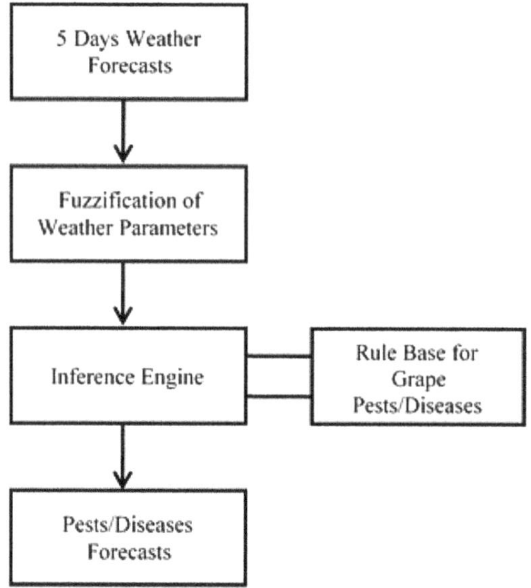


**FIGURE 5.1**
Flow of fuzzy inference engine for grape pests.

Following are some examples of rules for forecasting:

If Temperature IS Warm AND Humidity IS High AND Growth Stage IS Vegetation

Then Probability (Occurrence (Downy Mildew)) IS Very High

If Rainfall IS Moderate

Then Probability (Spread (Downy Mildew) IS Very Low

If Temperature IS Warm AND Growth Stage IS Bud-Break AND Humidity IS High

Then Probability (Occurrence (Mealy Bug)) IS Very High

If Temperature IS Hot AND Growth Stage IS Veraison AND Humidity IS Low

Then Probability (Occurrence (Mealy bug)) IS Low

Weather forecasts of weather station nearest to farmer's location are considered for pest forecasting. Details of minimum temperature, maximum temperature, rainfall and humidity are extracted from meteorology websites hosted by departments of government of India. Location-based weather data extraction is done by extracting longitude and latitude of farmer's location and then finding weather stations with closest co-ordinates to it.

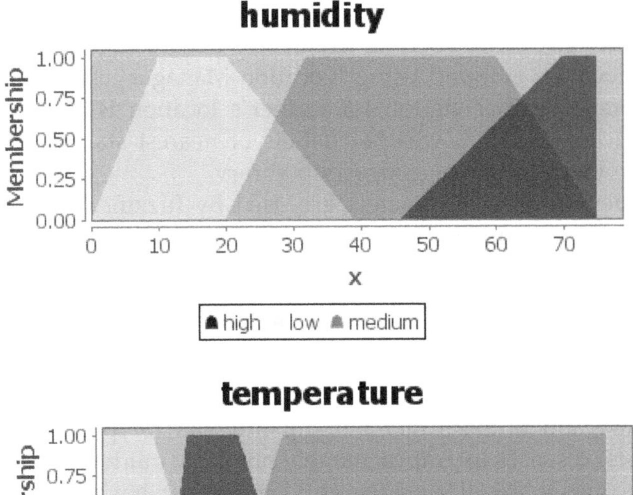


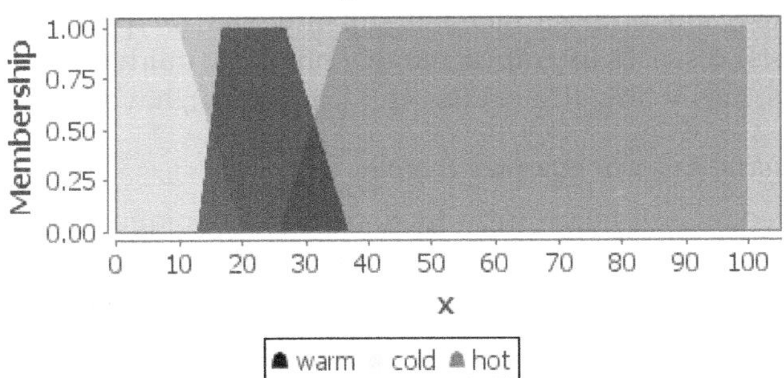


**FIGURE 5.2**
Membership functions for temperature and humidity.

#### *5.1.2.1 Implementation*

Details of tools and techniques used for implementation of decision support system are described here.

##### *5.1.2.1.1 jFuzzyLogic*

Fuzzy logic is a reasoning technique. It is used when parameters of decision making are fuzzy, i.e. not exact values but ranges are considered. jFuzzy-Logic is an open source framework developed in java for implementing fuzzy logic. It has functions to implement fuzzy control language. One can define membership functions, defuzzifiers, and fuzzy rules and use it in program using jFuzzyLogic. It is also possible to define parameterized functions with jFuzzyLogic. Eclipse plug-in is also available for jFuzzyLogic (Figure 5.2).

##### *5.1.2.1.2 JSOUP Library*

JSOUP is a library available in Java to work with HTML documents. One can traverse through HTML tags using DOM model. JSOUP API contains functions to extract required data from an HTML document. Both well-formed and rough HTML documents can be parsed using JSOUP.

Farmer's location is found using 'Location Manager' class from Android library. Nearest weather station for farmer's location is found from geographic coordinates. Then weather details of nearest station are extracted from meteorological website using jsoup library.

Exact values of these parameters are used by fuzzification module and appropriate member functions representing current weather conditions are derived. The system uses jFuzzyLogic open source library for developing inference engine. Fuzzy input variables defuzzify output variables. Rules are defined in fuzzy control language and stored in .fcl file. .fcl file is used for fuzzification.

Inference engine uses these membership functions and rules from grape pest rule-base and outputs membership function for pests. Rules for six types of pests/diseases in grapes, namely powdery mildew, downy mildew, anthracnose, mealy bug, flea beetles and leaf hopper, have been defined.

#### *5.1.2.1.3 Adding Rules to Inference Engine*

As mentioned in Section 5.1 'Introduction', IPM technique is decided considering environmental conditions. Probability of occurrence of particular pest changes with change in environmental conditions like rainfall, temperature and humidity and specific period of grape life cycle.

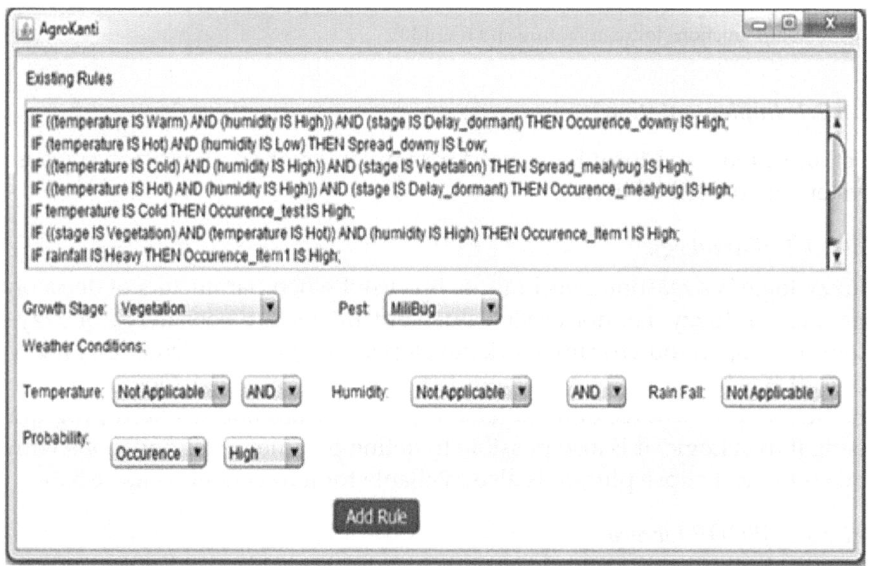


**FIGURE 5.3**
User interface for generating If-Then rules.

**FIGURE 5.4**
Grapes growth stages.

The relation between environmental changes and pests on grapes is studied and used for forecasting. These relations are entered as If-Then rules in the system. The user interface for entering these facts is shown in Figure 5.3. Figure 5.4 shows six growth stages of grapes. Weather details like temperature, humidity and rainfall are collected from website of Indian Meteorological Department. The information is accessed as JSON data using JSOUP library.

### 5.1.3 Semantic Web Rule Language

Semantic Web Rule Language (SWRL) is a rule mark-up language for OWL. It can be used to specify values of one object or data property based on values of other object and data properties in current OWL document. Any SWRL rule contains two parts as antecedent which is body of rule and consequent is a head of the rule. Specific syntax is followed to write SWRL rules. For example

$$\text{sister}(?q,?p) \wedge \text{parent}(?r,?q) \Rightarrow \text{mother}(?r,?p)$$

Favorable conditions for occurrence of pests and diseases are represented as Semantic Web Rule Language rules based on grape profile published by National Research Center for Grapes, India. Example rules are shown below.

1. Weather(?w) ^ Temperature(?w, ?t) ^ swrlb:lessThan(?t, 30) ^ swrlb: greaterThan(?t,20)^Disease(Powdery-Mildew)^Month(?m)^swrlb: member(?m, November, December, January, February, March) ➔ has Probability(Powdery-Mildew, High)
2. Weather(?w) ^ Temperature(?w, ?t) ^ swrlb:lessThan(?t, 36) ^ swrlb: greaterThan(?t, 25) ^ Relative-Humidity(?w, ?rh) ^ swrlb:greater Than(?rh, 90) ^ Insect-Pest(Thrips) ➔ hasProbability(Thrips, High)
3. Weather(?w) ^ Temperature(?w, ?t) ^ swrlb:lessThan(?t, 40) ^ swrlb: greaterThan(?t,24)^Relative-Humidity(?w,?rh)^swrlb:greaterThan (?rh, 90) ^ Insect-Pest(Mealybug) ^ Month(?m) ^ swrlb:member (?m, November, December, January, February, March) ➔ has Probability(Mealybug, High)
4. Weather(?w) ^ Temperature(?w, ?t) ^ swrlb:lessThan(?t, 27) ^ swrlb: greaterThan(?t, 23) ^ Disease(Anthracnose) ^ ➔ hasProbability (Anthracnose, High)
5. Weather(?w) ^ Temperature(?w, ?t) ^ swrlb:lessThan(?t, 33) ^ swrlb: greaterThan(?t, 16) ^ Disease(Downy-Mildew) ^ ➔ hasProbability (Downy-Mildew, High)

### 5.1.4 Extending Ontology

Along with forecasting of grape pests and diseases, mechanism is provided to extend the ontology by converting SWRL rules to ontology classes and attributes and adding it to ontology.

For example, from rule number 1 mentioned above, the new Individual will be added to class 'Favorable-Conditions-For-Pests' as 'FC-Powdery-Mildew-1'. Temperature and month values will be added as data property values. If any variable in antecedent part of rule is not data property of the class, then the new data property is created and value is assigned for that specific Individual.

### 5.1.5 Sensor Ontology

Many solutions are available for sensing environmental parameters. For using environmental readings for decision support, sensors need to be boarded on fields and be connected to computerized systems for measurement recording and manipulation. Arduino is an open-source platform for implementing wireless sensor networks. Using Arduino microcontroller, sensor inputs are read and sent to server using some connectivity technique like Wi-Fi, Zigbee or GPRS. Programs can be written to read inputs and to

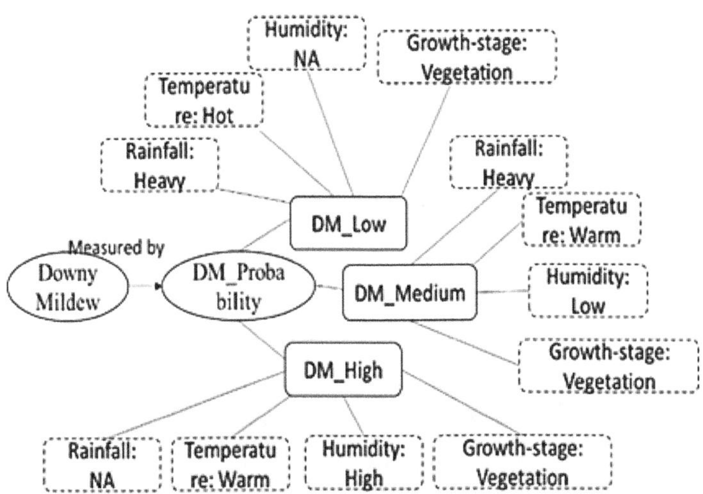


**FIGURE 5.5**
Extending ontology from rule-base.

**FIGURE 5.6**
ESP8266 Wi-Fi module.

write outputs to connected devices using Arduino IDE. Instructions can be sent on microcontrollers of Arduino kit to get the work done.

ESP8266 is a Wi-Fi module which can be used for transferring sensor outputs to server machines through GPRS or Zigbee. It can be mounted on Arduino microcontroller and programmed using AT commands. Figure 5.6 shows ESP8266 Wi-Fi module.

For sensing moisture in soil, soil moisture sensor can be used. Figure 5.7 is the soil moisture sensor used in this research.

As IoT is key player in precision agriculture, use of sensors is inevitable (Antonio-Javier Garcia-Sanchez et al., 2011). Some pesticides should be applied in the presence of soil moisture. The developed system uses soil

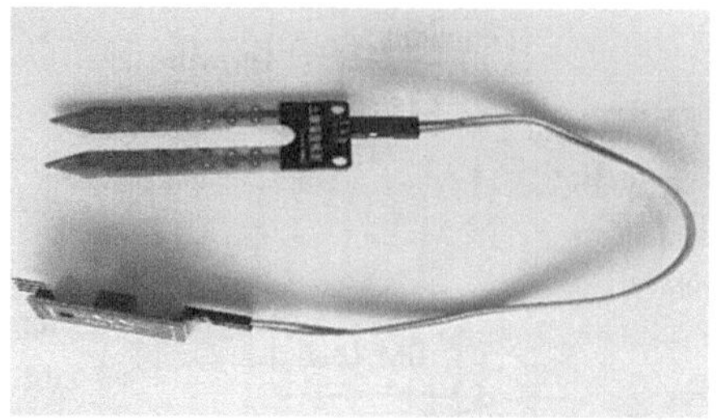

**FIGURE 5.7**
Soil moisture sensor.

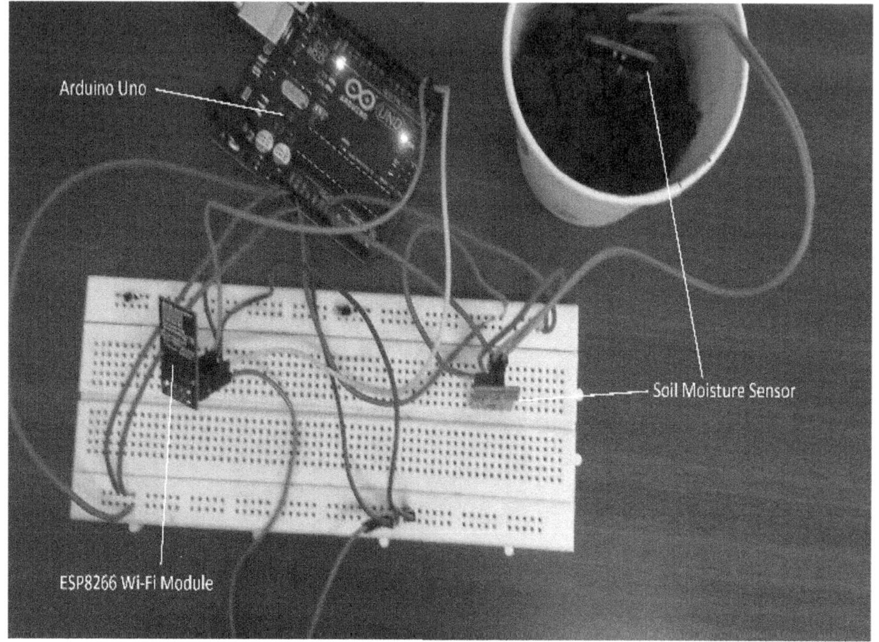


**FIGURE 5.8**
Arduino + ESP8266 Wi-Fi Module for sending soil moisture readings to PDMGrapes server.

moisture sensors on grape fields. Four basic steps are followed as sensing, networking, analyzing and application (Ciprian-Radu Rad et al., 2015). On-field sensor nodes having sensors deployed on Arduino UNO kits are deployed in grape farms; each node having soil moisture sensor and ESP8266 Wi-Fi module. Sensor measurements are collected on hourly basis. Data is collected on base station computer using Wi-Fi. Experimental design of module is shown in Figure 5.8. Collected data is sent to PDMGrapes server using 3G internet connection.

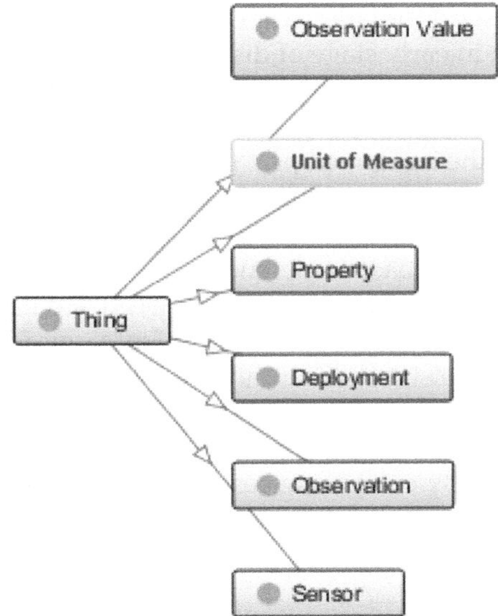


**FIGURE 5.9**
Classes in sensor ontology for soil moisture sensors information.

Data collected from sensors is stored in observations database. To use it along with pest management ontology, this information is converted to ontology. Semantic sensor network (SSN) ontology has become a standard for storing sensor data as ontology. So the sensor data collected here is mapped to SSN ontology.

Classes and attributes mentioned by incubator group are used for this purpose. Mapping rules are defined explicitly. Unique identification of sensor, type of sensor, location of sensor, sensor's measurement unit, sensor observation time and value are stored in ontology.

Classes from SSN ontology like Sensor, Property, Deployment, UnitOf Measure, Observation and ObservationValue are used for this purpose. Information available in SSN ontology about soil moisture is used to advise grape grower about pesticide to be used in the presence of soil moisture.

### 5.1.6 Conclusions

The chapter describes development of decision support system for controlling pests and diseases on grapes specifically in hot tropical region of India. It demonstrates use of ontology for maintaining knowledge about integrated pest management and treatment of diseases on grapes. Such ontology is the efficient way to represent, share and evolve knowledge in any agricultural sector. Use of image processing techniques for identification of disease from remote location is useful for large grape wine yards. It also helps farmers to take remedial action in early stage of disease and minimize use of fungicide. It is discussed how diseases on grapes can be identified using image processing technique.

It is observed that the integrated pest management using decision support system minimizes environmental loss and improves export quality of grapes as use of agrochemical can be reduced with such system. Examples of rules to be used by fuzzy logic based inference engine are discussed here. Use of SWRL for incorporation of relationship between environment and grape pest is discussed. Use of concepts from SSN ontology for storing information collected by soil moisture sensors adds to semantic content of grape pest management.

The experimental results show satisfactory results on pest forecasting and disease identification. By comparing results from DSS with expert's knowledge and farmer's experience, it is concluded that system provides forecasting with satisfactory accuracy.

## 5.2 Disease Detection on Grape Crop

### 5.2.1 Introduction

Use of image processing technique for agricultural decision support system is unavoidable. It can be used under all fields mentioned in the motivation. For quality management of pests and diseases on grapes, along with forecasting, detection and remedy of diseases is equally important. Corrective action taken in time helps a lot to grape grower. An attempt is made in this work to detect diseases using image processing techniques. Basic image processing steps are shown in Figure 5.10. First image to be processed is acquired using camera. It is then pre-processed to remove any noise if it exists and to enhance the quality of image. Image is then partitioned into segments by using one or more image features as color, texture and intensity. These features can be used under edge detection, thresholding, clustering or histogram-based methods. As color and texture of grape leaves changes because of disease, the leaf images can be processed for detection of color and text transformations. Machine learning techniques like K-nearest neighbor classification, K-means clustering, Bayesian network and artificial neural networks can be used here.

In this work, leaf image is categorized into one of the disease types using multi-class support vector machine. Support vector machine is a classification technique used for classifying unclassified data in one of the classes based on attribute values. SVM finds maximum separating hyperplane

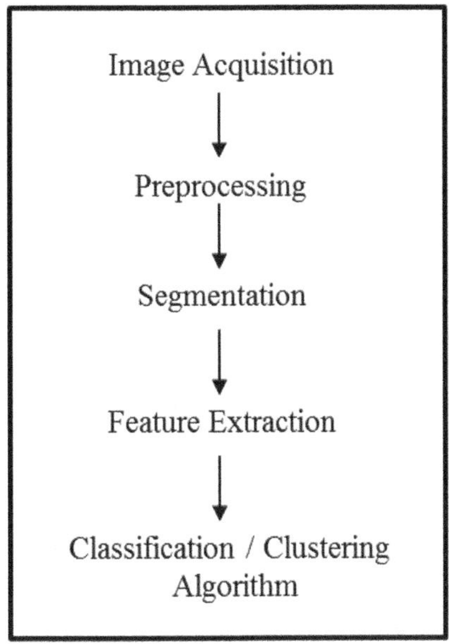


**FIGURE 5.10**
Basic leaf image processing steps.

between two classes. Kernel density functions are used for using SVM as multi-class classifier.

### 5.2.2 Literature Survey

Many approaches are proposed by researchers to detect diseases on crops using image processing techniques namely original data-based query, use of perceptual hash algorithm or hamming distance, color-based retrieval, color histogram, shape-based retrieval, texture-based retrieval and content-based multi-feature retrieval. Techniques used by researchers are reviewed in this chapter.

Detection of six types of wheat diseases is done using support vector machine (SVM) (Punnarari Siricharoen et al., 2016). It is a mobile system developed using Android and openCV. System first rotates captured image using 2-D Discrete Fourier transform. It also allows for manual rotation of image. Background is removed using crop interface and then interested features are extracted. Three types of features, namely texture, color and shape, are used. Under texture features, local homogeneity and local linear-dependency measures, contrast and entropy are considered. These features are derived from co-occurrence matrix. Cr component from YCbCr is used for color feature extraction. Mean standard deviation and skew-ness is measured from histogram of intensity values. Otsu thresholding is applied to

Cb and Cr components to extract disease areas from main leaf. Contours of disease patches are extracted using two shape features as elongatedness and hydraulic radius. After extracting all nine features, support vector machine is used initially to remove non-disease leaves and then to predict disease on leaf.

Disease detection by segmenting image using histogram analysis can also be done (J. G. A. Barbedo, 2016). The rules are formed based on H channel from HSV transformation and A channel from L*a*b* transformation to distinguish healthy pixels from disease pixels. Detection of borer in tomato image is done by defining threshold values for Y, Cb and Cr (Prathibha G P et al., 2014). Leaf image is converted from RGB to HIS. Then spatial gray-level dependence matrix is used and masking of green pixels is done for detection of disease on grape leaf (Pradnya Narvekar et al., 2014).

Use of deep learning technique for counting moths from trap images is done (Weiguang ding, Graham Taylor 2016). Convolution neural network is used as classifier under sliding window approach. Detection of powdery mildew, downy mildew, black rot and leaf roll is done using back propagation neural network.

Energy, entropy, cluster shade, cluster prominence and correlation are the features extracted from image and stored as gray-level co-occurrence matrix (Nivedita Kakade, Dnyaneshwar Ahire, 2015).

Efforts are taken by various researchers to detect pests and diseases by processing crop images for various crops like maize (Ding and Taylor, 2016). Techniques based on data, color, shape, texture or context features of images are used for pest and disease diagnosis. Hamming distance is considered in data-based technique whereas color space histograms are matched in color-based retrieval (Wang Zhi-jun et al., 2014). In shape-based methods, edges and region are considered. For edge extraction, Canny, Robert, Prewitt, Sobel or Wavelet operators can be used. One of the statistical, structural, model-based method, space method or frequency domain analysis method can be used for texture-based image analysis. Combination of multiple features is mostly used for pest and disease detection from image. After feature extraction, one of the classification or clustering techniques can be used for disease detection. e.g. artificial neural networks (Weiguang and Graham, 2016, P. Boniecki et al., 2015, Karlos Espinoza et al., 2016, Sachin D. Khirade et al., 2015), spatial gray-level dependence matrices (Wang Zhi-jun et al., 2014), fuzzy logic (SS Sannakki et al., 2011, Archana Chougule et al., 2016), Bayesian decision theory (Jing-Lei Tang et al., 2016) and SGDM matrix (Pradnya Ravindra Narvekar et al., 2014).

### 5.2.3 Disease Detection Using Image Processing Techniques

Image processing techniques can be used for the identification of diseases on crops from remote location. By capturing crop image, basic image processing

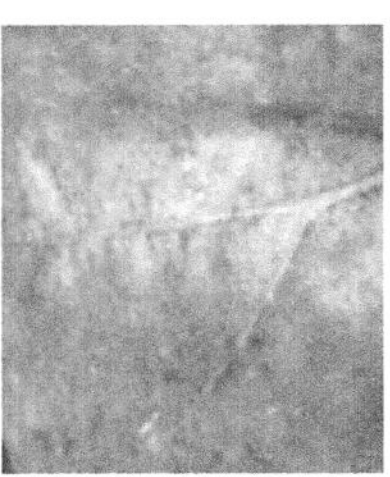

**FIGURE 5.11**
Effect of diseases on grape leaves.

steps can be applied and then one of the machine learning techniques can be used for disease identification.

Detection of three types of grape diseases by PDMGrapes is done by processing images of grape leaves. Occurrence of diseases causes appearance of different symptoms on grape leaves like change in color and texture of leaf. Occurrence of disease on grape can be detected by processing images of grape leaves.

Detection of three major diseases on grapes, namely anthracnose, powdery mildew and downy mildew, is provided. Images of leaves are captured using smart phone camera by grape grower and uploaded for disease detection using 'PDMGrapes' – farmer's app on smart phone. As the image is captured under uncontrolled light conditions, it contains noise. Further processing of image is done on server side.

Two separate databases of images are maintained for training and testing. Training database contains already stored images of diseases and second database is of captured images to be tested for disease occurrence. Disease detection is carried out using the following steps:

**Step 1:** The captured image is preprocessed for removing noise and improving color contrast. Noise is removed using Fourier filtering.

**Step 2:** The leaf is segmented from background using histogram thresholding on green pixels.

**Step 3:** Histogram equalization is done using cumulative distribution function for enhancing the image. Image intensities get distributed and contrast is enhanced from local to higher. Histogram of the output image becomes uniform.

**Step 4:** Image is segmented using k-means clustering algorithm. Value of K is set to three. Euclidean distance metric is used as distance measure. Each pixel in the image is assigned to the cluster that minimizes the distance between the pixel and the cluster center. As leaf color changes because of disease infection, green pixels are considered first. Pixels with intensity less than threshold are removed. The threshold is calculated using Otsu's method. Interesting features are then extracted from image. Luminosity and chromaticity layers of image are used for k-means clustering. For this purpose, image is converted from RGB color space to L*a*b color space. After creating clusters, cluster containing features of interest is selected and converted to gray scale. Gray-level co-occurrence matrix is constructed.

**Step 5:** Gray-level co-occurrence matrix is used for feature calculation which works on spatial relationships between pixels. Features like entropy, standard deviation, contrast and correlation are used here.

**Step 6:** Using features of training images and query image features under support vector machine, query image is classified in one of the disease category or it is labeled as healthy leaf. Multiclass SVM classification is used here.

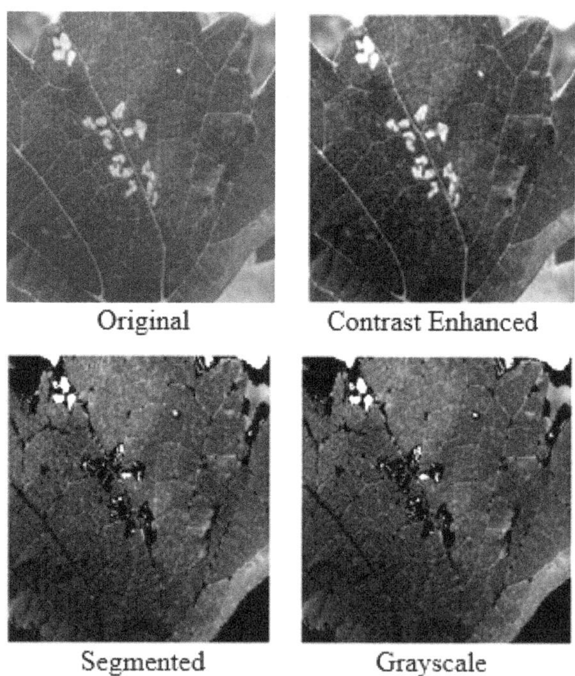


**FIGURE 5.12**
Grape leaf image segmentation by K-means clustering.

Detected disease is intimated to the farmer. All details of the disease are extracted from IPM ontology and provided to the farmer. For each grape disease, 100 training images are captured and saved in database. The proposed approach can also be extended to detect diseases on stems of plants.

### 5.2.4 Implementation and Analysis

This subsection describes tools used and performance evaluation for the implementation of disease detection using image processing.

#### *5.2.4.1 OpenCV*

Open source computer vision library has so many image processing functions. It supports many languages including C, C++, Python and Java. Java language is used in current research. Functions for all steps in image processing like image reading, smoothing, noise removal, thresholding and classification/clustering are supported by OpenCV.

Accuracy of disease detection using image processing technique was tested for all three diseases. The accuracy cannot be guaranteed to 100% as images are captured from smart phone cameras in uncontrolled environment. Images captured in controlled environment can give much better results. Table 5.1 shows confusion matrix for 15 images classified as one of the three diseases or as unaffected leaf. It can be concluded from confusion matrix that multiclass support vector machine gives most accurate results for the detection of powdery mildew disease. The precision values for powdery mildew, downy mildew and anthracnose are 73.33%, 60% and 46.66%, respectively. Farmers who experimented the use of PDMGrapes mentioned that the use of fungicides on grape fields for pest management is reduced to some extent; information provided on pests and diseases was useful, but accuracy of pest forecasting is not much.

**TABLE 5.1**
Confusion Matrix of Disease Detection using Image Processing

| | | Predicted | | | |
|---|---|---|---|---|---|
| | | Powdery Mildew | Downy Mildew | Anthracnose | Unaffected |
| Actual | Powdery Mildew | 11 | 02 | 0 | 02 |
| | Downy Mildew | 04 | 09 | 00 | 02 |
| | Anthracnose | 01 | 06 | 07 | 01 |
| | Unaffected | 00 | 00 | 00 | 15 |

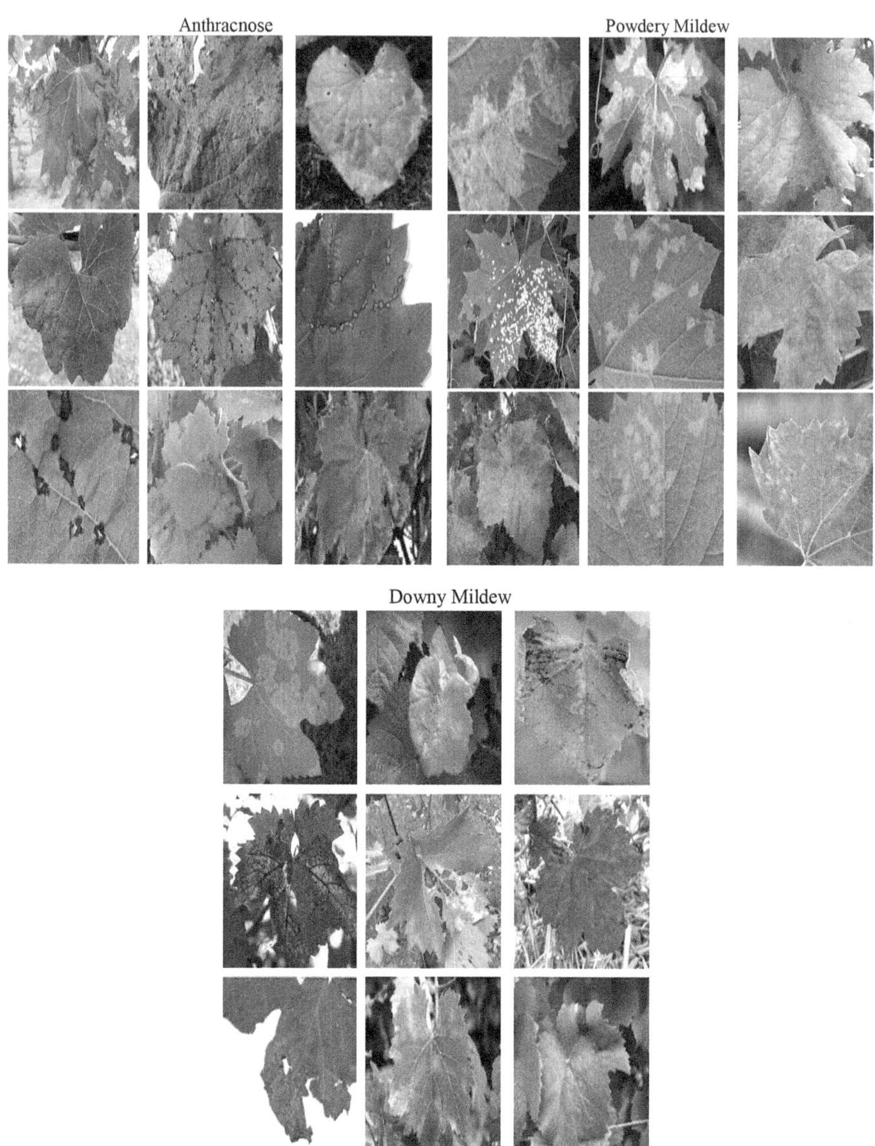


**FIGURE 5.13**
Sample leaf disease images used for training SVM.

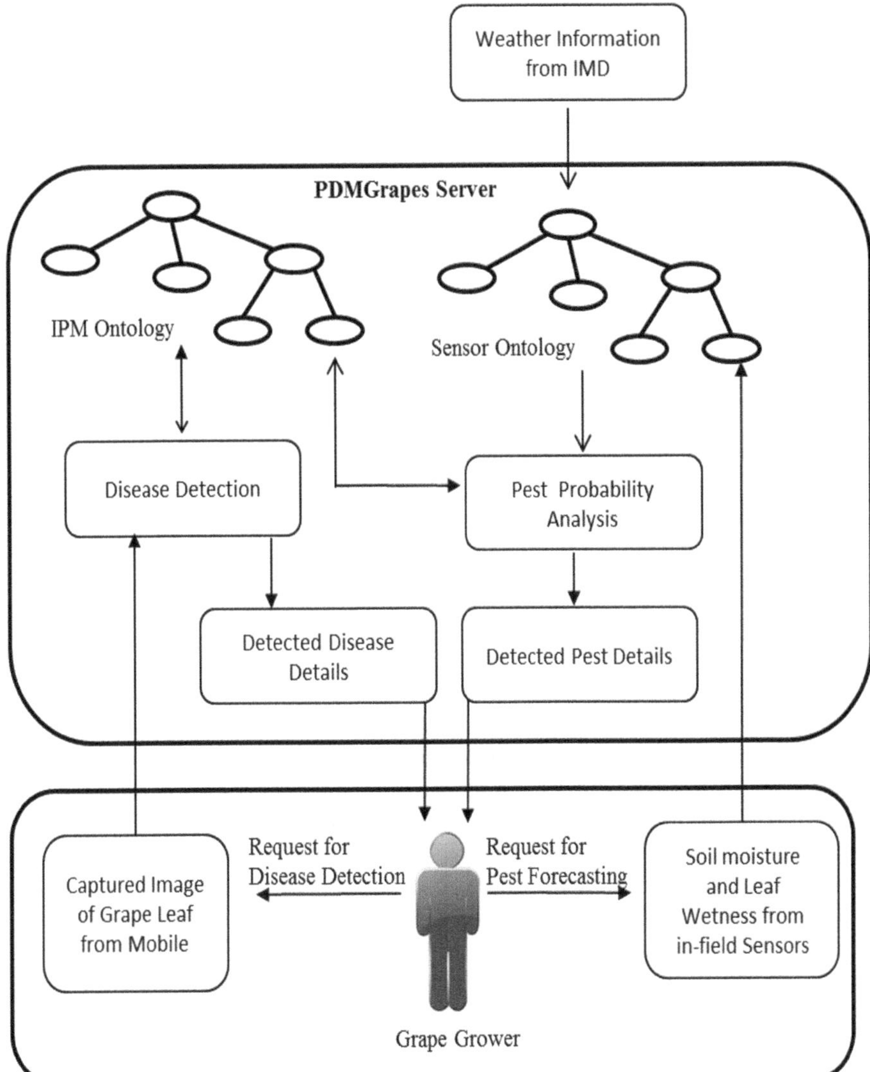


**FIGURE 5.14**
General architecture of PDMGrapes.

### 5.2.5 Pest and Disease Management Using PDMGrapes

PDMGrapes is an integrated decision support system which includes pest forecasting and disease detection as described in previous chapters. A grape grower interacts with PDMGrapes using Android-based application shown in Figure 5.16. The grape grower can ask for probable occurrence

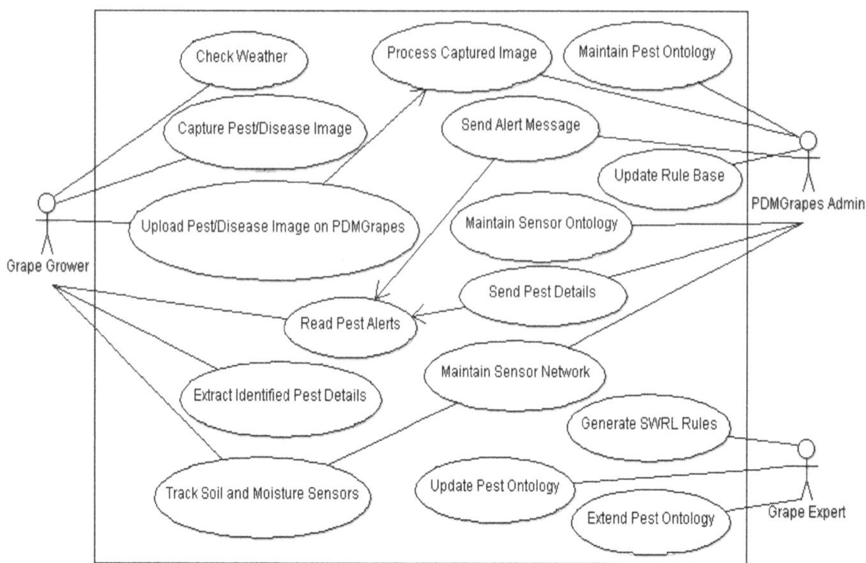


**FIGURE 5.15**
Use cases for PDMGrapes.

of pest/disease by selecting his location. Using data stored in IPM ontology and SWRL rules, occurrence of pest is forecasted to farmer. It is sent as an alert message on mobile application. The grape grower can capture image of doubtful grape leaf from smart phone and upload to PDMGrapes. PDMGrapes will reply if one of the diseases mentioned above is detected or it will return it as healthy leaf.

Using knowledge stored in ontology described in previous chapters, the decision support system is developed for forecasting of probable occurrence of pests and diseases and identification of diseases on grapes. Figure 5.14 shows general architecture of the developed decision support system. Figure 5.15 shows use cases of PDMGrapes. PDMGrapes works as follows:

Pest Forecasting:

1. Grape grower sends request to system for forecasting occurrence of probable pests.
2. Server extracts weather details from website of Indian meteorological department. Server analyses it in two ways:
   a. Using SWRL rules for probability of occurrence of any pest
   b. Using fuzzy logic based inference engine

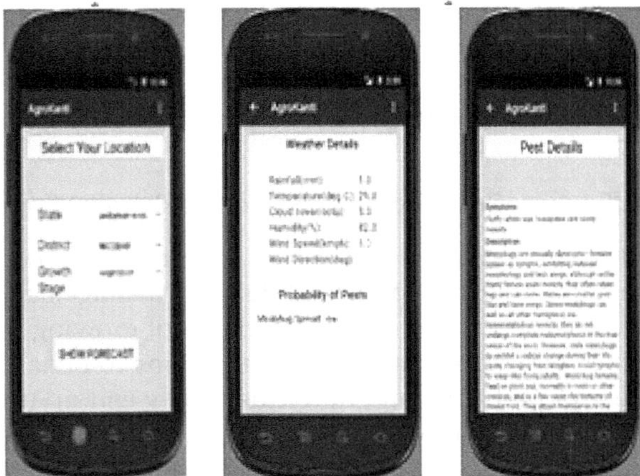


**FIGURE 5.16**
Android-based smart phone application for grape growers.

3. IPM details of probable pests are extracted from IPM ontology and provided to grape grower. If recommended pesticide needs presence of soil moisture then soil moisture status is extracted from soil sensor ontology and intimated to grape grower.

Disease detection:

1. Grape grower captures image of grape leaf using smart phone and sends it to PDMGrapes server through Android app.
2. Received image is processed on server for disease detection.
3. If disease is detected on grape leaf, then grower is provided with details of detected disease. Details are extracted from IPM ontology stored on server.

### 5.2.6 Smartphone App

#### *5.2.6.1 Android Studio*

Applications to work on Android-based smart phones can be developed using Android Studio. Android is java-based language and contains functions required specifically for mobile applications. Interface design, development and simulation of Android applications are possible using Android studio. It is available for free. Sample codes, emulators and testing tools are available in Android Studio framework. Providing access of any decision support system available on server to end users on their smart phones is possible through Android apps. Android Studio 2.2.1 is used for developing farmer's interface to PDMGrapes.

### 5.2.7 Existing Practice versus Developed Decision Support System

In India, traditional approaches are used by most of the farmers for agriculture management. Specifically, pests and diseases management depends on farmer's awareness, observations and experience of growing that particular crop. Many times farmers do not know precautions to be taken for avoiding excessive use of pesticides and fungicides. They end up using excessive chemicals which affect quality of grapes and in turn affect human health. Sometimes exported grapes get rejected due to chemical residue above specified threshold. For finding new updates on agricultural practices, farmers in India watch television shows, use telephone services provided by government of India, magazines and communication with other expert farmers. But on field, location aware systems for precision agriculture are rarely used by farmers in India.

For storing and using the expert knowledge, traditional approaches like article publications and relational databases are used. Hence, the expert's knowledge remains restricted to the particular application, division and reaches to only limited farmers in the country.

The research work carried out here helps farmers to overcome problems mentioned above. Advantages of developed decision support system are as follows:

1. Knowledge preservation and easy sharing
2. Reuse of existing expert's knowledge on pest and disease management
3. Reduction in loss due to pests and diseases on grapes
4. Reduction in use of pesticides and fungicides
5. Reduction in side effects of chemicals on environment
6. Increase in total yield of grapes
7. Connectivity of agricultural experts with grape growers through smart phone application

### 5.2.8 Performance Evaluation of PDMGrapes

For checking validity of PDMGrapes and to verify its results, farmers at 20 different locations of India are asked to use PDMGrapes.

Pests/diseases forecasted by PDMGrapes are recorded and compared with actual pests/diseases and techniques used by farmers at respective

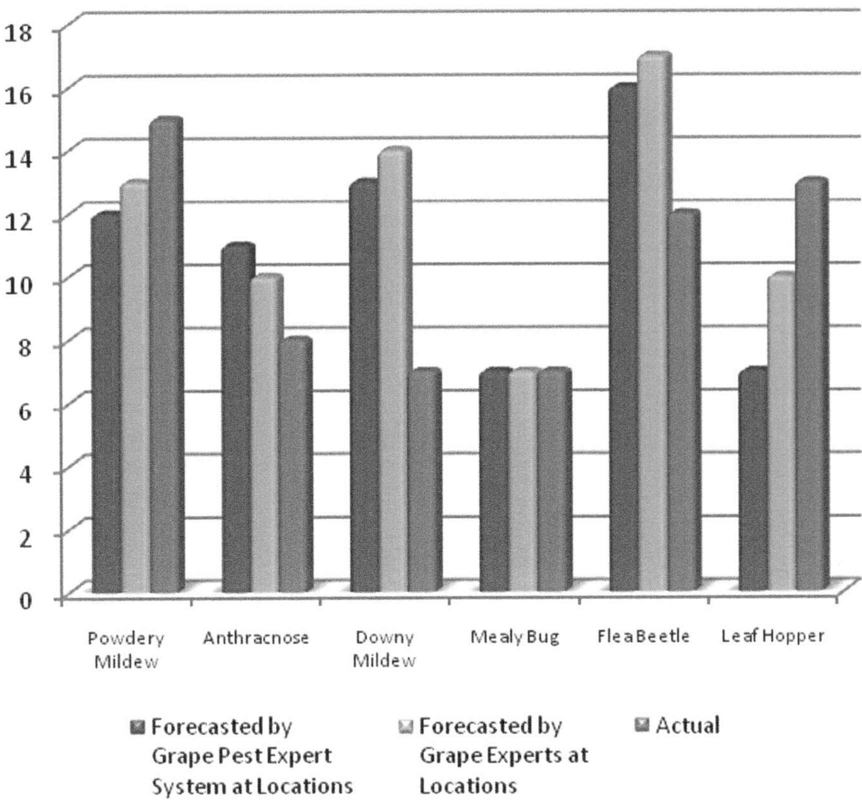


**FIGURE 5.17**
Pest forecasting by PDMGrapes.

locations. The work also considers expert's opinion about probable pests during given weather conditions. Probable occurrence of six pests on grapes, namely powdery mildew, anthracnose, downy mildew, mealybug, flea beetle and leafhopper, is compared. Figure 5.17 shows the graph of results of this comparison.

PDMGrapes is experimented for functionality and performance on 15 grape farms in Pune, Sangli and Kolhapur districts of Maharashtra, India. It was tested for two seasons from October 2016 to March 2016 and from April 2017 to March 2017. Table 5.2 shows weather conditions and pests and diseases forecasted by PDMGrapes in three weeks of March 2016.

Access of PDMGrapes was provided for use to 120 grape growers and 10 grape experts. The parameters for evaluation are user friendliness, pest forecasting accuracy, disease detection accuracy and correctness of information provided from IPM ontology. Grape growers and grape experts were asked

**TABLE 5.2**

Example of Pest Forecasting in the Month of March 2016 at Grape Farm in Pune District

| Date | Temp Max (°C) | Temp Min (°C) | Humidity (%) | Rainfall (mm) | Average Weather for Weak | Pest/Disease Forecasted | Probability |
|---|---|---|---|---|---|---|---|
| 01/03/16 | 35 | 19 | 6 | 7 | | | |
| 02/03/16 | 32 | 17 | 74 | 0 | Max Temp: 33 | | |
| 03/03/16 | 34 | 18 | 85 | 9 | Min Temp: 17.14 | Thrips | Low |
| 04/03/16 | 33 | 17 | 75 | 0 | | Downy Mildew | High |
| 05/03/16 | 31 | 18 | 71 | 3 | Humidity: 68.57 | Anthracnose | Medium |
| 06/03/16 | 33 | 16 | 90 | 0 | Rainfall: 2.71 | | |
| 07/03/16 | 33 | 15 | 79 | 0 | | | |
| 08/03/16 | 35 | 16 | 60 | 0 | | | |
| 09/03/16 | 35 | 16 | 65 | 0 | Max Temp: 35.57 | | |
| 10/03/16 | 36 | 17 | 63 | 0 | Min Temp: 16.43 | Thrips | Low |
| 11/03/16 | 36 | 17 | 63 | 0 | | Mealy bug | High |
| 12/03/16 | 38 | 18 | 65 | 0 | Humidity: 58.29 | Anthracnose | Medium |
| 13/03/16 | 36 | 18 | 45 | 0 | Rainfall: 0 | | |
| 14/03/16 | 33 | 13 | 47 | 0 | | | |
| 15/03/16 | 33 | 15 | 75 | 0 | | | |
| 16/03/16 | 35 | 17 | 65 | 0 | Max Temp: 36.14 | | |
| 17/03/16 | 35 | 17 | 55 | 0 | Min Temp: 17.14 | Thrips | Low |
| 18/03/16 | 37 | 18 | 55 | 0 | | Mealy bug | High |
| 19/03/16 | 38 | 18 | 58 | 0 | Humidity: 56.86 | Anthracnose | Medium |
| 20/03/16 | 38 | 18 | 47 | 0 | Rainfall: 0 | | |
| 21/03/16 | 37 | 17 | 50 | 0 | | | |

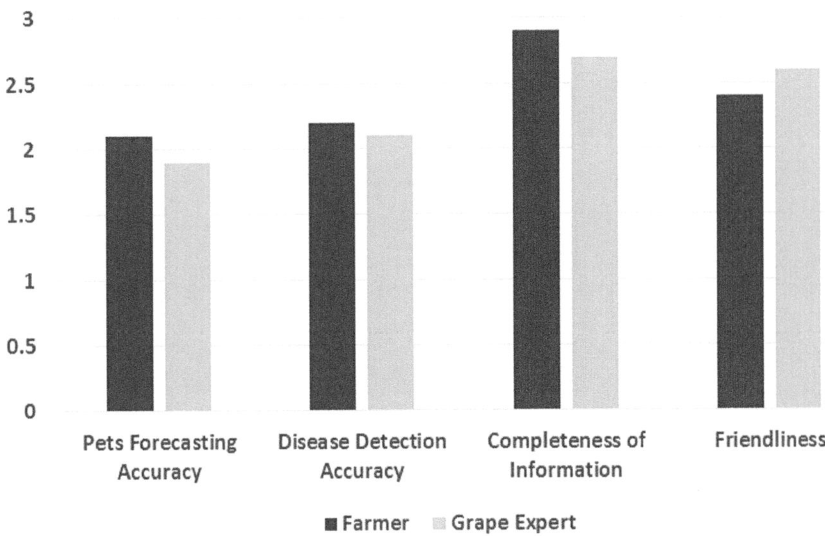


**FIGURE 5.18**
Evaluation of PDMGrapes by farmers and grape experts.

to rate system between 0 and 3 for each criterion. Figure 5.18 shows the evaluation graph.

Accuracy of disease detection using image processing technique was tested for all three diseases. The accuracy cannot be guaranteed to 100% as images are captured from smart phone cameras in uncontrolled environment.

# 6

# Nutrient Management

## 6.1 Introduction

Researchers in agricultural research centers across India work on various aspects of production of major crops. As outcomes of these researches, automated systems and research documents are generated. To have integration of such systems and sharing and reuse of generated knowledge, it must be represented in interoperable format.

In data-driven models, knowledge of processes carried out in a domain, relationship between processes and reasoning representation should be convincing and easy to understand by domain experts. In data-driven decision support model, representation of knowledge in a format which can be reasoned and shared seamlessly makes life of domain experts easier. In technologies where semantics and context awareness is required, ontology is used. Semantics of a domain can become clear through the use of ontology. Many times, experts at various organizations work collaboratively on research projects. For collaborative research work, sharing of data is must. Knowledge and information between heterogeneous systems can be shared using ontology. In precision agriculture, various automated devices are used and need to interact with each other for controlling processes. Meaningful representation of metadata about such devices and information required for controlling processes in agriculture can be done using ontology. IoT-based systems can be easily integrated by sharing knowledge in terms of ontology. The work discussed in this chapter shows how ontology can be built for preparing knowledge base for nutrition management of grapes. Information about ontology Classes, Individuals, Object and Data Properties and Relationships used for knowledge base is described here.

With increased use of ontologies, maintenance and evolution of ontologies become important. Understanding of domain by experts improves with time, so experts need to incorporate those changes in existing ontology. New information is captured and accommodated in ontology evolution process. Ontology versioning, integration, merging and maintenance are parts of ontology change management. With accommodation of changes in ontology,

DOI: 10.1201/9781003408253-7

preserving consistency is also important. Manual matching and evolution of ontologies can be time consuming, complex and error prone. Using decision tree algorithm C4.5, one can find important rules about ontology evolution from knowledge base. The objective of this work is to demonstrate application of decision tree to dataset tuples and find out the knowledge to be extended or changes to be done in nutrition management ontology.

Using decision support in agriculture helps producing better crop yields, lowering costs and help minimizing environmental pollution. Grape is one of the important crops in India. Grapes are exported from India to Middle East and European countries on a large scale. To maintain quality of grapes and gain more profit, nutrition management of vineyards is important. Primary nutrients in grapes are N, P and K. Secondary nutrients are Ca, Mg, S, Fe, Mn, Zn, Cu, B, Mo and Cl. Farmers make use of organic and inorganic fertilizers to fulfill requirements for nutrition management. To reduce soil pollution and chemical content in crops, use of inorganic fertilizers should be minimized and use of organic fertilizers should be motivated. This can be achieved if farmers get precise knowledge about application and effects of organic and inorganic fertilizers. With the help of expert's knowledge in decision support system, healthy and productive vine growth is possible. Machine learning techniques like fuzzy logic, artificial neural networks, Bayesian networks and decision trees can be used for developing such recommendation systems. Interpretable model can be developed using decision trees. When ontology is used as knowledge base instead of simple if-then rules, Semantic Web Rule Language (SWRL) is a good option for developing such interpretable model. Second objective of the work described in this chapter is to demonstrate advantage of decision tree machine learning technique and its use for formation of SWRL rules. These rules can then be used by decision support system for integrated nutrient management.

This chapter is organized as follows: Overview of ontology management systems and approaches along with nutrition management systems developed by other researchers is described first. Next section details the approach proposed for building NM ontology and its evolution from decision trees. After that it is discussed how formation of SWRL rules for decision support can be automated using decision trees.

### 6.1.1 Literature Survey

The brief about articles published and tools developed on nutrition management of grapes are published worldwide. Researchers from National research center for grapes, India, also publish research documents and information on websites about application of fertilizers on grapes. Farmers need to read these documents for decision support on fertilizer application. Author of this book did not find a decision support system for nutrient management of grapes in India.

Spectrum analytics Inc., Washington, provides soil, plant tissue and fertilizer analysis services (www.spectrumanalytic.com). They provide information about nutrition requirements and application of fertilizers on grape farms at different growth stages.

SMART (www.smart-fertilizer.com) is a fertilizer management platform which provides optimized fertilizer application program to its customers based on the analysis of on-field data. It works for 250 types of crops. It contains crop database and fertilizers database. Different kinds of reports, including fertilizer schedule is provided by SMART. Names of fertilizers to be used along with its amount are recommended for each growth stage of crop.

Precision Fertilization Management Information System (PFMIS) (Zhimin et al., 2012) uses GIS and GPS technologies for fertilization recommendation. Artificial neural network technique is used for data processing. Three-dimensional co-ordinates system on GPS is used for getting soil attributes of nutrients. Web-based expert system is connected to ArcGIS server containing spatial data grid maps about soil resources.

Representation of production knowledge for citrus in hilly areas is explained (Ying Wang et al., 2015). Conversion of production knowledge from text and reports to fertilization and irrigation ontology is elaborated in the paper. They have developed and evaluated support system which uses developed ontology. They have represented nutrition deficiency symptoms and soil moisture observations as triples and relations between triples.

## 6.2 Methods

### 6.2.1 Building NM Ontology

Formal representation of domain knowledge is done using ontology. It facilitates the interaction with domain experts. So the system proposed here uses ontology as knowledge base. Ontology is represented as a tuple $T(C, I, P, R)$, where C is a set of classes, I is a set of individuals, P is a set of properties and R is as a set of relationships between classes, individuals and properties. Various management aspects of crops can be represented in ontology such as fertilization management, pest and disease management, irrigation management, soil and land management and crop life cycle information management.

Here effort has been taken to represent nutrition management knowledge of grapes using ontology known as NM ontology. The information is collected from research documents published by researchers on grape cultivation. NM ontology is built in Web Ontology Language (OWL) using Protégé 5.1 editor.

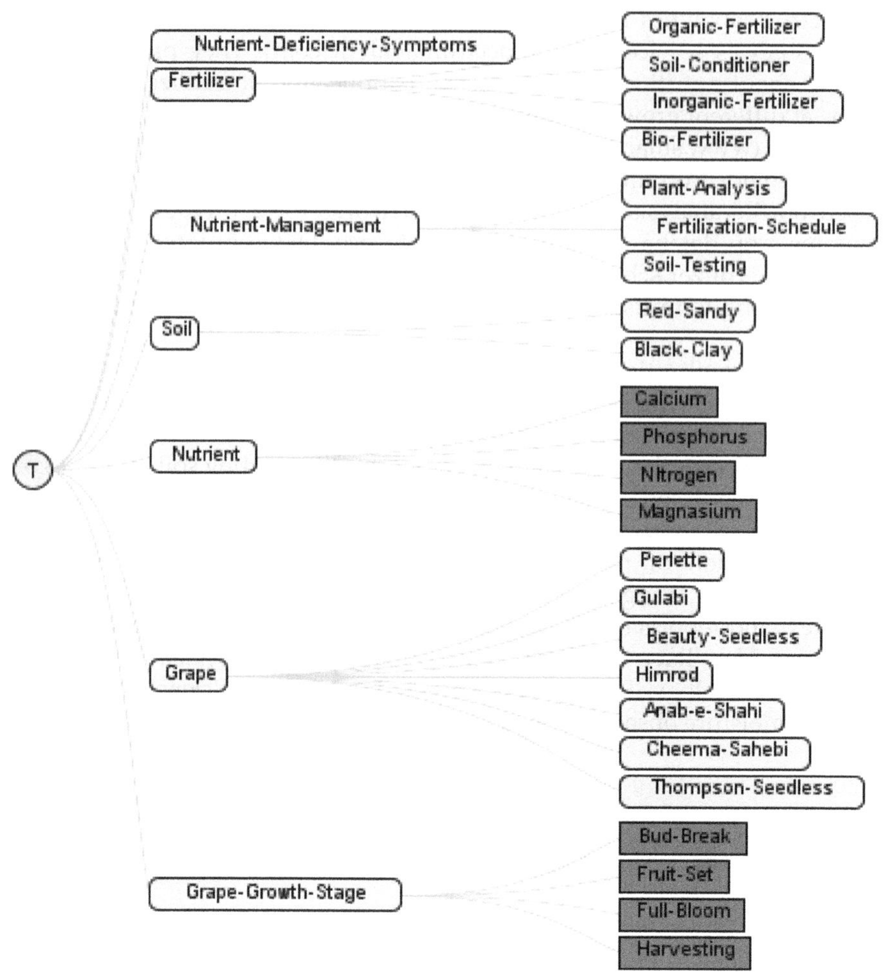


**FIGURE 6.1**
Nutrition management ontology concepts.

Figure 6.1 shows classes, subclasses and few individuals in NM Ontology. After defining classes, appropriate Individuals, Object properties and Data properties are also added to NM ontology. Figure 6.2 shows relationships between classes based on hierarchy and object properties.

As nutrition requirement is not the same at all growth stages of crop, growth stage should be considered along with soil and petiole testing results for nutrient recommendation. Hence, 'Growth-Stage' is added as a class in ontology and all types of growth stages as individuals of growth-stage class.

Deficiency symptoms and deficiency levels for nutrients are stored in NM ontology as object property values of Nutrition-Deficiency-Symptom and

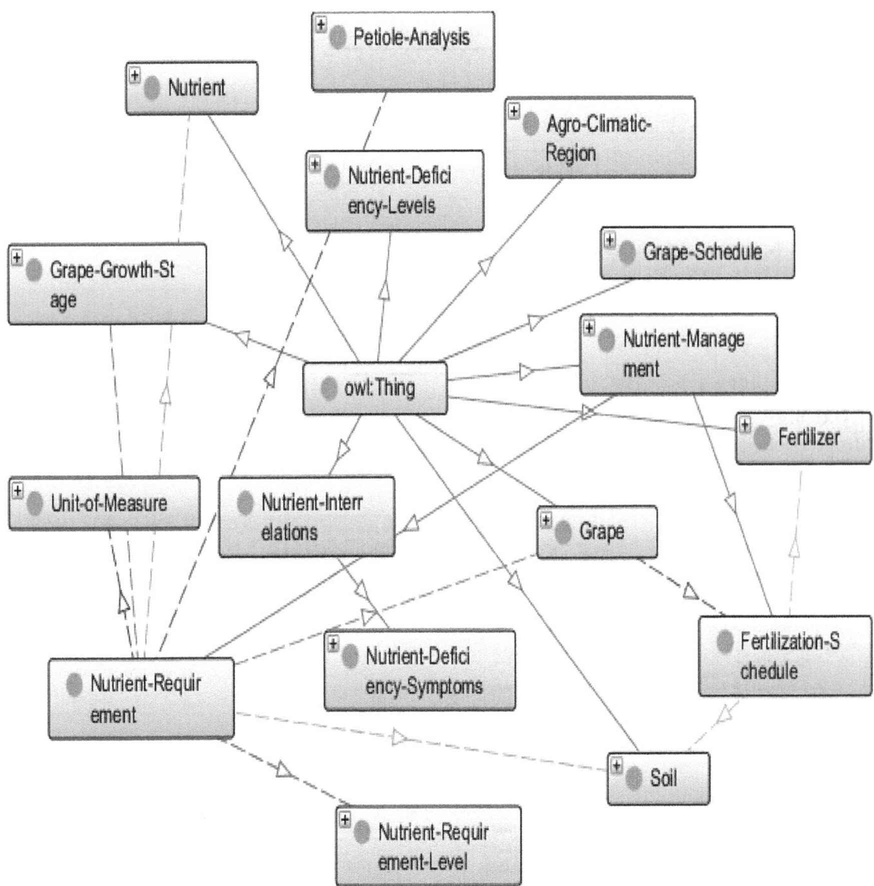


**FIGURE 6.2**
Relations between nutrition management ontology classes.

Nutrition-Deficiency-Level classes. Figure 6.3 is an example of deficiency symptoms of nitrogen.

Detailed information about all fertilizers used for nutrition management of grapes is stored in NM ontology. Figure 6.4 gives snapshot of ontology in protégé editor showing details of Calcium-Nitrate Fertilizer.

Along with built ontology, expert's advice is considered for constructing and updating decision tree.

### 6.2.2 Mapping of Concepts from Decision Tree for Ontology Evolution

Decision tree is a supervised data mining technique. It is used for classification and regression tasks in machine learning domain. Advantage of

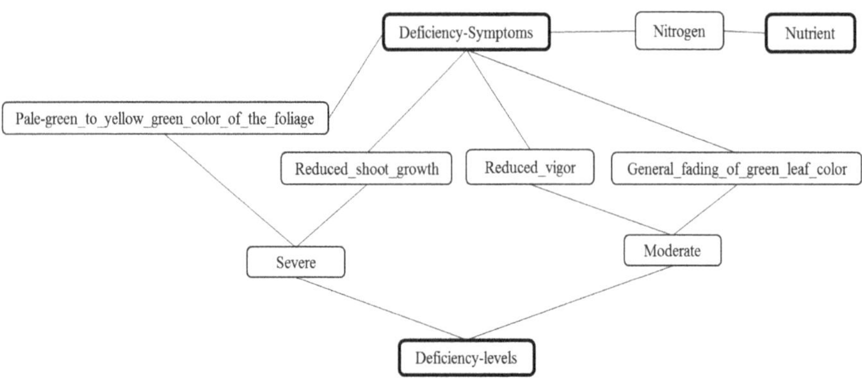


**FIGURE 6.3**
Nitrogen deficiency symptoms.

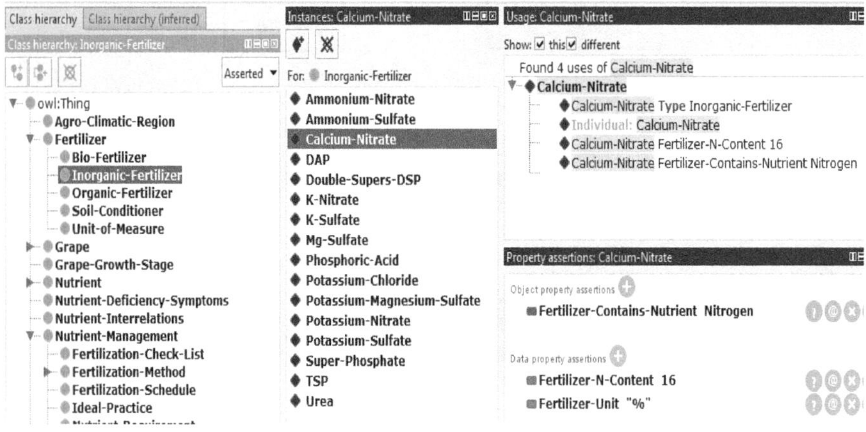


**FIGURE 6.4**
Calcium-Nitrate details stored in NM ontology.

decision tree is that DTs are readable and do not require any assumptions. Classification rules for domain-specific data can be represented in structural form using decision trees. Decision trees are extracted from knowledge stored in datasets using decision tree algorithms. Being readable, decision trees can be interpreted by agricultural experts. There is no need of a priori assumptions for decision trees. Decision trees can be used for finding out unknown relationships from data.

Taking above-mentioned advantages into consideration in this work, decision trees derived from nutrition management knowledge are used for the evolution of NM ontology. Hierarchies to be maintained in NM ontology are

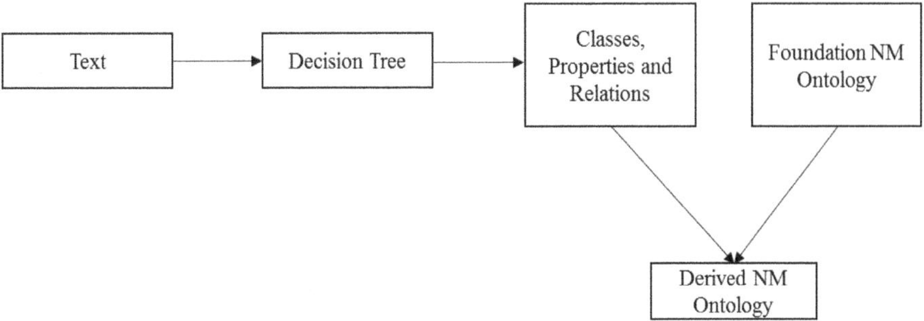


**FIGURE 6.5**
Using decision trees for ontology evolution.

found from levels among decision nodes in decision trees. Along with ontology built in protégé editor, expert's advice is considered for constructing and updating decision tree. As research and experience of experts increase with time, system needs to be added with new information published by grape experts. Therefore, periodic evolution of ontology is required. While evolving ontology, some concepts may overlap or some concepts may be missing. To resolve these issues, rules derived from induction of decision trees can be used. By using decision trees, it is checked if two or more properties (sub-property) can be replaced by one property (super-property) without any data loss. It is made sure that there is an element in NM ontology corresponding to leaf nodes of decision trees derived from NM knowledge. It can be an Individual, a data property value or object property.

NM ontology is revised with rules derived from Realizers decision tree. It is built using Weka machine learning tool applied on fertilizers knowledge base. Following acronyms are used in subsequent part for describing issues that are considered while evolving NM ontology:

```
NMO: NM Ontology
C = {c | c ϵ Concept in NMO}
D = {d | d ϵ Data Property in NMO}
IN = {in |in ϵ Individual in NMO}
OB = {ob | ob ϵ Object Property in NMO}
DT: decision tree
BDT = {bdt | bdt ϵ Branch conditions of DT nodes}
NDT = {ndt | ndt ϵ Nodes of DT}
LV = {lv | lv ϵ Value at leaf node of DT}, then
```

for current NM ontology

1. When a node from decision tree is to be added as a new Concept in NMO, Check change in structure of existing ontology due to

addition of new Concept against its value addition (importance) to knowledge base.

$$\text{IF}\left(\text{Addition}(\text{ndt})\rightarrow \text{C}\right)\wedge \text{Value}\times\left(\text{Addition}(\text{ndt})\right) > \text{Cost} \times\left(\text{Addition}(\text{ndt})\right) \text{ THEN Add}(\text{ndt})\rightarrow \text{NMO}$$

For value addition, the value is taken as information gain value from decision tree for the respective concept. In decision tree, attributes with highest information gain are chosen as decision nodes. Hence, if Concept to be added is node in decision tree, it is directly added to hierarchy.

2. Check for inheritance relationship by generating set of nodes

```
For each ndt ϵ NDT
Check hypernyms and hyponyms relation of ndt with each cϵ C
                 If ndt ≈ hypernym, Then Add(ndt) as parent
                 node of c
                       Else If ndt ≈ hyponym, Then
                       Add(ndt) as child node of c
```

3. Handle side effects after deleting Concept or Property

   After deleting a Concept or Property from hierarchy which is a sub node, tree can be adjusted in two ways as removing all nodes below sub node to be deleted and deleting only a sub node and adding descendant nodes to parent node.

```
DELETE (c) => C {c1…ck-1, ck+1…cn-1}
OR
DELETE (c) => C{c1…..ck-1}
```

4. Check for Data Property values and Object Properties

   For each bdt in BDT,

```
If NOT (bdt ϵ D v bdt ϵ OB)
Then
 If (bdt is a Value) Then Add (bdt) ➔ D
Else If (bdt is a Category) Then Add
(bdt) ➔ Ob
```

5. Add leaf node values as Data property value or as an Individual in NMO if it does not already exist:

   For each lv in LVDT,

```
If NOT (lv ϵ D V lv ϵ OB)
```

Then

```
 If (lv is a Number) Then Add (lv) →
 VAL(d)
Else Add (lv) → LABEL(in)
```

6. Merge common Properties to remove redundancy
   For each p ϵ (D ∨ OB)

```
        If (Synonym (Pi, Pj) is TRUE)
             Then
    Merge (Pi, Pj)
```

7. Maintain log of changes done by experts as:
   Add record to log as (E, d, t, N, Told, Tnew), where E is expert name, d is Date, t is Time, N is Node type, Told is Old status and Tnew is New status

Following are examples of use of decision tree:

A decision tree about nutrient contents in different fertilizers is taken as the first example. Table 6.1 lists fertilizers used in vineyards along with their nutrient contents in percent. The decision tree shown in Figure 6.6 is derived from Table 6.1 by applying C4.5 algorithm using Weka tool. From decision

**TABLE 6.1**

Fertilizers with nutrient content in %

| Fertilizer | Nutrient | % Content |
|---|---|---|
| Urea | Nitrogen | 46 |
| Ammonium Nitrate | Nitrogen | 35 |
| Ammonium Sulfate | Nitrogen | 21 |
| Di-ammonium Phosphate | Nitrogen | 18 |
| Calcium Nitrate | Nitrogen | 16 |
| Super phosphate | Phosphorus | 11.3 |
| TSP | Phosphorus | 19.6 |
| Phosphoric acid | Phosphorus | 26 |
| DAP | Nitrogen | 18 |
| DAP | Potassium | 19 |
| Potassium chloride | Potassium | 50 |
| K-sulfate | Potassium | 40 |
| K-nitrate | Potassium | 37 |
| K-nitrate | Nitrogen | 13 |
| Mg-sulfate | Magnesium | 20.2 |

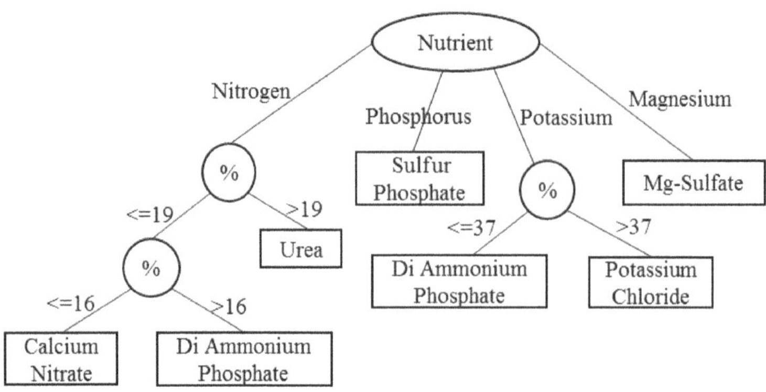


**FIGURE 6.6**
Decision tree for fertilizer selection based on nutrient content/requirement.

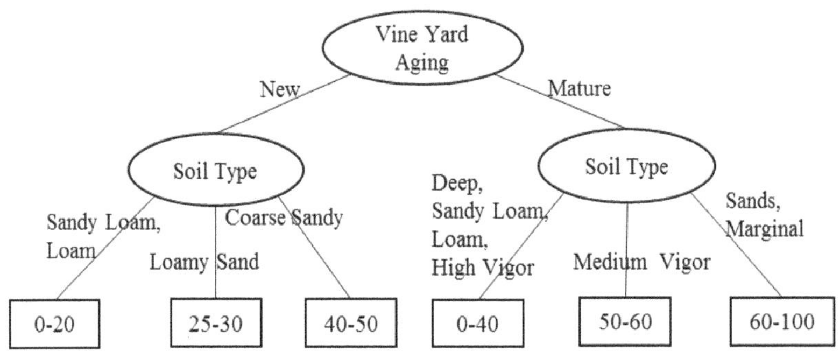


**FIGURE 6.7**
Decision tree for annual rate of nitrogen requirements in lbs/acre based on vine yard aging.

tree in Figure 6.6, it is checked whether all fertilizers from leaf nodes exist as individuals in current NM ontology.

The second example is about addition of new concept in NM ontology. 'Vineyard Aging' is one of the important factors in making decision about fertilizer application. In existing NM ontology, vineyard aging was not considered by experts. The Class 'Vineyard-Aging' and its Individuals as 'New' and 'Mature' are added in the ontology after getting decision tree about annual rate of nitrogen requirements as shown in Figure 6.7.

**Algorithm:** Ontology Evolution from Decision Tree

**Input**: `Datasets on nutrient management of grapes, Existing NM Ontology`
**Output**: `Updated NM Ontology`

```
    Step 1: Pre-process data for removing blank spaces
            and missing values
    Step 2: Select attributes for classification with
            maximum information gain
    Step 3: Classify data using C4.5 decision tree
            learning algorithm
    Step 4: Sort existing Classes in ontology in
            alphabetical order and assign unique
            identifiers to each Class
Repeat
    Step 5: Compare node of decision tree(ndt) with
            Classes(C) in NM ontology
    If Class (c) does not already exists
              Check for inheritance relationship
              If class is hyponym for existing class,
                  Add new (ndt) as subclass
                  Update descendent Class (c) as subclass
                  of newly added Class
              Else if node (ndt) is hypernym for existing
              class
                        Add node (ndt) as new subclass of
                        current Class (c)
    End If
    Step 6: Define new Object or Data Property from
            branch value of decision tree
    Step 7: If leaf node label is numeric value
                      Add label as Data Property Value
              Else
                      Add label as an Individual
    Step 8: Add Log Record of decision tree label → NM
            ontology label
Until it reaches the last leaf node
```

In example 3, the class 'Region' and its objects like 'North India', 'Telangana' and 'Maharashtra' are derived from decision tree in Figure 6.8 and added in the NM ontology as new concepts and individuals.

## 6.3 Decision Support

Decision support in any field can be provided by applying inference logic to domain knowledge. There are two types of inferences as forward inference and backward inference (Chen R. et al., 2005). This work uses forward inference approach as recommendations will be made based on knowledge

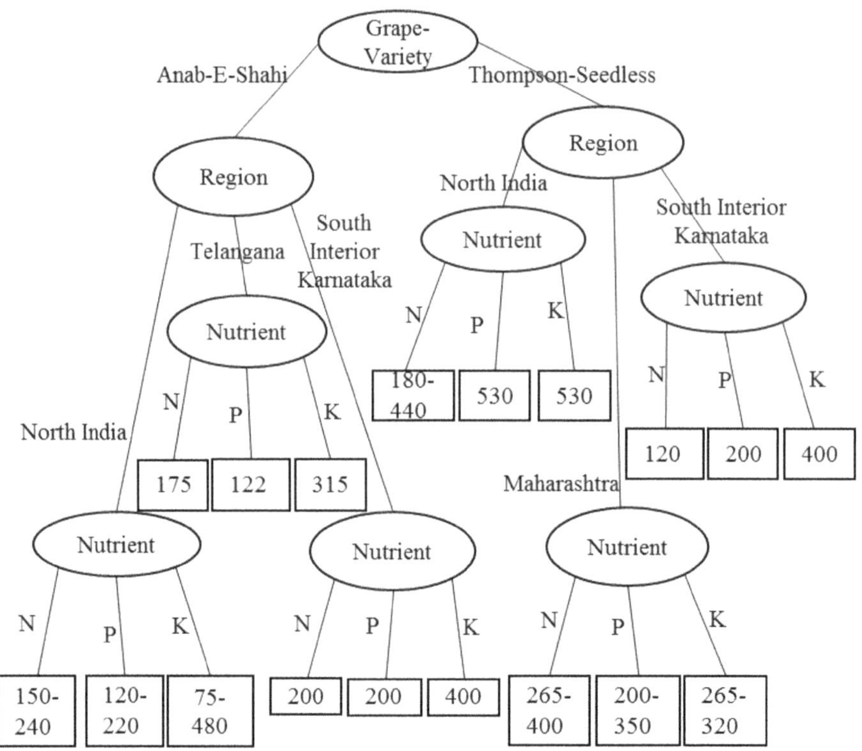


**FIGURE 6.8**
Decision tree for recommended doses of nutrients (Kg/acre) for different varieties under different agro-climatic regions.

in ontology. Rich and well-structured rule set is heart of any decision support system. Semi-automatic generation of rule base for inference engine is discussed in the following sections.

### 6.3.1 Mapping of Concepts from Decision Tree for Rules Formation

For decision support on nutrient management, knowledge representation in terms of rules is must. This sub-section describes how these rules can be formed using decision trees. -This research uses SWRL for representing rules of decision support. SWRL is a standard rule language based on RuleML (Martin O'Conner, 2009). Reasoning on knowledge present in ontology can be done using SWRL. To reduce time required to form these rules and to increase accuracy, decision trees extracted from nutrition management datasets are used. These rules can be derived from NM ontology as shown in Figure 6.9. Class individuals; object properties and data property

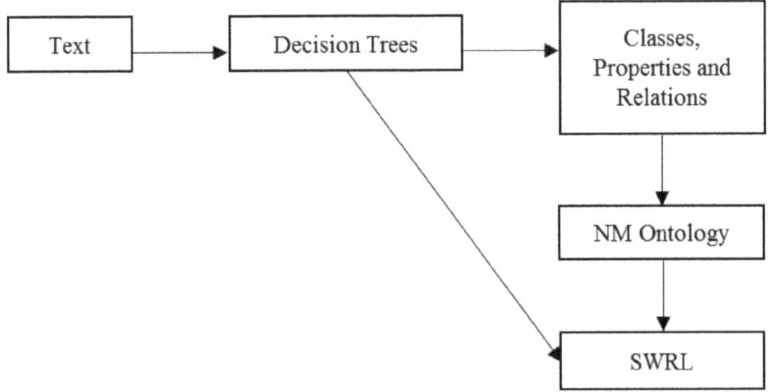


**FIGURE 6.9**
Using decision trees for generating SWRL rules.

values are used by SWRL for reasoning. The rule has two parts as antecedent and consequent.

$$\text{antecedent} \rightarrow \text{consequent}$$

Decision on which object or data properties should be antecedent of rules and which should be consequent of rules can be very well understood by parsing decision trees of related knowledge. SWRL built-ins like SWRL:greaterThan and SWRL:lessThan are available for mentioning conditions. Choice of SWRL built-in for rule formation becomes explicit from decision tree. Example of SWRL rules extraction is discussed in the following sections.

Nutrient requirement of grapes varies at different growth stages and between different days of growth stages. Hence, rules for nutrient requirements need to be formed based on grape growth stages and growth days. This knowledge is represented as decision tree shown in Figure 6.10. It shows requirement for four types of nutrients as nitrogen, phosphorus, potassium and magnesium. The class 'Grape-Schedule' and its two individuals 'before-pruning' and 'after-pruning' are added in NM ontology after parsing this decision tree. The 'Days' attribute is added as data property of 'Grape-Schedule' class. It is known as 'Days-After-Pruning'. Domain for the attribute is Grape-Schedule and range is xsd:integer. Requirement levels are added as individuals of Requirement-Levels class and an object property is defined for it specifying Nutrient-Requirement as its domain. The Java program is written for auto-generation of SWRL rules. Seventy-two such rules are generated about nutrient management of grapes. Table 6.2 lists the SWRL rules extracted from this decision tree.

Petiole content analysis is very important for deciding nutrient requirement. SWRL rules for recommendation of nutrients based on petiole contents

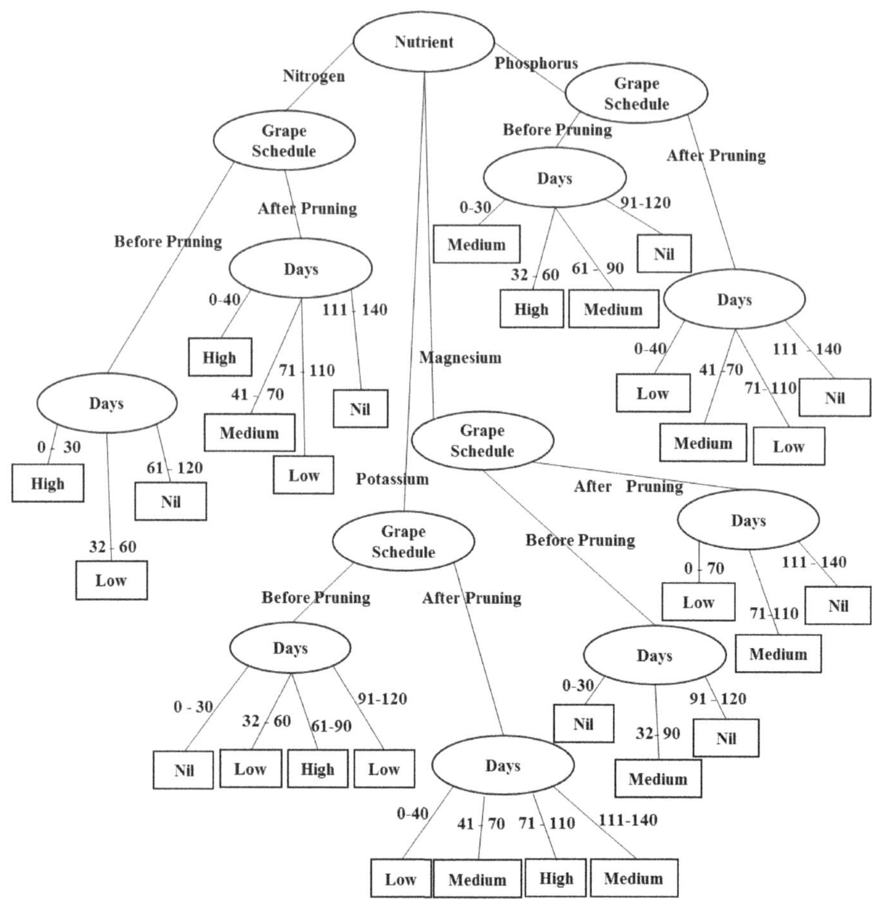


**FIGURE 6.10**
Schedule-wise decision tree for nutrient requirements of grapes.

tests and soil analysis (K.L. Chadha, S.D. Shikhamany, 2002) are derived from decision tree shown in Figure 6.11. Examples of extracted rules are listed in Table 6.3.

## 6.3.2 Decision Support System

The developed ontology and SWRL rules are used to develop decision support system to be used by grape growers. Figure 6.12 shows overall architecture of developed system known as Grapes Nutrition Management Support System (GNMSS). Nutrition requirements of grapes can be predicted by measuring soil content and petiole content of specific nutrient. Petiole contains optimum quantity of nutrient at bloom to veraison stage of grape growth.

**TABLE 6.2**

Example SWRL rules generated from decision tree in Figure 6.10

| Rule | Rule Content | Rule Meaning |
|---|---|---|
| Rule 1 | Grape-Schedule(Before-Pruning) ^ Macro-Nutrient (Nitrogen) ^ Nutrient-Requirement-Level(?l) ^ Days-Before-Pruning(?d) ^ SWRLb:lessThanOrEqual (?d, 60) ^ SWRLb:greaterThanOrEqual(?t, 32) ➔ hasRequirementLevel(Nitrogen, Low) | IF Grape Schedule is Before Pruning and Days between 32 and 60 THEN Requirement of Nitrogen is Low |
| Rule 2 | Grape-Schedule(After-Pruning) ^ Macro-Nutrient(Potassium) ^ Nutrient-Requirement-Level(?l) ^ Days- After-Pruning(?d) ^ SWRLb:less ThanOrEqual (?d, 40) ^ SWRLb:greaterThan(?t, 0) ➔ hasRequirementLevel(Potassium, Low) | IF Grape Schedule is After Pruning and Days between 0 and 40 THEN Requirement of Potassium is Low |
| Rule 3 | Grape-Schedule(Before-Pruning) ^ Macro-Nutrient (Magnesium) ^ Nutrient-Requirement-Level(?l) ^ Days-Before-Pruning(?d) ^ SWRLb:lessThanOrEqual (?d, 90) ^ SWRLb:greaterThanOrEqual (?d, 32) ➔ hasRequirementLevel(Magnesium, Medium) | IF Grape Schedule is Before Pruning and Days between 32 and 90 THEN Requirement of Magnesium is Medium |
| Rule 4 | Grape-Schedule(Before-Pruning) ^ Macro-Nutrient(Phosphorus) ^ Nutrient-Requirement-Level(?l) ^ Days-Before-Pruning(?d) ^ SWRLb:less ThanOrEqual (?d, 30) ^ SWRLb:greaterThan(?t, 0) ➔ hasRequirementLevel (Phosphorus, Medium) | IF Grape Schedule is Before Pruning and Days between 0 and 30 THEN Requirement of Phosphorus is Medium |

Hence, site-specific soil testing results and petiole content analysis are used as input for inference engine of decision support system.

Knowledge base for decision support system is NM ontology described in Section 6.3. These observations are generally stored in excel sheets. The records are converted to ontology elements and added to NM ontology to be used by SWRL rules. Inference engine provides recommendations about names and quantity of fertilizer application at that site. It is based on rules written in SWRL some of which are mentioned in Chapter 5.

Nutrition requirements based on soil test results and petiole test results using SWRL are forecasted to grape growers on demand basis. OWL APIs are used for implementation of inference engine. For reasoning on SWRL rules, pellet reasoner is used. Not just requirements but also suitable fertilizers for fulfilling nutrient requirements are recommended by GNMSS.

## 6.4 Evaluation

Evaluation of proposed algorithm and of decision support system is done by performing both quantitative and qualitative analysis as described in the following section.

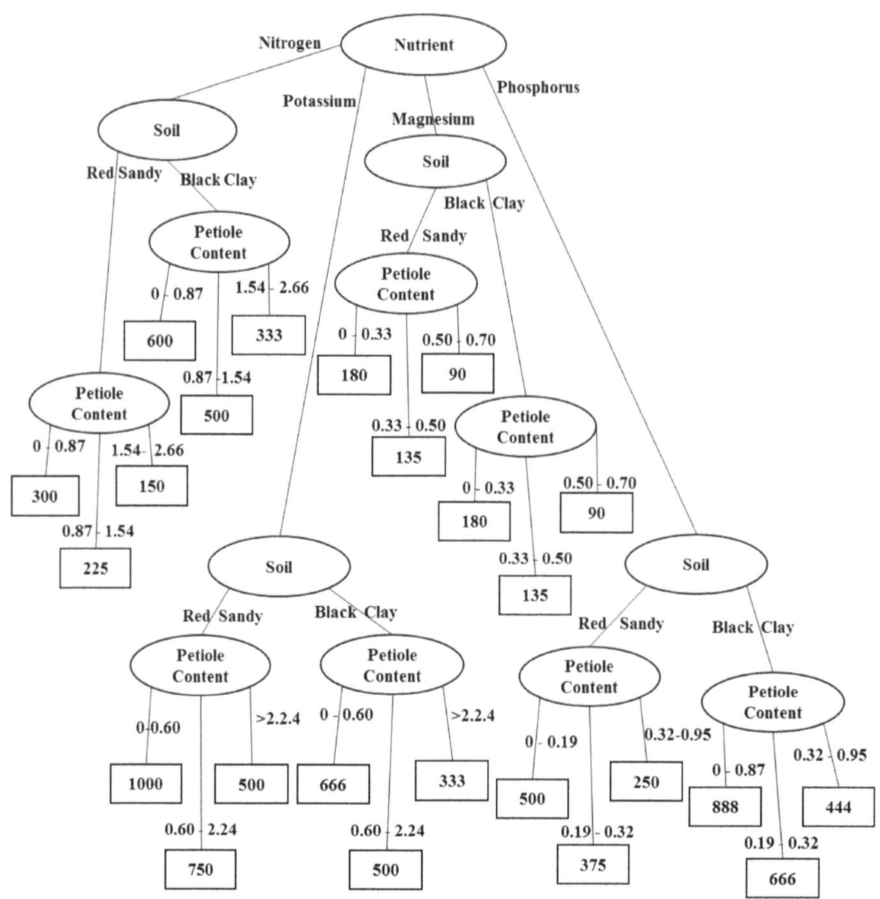


**FIGURE 6.11**
Decision trees based on petiole contents and soil types (Source: Pre-harvest manual for production of table grapes for exports- APEDA, New Delhi).

## 6.4.1 Quantitative Analysis

The proposed algorithm was tested by using 18 different decision trees extracted from documents on nutrient management of grapes and then applying all the steps mentioned in algorithm to evolve foundation NM ontology. The same documents are used directly without any pre-processing and the ontology is built using conventional method where all elements are added manually. Evaluation of its accuracy is calculated based on how many classes, data properties, object properties and hierarchical relations between classes are correctly identified by decision trees.

**TABLE 6.3**

Example SWRL rules generated from decision tree and used by decision support system

| Rule | Rule Content | Rule Meaning |
|---|---|---|
| Rule 1 | Observation(?o) ^ Macro-Nutrient(Nitrogen) ^ Petiole-Content(?o, ?p) ^ Soil(Red-Sandy) ^ SWRLb:lessThanOrEqual(?p, 0.87) ➔ has RequirementQuantity(Nitrogen, 300) | IF petiole content is between 0 and 0.87 and soil is red sandy THEN Requirement of Nitrogen is 300Kg/Ha |
| Rule 2 | Observation(?o) ^ Macro-Nutrient(Potassium) ^ Soil(Black-Clay) ^ Petiole-Content(?o, ?p) ^ SWRLb:GreaterThan(?p, 0.60) ^ SWRLb:lessThan OrEqual(?p, 2.24) ➔ hasRequirementQuantity (Potassium, 500) | IF petiole content is between 0.60 and 2.24 and soil is black clay THEN Requirement of Potassium is 500Kg/Ha |
| Rule 3 | Observation(?o) ^ Macro-Nutrient( Magnesium) ^ Soil(Black-Clay) ^ Petiole-Content(?o, ?p) ^ SWRLb:GreaterThan(?p, 0.50) ^ SWRLb:lessThanOrEqual(?p, 0.70) ➔ has RequirementQuantity(Magnesium, 90) | IF petiole content is between 0.50 and 0.70 and soil is red sandy THEN Requirement of Magnesium is 90Kg/Ha |
| Rule 4 | Observation(?o) ^ Macro-Nutrient(Potassium) ^ Petiole-Content(?o, ?p) ^ Soil(Red-Sandy) ^ SWRLb:lessThanOrEqual(?p, 0.19) ➔ has RequirementQuantity(Potassium, 500) | IF petiole content is between 0 and 0.19 and soil is red sandy THEN Requirement of Potassium is 500Kg/Ha |

Precision and recall values are calculated using the following formulae:

$$\text{Precision} = \frac{\text{Rightly Classified Elements}}{\text{Rightly Classified Elements} + \text{MisClassified Elements FROM Other Terminology}}$$

Recall is calculated as:

$$\text{Recall} = \frac{\text{Rightly Classified Elements}}{\text{Rightly Classified Elements} + \text{MisClassified Elements TO Other Terminology}}$$

Precision and Recall values for Classes, Object Properties, Data properties and Individuals retrieved from decision trees and those in ontology built using conventional manual method are as mentioned in Table 6.4.

As use of smart phones is very common among grape growers and using decision support system on smart phone is easier than on computers, GNMSS was made available to users as an application on Android smart phone. The system was tested by 15 grape growers and 3 grape experts for one year from September 2015 to October 2016.

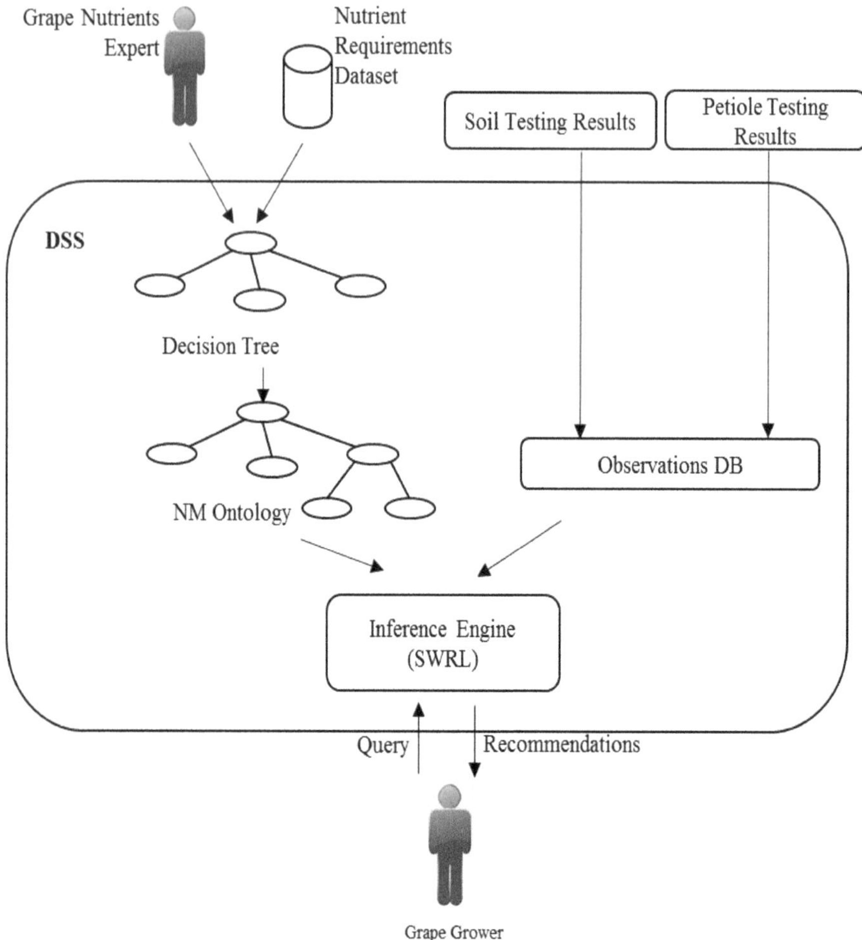


**FIGURE 6.12**
Grapes Nutrients Management Support System (GNMSS).

To improve the accuracy of GNMSS, the SWRL Rule-base is revised again and feedback from experts is incorporated to update some SWRL rules and 16 new SWRL rules are added to knowledge base of GNMSS. Same experts are again asked to test GNMSS on same parameters. GNMSS is used and evaluated for the second time from July 2017 to November 2017 for five months after improving knowledge base. Figure 6.13 is the line chart showing accuracy of predictions by GNMSS at different regions, when soil analysis results and petiole content analysis results were highly accurate.

**TABLE 6.4**

Comparison of precision and recall values for conventional ontology building versus use of proposed approach

| | Conventional Method | | Using Decision Trees | |
|---|---|---|---|---|
| | **Precision (%)** | **Recall (%)** | **Precision (%)** | **Recall (%)** |
| Classes | 79.51 | 79.88 | 92 | 90 |
| Object Properties | 52 | 48 | 73 | 80 |
| Data Properties | 78 | 76 | 88 | 87 |
| Individuals | 72 | 70 | 91 | 91 |

### 6.4.2 Qualitative Analysis

The algorithm is tested for its quality attributes as reduction in ambiguity, user friendliness and efficiency with the help of agriculture experts. Fifteen agriculture experts were asked to use the algorithm and opinion was taken on three parameters as reduction in ambiguity of used terminologies, ease of development and reduction in time required for developing ontology in scale of 0 to 3. 0 means very low and 3 means very high. The review results are recorded. Figure 6.14 shows results of the review. The survey showed that decision tree approach for ontology evolution minimized the time required for building ontology. It helped experts in having visual clarity of domain knowledge to be mentioned as ontology and minimized number of ambiguous terminologies in the ontology.

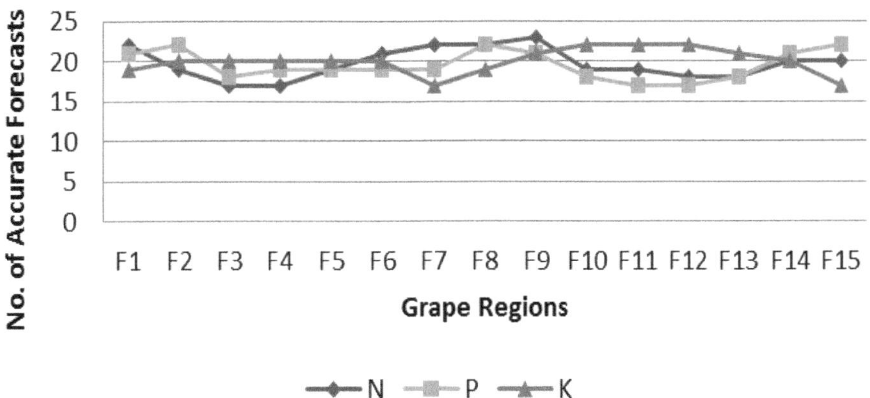


**FIGURE 6.13**
Nutrient requirements forecasts by GNMSS at different vineyard regions.

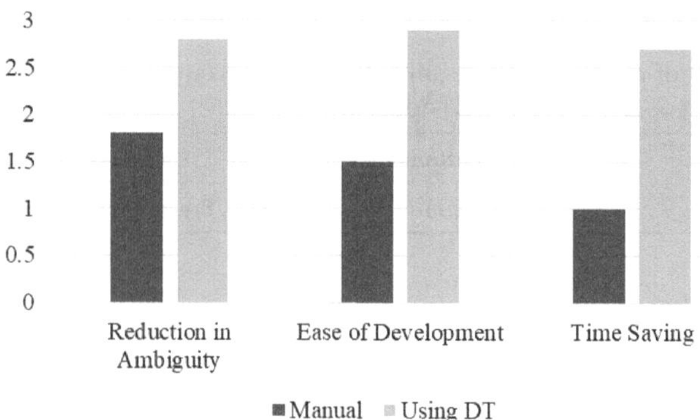


**FIGURE 6.14**
Effect of using decision tree for ontology building

## 6.5 Conclusions

The chapter describes building of ontology for nutrition management of grapes. Using ontology in agriculture field helps grape experts in knowledge dissemination and use. It also describes how use of decision tree reduces time required for developing SWRL rules and improves quality of context information. Developed knowledge base can be reused by existing expert systems on grape production because of semantic interoperability of ontologies. It also describes how decision tree technique under machine learning can be used for building and evolution of ontology and formation of SWRL rules for nutrition management of grapes. Validation of the proposed approach under decision support system is demonstrated in the chapter. It can be concluded that machine learning techniques help in minimizing efforts in knowledge building using OWL, and SWRL and using ontology in agriculture field helps experts and farmers in knowledge dissemination and use. It reduces time required for developing SWRL rules and improves quality of context information. Developed knowledge base can be reused by existing expert systems on grape production because of semantic interoperability of ontologies. As both knowledge base and inference logic are represented in OWL, the system ensures full semantic interoperability. The limitation of decision support system is that it depends on accuracy of soil testing results and petiole testing results.

# 7

# Irrigation Management

## 7.1 Introduction

Water is the most important resource in agriculture. Irrigation scheduling is deciding about frequency and duration of water supply to any crop. Proper scheduling of irrigation can minimize wasting water and can also help to improve quality of grapes. There are different methods of irrigation. Drip irrigation is used by almost all vineyards in India. 'Manerajuri' is a village in India famous for grapes but more than 10,000 bore wells have run dry in year 2016. This fact motivated to develop knowledge base and decision support system which can be used for micromanagement of available water.

Knowledge base generation is done for scheduling water supply to grapes in hot tropical region of India. It is developed in terms of ontology as good irrigation practices in ontology will be good education material for farmers.

Structured representation of knowledge is more useful than unstructured one. Ontologies can be used for structured representation of concepts in any domain. Along with concepts, relationships between concepts can also be mentioned using ontology. Maintenance and sharing of information can be facilitated using ontologies. Manual construction of domain ontology is time consuming and error prone. Semi-automated approach will help in enriching ontology building, reducing required time and enhancing quality of built ontology. For IoT-based automation of irrigation systems, formal representation and management of IoT techniques and devices used is important.

Automated irrigation system needs information like ambient temperature and humidity, atmospheric pressure, soil temperature, soil moisture and leaf wetness. System can be built with such information using sensors, actuators, monitors, collectors and transmitters. Data generated and required from such varying sources can be easily integrated using ontology. This chapter describes building ontology for developing IoT-based automated irrigation systems. It details mechanism used for constructing ontology. Two types of ontologies, namely vineyard ontology and smart irrigation ontology, are described here. These ontologies can be used for generating knowledge

DOI: 10.1201/9781003408253-8

base and establishment of automated irrigation system based on available resources. It can also be used to educate grape growers about principles of vineyard irrigation.

## 7.2 Literature Survey

Ontology is developed for irrigation systems (J. I. Toledo-Alvarado et al., 2012). It is generic ontology and does not consider any crop-specific details for irrigation. As it was built long back, it does not consider IoT-related concepts for automated irrigation system.

Smartvineyards (www.smartvineyards.net) is an irrigation management system that uses soil water tension to monitor vine and water stress in each vineyard block. Readings of sensors are displayed on web browser in graphical form. It uses soil tension sensors for the same purpose. Irrisoft (www.irrisoft.net) provides software for irrigation scheduling known as InSite Irrigation Scheduling. It provides summary of evapotranspiration (ET) values and station-wise irrigation schedules based on various parameters like weather details, plant type and soil type. Basic Irrigation Scheduling (BIS) is an excel application for irrigation scheduling. It is developed for crops in California. It estimates annual trends of ET. C. Cornejo et al. have developed irrigation ontology which is used for educational purpose. Cropx is one of the leading IoT-based irrigation automation systems (cropx.com). Netafim (www.netafim.com) is a smart drip irrigation system that can be controlled by application on smartphone. It requires the irrigation schedule to be defined explicitly by farmers.

## 7.3 Methodology

Building ontology consists of five basic steps as defining domain, scope and objective of ontology, listing important keywords from the domain, finding hierarchies between keywords, defining relations between them and adding those keywords as concepts in ontology and defining relationships between concepts. Various formats for building ontology are available as RDF, RDF-S, OWL and OWL-DL. Here, ontology is developed in Web Ontology Language (OWL) format. Classes, individuals, data properties, object properties and axioms are the main parts of OWL ontology. Classes represent core concepts in the domain. Individuals are instances of any specific class. Data properties are attributes of a class with specific values, and object properties hold values as objects of some other class. Two ontologies are maintained separately as vineyard ontology and smart irrigation ontology.

### 7.3.1 Building Vineyard Ontology

Water management is important to maintain yield and quality of grapes. This chapter details how water management knowledge is represented in ontology form. Knowledge about irrigation scheduling of grapes is available in various documents published by researchers from organizations like national research center for grapes (http://nrcgrapes.nic.in). To make use of this knowledge in decision support system, it must be transformed to accessible form. As mentioned earlier, knowledge stored in ontology can be accessed and shared by automated systems. This chapter discusses about converting the irrigation scheduling details available in text documents to ontology. AGROVOC is used as reference ontology. AGROVOC is available in resource description framework (RDF) format.

Documents for irrigation scheduling are taken as input and the most relevant documents are only considered. Relevance of documents is ranked using TF-IDF algorithm. Natural language processing techniques are used then to extract important keywords from text. The text is converted to a number of tokens using String tokenizer. After that, stop words are removed from list of tokens. There can be same words with different forms. Such words are converted to common form using Porter's stemmer. OpenNLP POS tagger is used for extracting important keywords from tokens. POS tagger assigns labels to keywords as NN for noun and NNP for proper nouns. Assigned labels are then considered for probable classes, data properties, individuals or object properties. Along with concepts, relationships between concepts are also found by processing sentences. Extracted relations are used for defining hierarchy among classes and among properties.

The ontology is built using Protégé APIs available in Java language. The fundamental concepts related to irrigation are added as classes in ontology. The ontology is built using top-down approach. More general terms are added at higher level in hierarchy, followed by more specific concepts at lower levels.

Vineyard ontology contains 16 classes, 56 individuals, 12 object properties and 19 data properties. The built ontology is further edited using Protégé 5.1 ontology editor. Protégé editor has facilities to add, edit and delete concepts, change hierarchy, view ontology and use reasoners to ontology. The irrigation knowledge is extracted from research documents published by national research for grapes, Pune, India. Irrigation schedule can be decided based on knowledge stored in vineyard ontology in terms of individuals, object properties and data property values. Requirements of irrigation for grapes

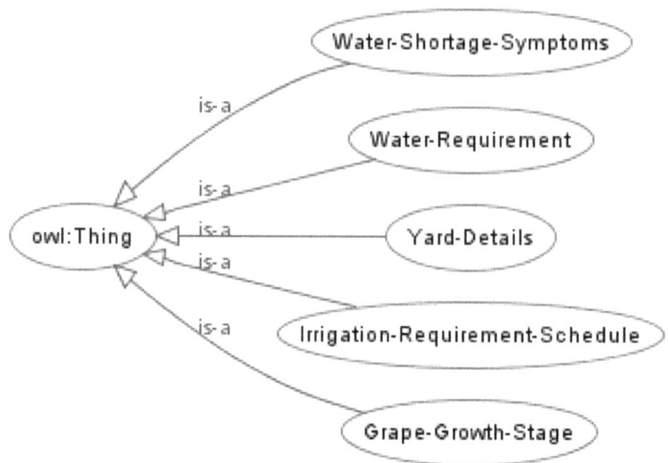


**FIGURE 7.1**
Classes in Vineyard_Ontology.

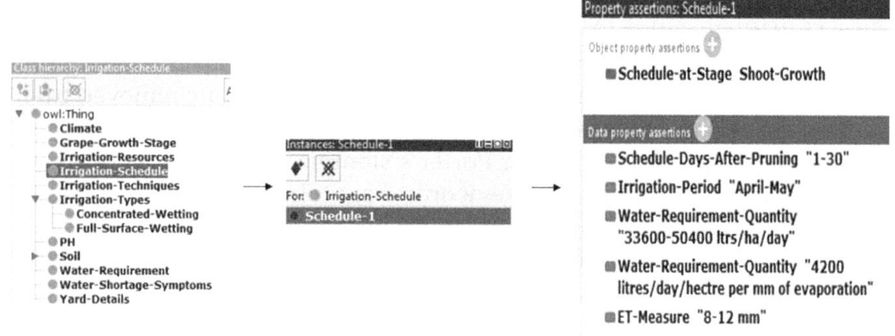


**FIGURE 7.2**
Example of irrigation schedule defined in Vineyard_Ontology as data and object property assertions.

are mentioned as individuals of Irrigation-Schedule class. Under each object, water requirement is specified as data property value. Growth-stage wise water requirements of grapes are considered and mentioned for each irrigation schedule. Figures 7.1 and 7.3 show classes under Vineyard_Ontology and Smart_Irrigation_Ontology, respectively. Water-Shortage-Symptoms class stores all symptoms shown on grape leafs, stems, berries and in soil due to shortage of water. Specific information about yard like root depth, soil type and available water resources are covered by Yard-Details class. All stages of vine growth are stored as individuals of Grape-Growth-Stage class and are referenced by irrigation requirement schedule.

**FIGURE 7.3**
Classes in Smart-Irrigation-Ontology.

Irrigation-Requirement-Schedule is the most important class for modeling and predicting irrigation requirements. It contains water requirement schedules as individuals detailing days after pruning of schedule, water requirement quantity in liters per day per hectare, growth stage of vines, irrigation period in terms of months and evapotranspiration measure. Figure 7.2 shows example of irrigation schedule defined in Vineyard Ontology.

### 7.3.2 Smart Irrigation Ontology

In order to provide knowledge base of tools and techniques that can be used for automation of irrigation scheduling, Smart-Irrigation-Ontology is built. It contains all concepts including IoT, for creating and managing smart irrigation system for vineyard. The time and amount of water to apply to vineyard is generally based on four methods: monitoring of soil moisture levels, measuring water status in plants, evapotranspiration measurement and the estimated vineyard water use rate and soil water storage. As irrigation decision depends on various factors in vineyard, sensors are used for such measurements. Figure 7.4 shows types of sensors that can be used for smart irrigation. Unit-of-measure, type-of-sensing, locating-of-sensing and sensor-description are data properties of Sensor class. The ontology provides all support for storing information about IoT-based tools. It also provides data and object properties for storing measurements read by such tools. It comes under Devices and Communication-Techniques classes and their sub-classes. Knowledge about irrigation techniques that can be used under vineyards and possible water resources comes under Irrigation-Techniques and Water-Resources

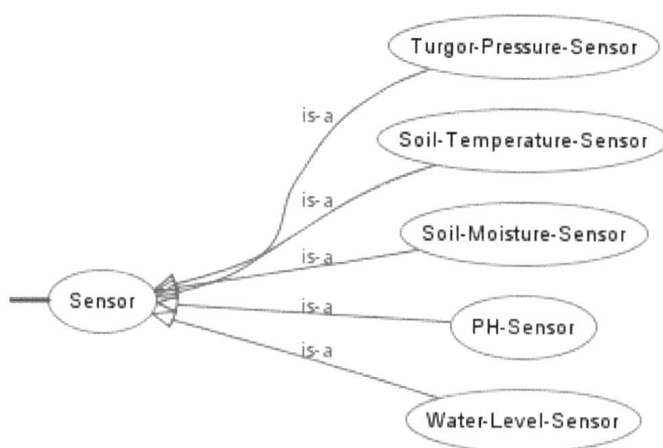


**FIGURE 7.4**
Sensor class in Smart-Irrigation-Ontology.

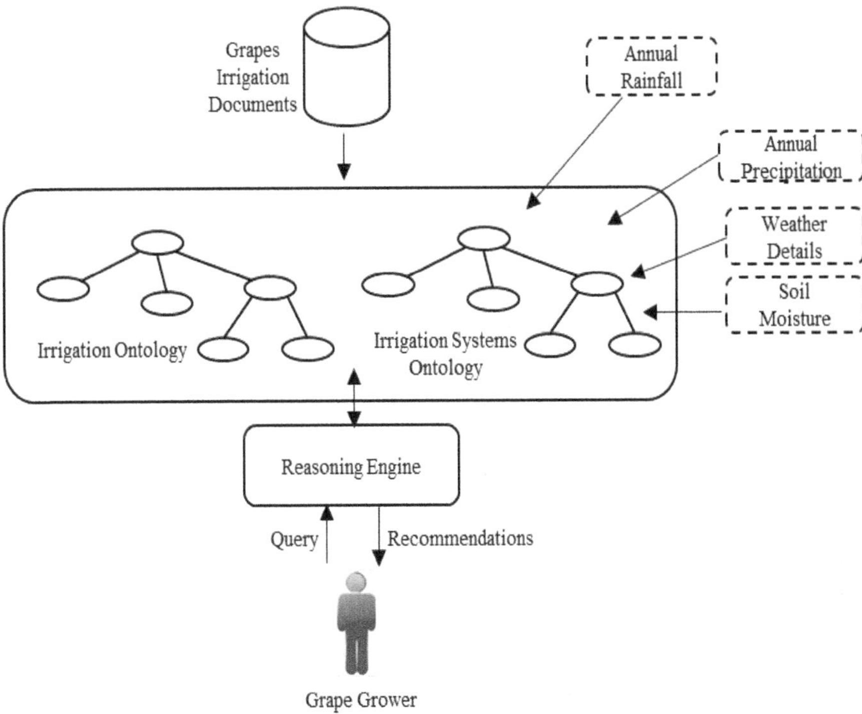


**FIGURE 7.5**
Use of developed ontology for smart vineyard irrigation system.

classes. Observations class contains subclasses, data and object properties for storing measurements taken by sensors. System-Design and User-Interface are the classes suggesting options for building irrigation automation system using available resources. As irrigation management depends on climate and weather details in specific region; two classes, namely Climate and Weather-Details, are added in the ontology. Annual-Precipitation and Annual-Rainfall are data properties of Climate class. Rainfall, humidity and temperature are parts of Weather-Details class.

Developed ontology can be used for developing IoT-based irrigation systems and educating grape growers about irrigation techniques as shown in Figure 7.5. Smart-Irrigation-Ontology can be used to decide on irrigation automation devices and configuration. Based on available resources, specific ontology can be extracted from Smart-Irrigation-Ontology and can be used as knowledge base for smart irrigation system. By using knowledge stored in ontology and automating irrigation, quality of grapes can be improved and water wastage can be minimized.

## 7.4 Conclusions

Ontology plays an important role in IoT-based automation of agricultural systems. The chapter demonstrates how ontology can be built by using natural language processing techniques and formal concept analysis. The work described in the chapter demonstrates how irrigation details about vineyards can be very well represented using ontology. The information about sensors can also be stored in ontology and used for automated systems building is shown in smart irrigation ontology. Based on given water requirements automated irrigation system can be built using knowledge from vineyard ontology and smart irrigation ontology as proposed in the chapter.

# 8

# *Crop Suitability Recommendation*

## 8.1 Introduction

Agriculture is the main source of income and survival in India for the majority of population. Agriculture is done from ages in India. Hence, a rich collection of historical data about agriculture is available. Information Technology can be used to process such a large amount of data and then for recommendation. Various data mining techniques can be used for finding recommendations about crops and fertilizers. Outputs of these techniques can be communicated on smart phones. This chapter focuses on the implementation of data mining algorithms which can help in building an efficient recommendation system using available observation data.

This chapter describes a system which recommends to farmers crops suitable for a particular region based on crop yield history of last three years in that region and the fertilizers suitable for a specific crop based on soil measurements. It can help farmers for increasing their crop production. The described work shows how information available with government about yearly production in various areas can be used for crop recommendations to farmers. As information represented in the form of ontology can be easily shared and reused, the knowledge base of recommendation system is maintained in the form of ontology. The system uses random forest algorithm for crop recommendation as it works efficiently on huge dataset and can handle missing values. This chapter describes how k-means clustering can be used for predicting best suitable fertilizer for the crop based on given available NPK content in the soil.

## 8.2 Design and Implementation

The recommendation system is developed as Android-based application connected to server and having ontology as knowledge base. Architecture of knowledge base is shown in Figure 8.1. The farmer has to create an account

DOI: 10.1201/9781003408253-9

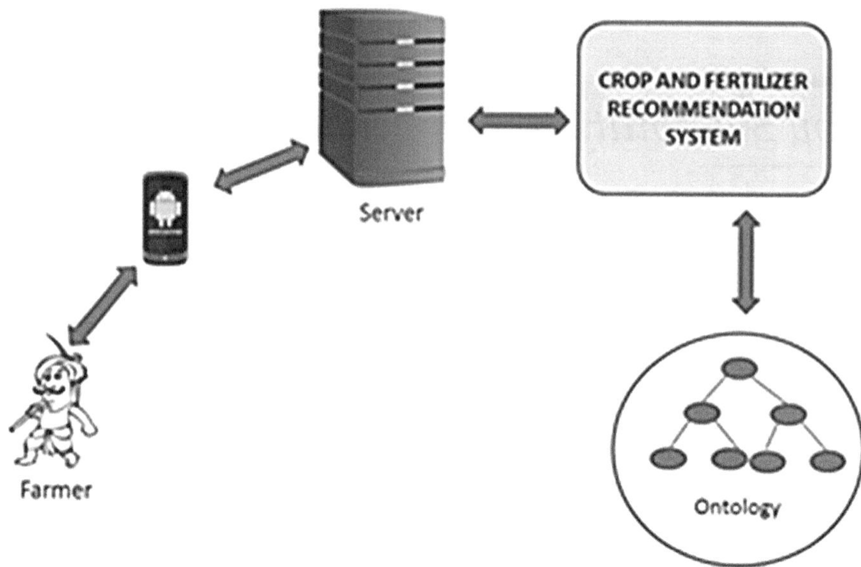


**FIGURE 8.1**
Crop suitability recommendation system architecture.

and log into the Android application for accessing the system. After that, famer can get two services as crop recommendation and fertilizer predictions.

Crop prediction is done using random forest algorithm. Fertilizer recommendation is done through k-means clustering algorithm. For getting these outputs, farmers need to enter some input values which acts as test data. The trained data is stored in the ontology which helps in creating a machine learning model for crop prediction. All these processes take place at the server end and output is displayed back to farmers on their Android device.

### 8.2.1 Crop Recommendation

Specific regions in Maharashtra state of India have specific soil characteristics, weather conditions and crop production history. Information about types of crops harvested and yield of those crops in those areas can be used for taking decision on which crops give maximum yield in specific region. For recommending the most suitable crop for the field, knowledge base containing past 3 years data about yields of crops in Maharashtra is used. It is taken as training set. This knowledge is collected from Department of Agriculture, Government of Maharashtra. This knowledge is stored in the form of ontology. Web Ontology Language (OWL) is used for ontology representation.

OWL is a Semantic Web language. It is designed to represent rich and complex concepts, groups of concepts and relationships between concepts.

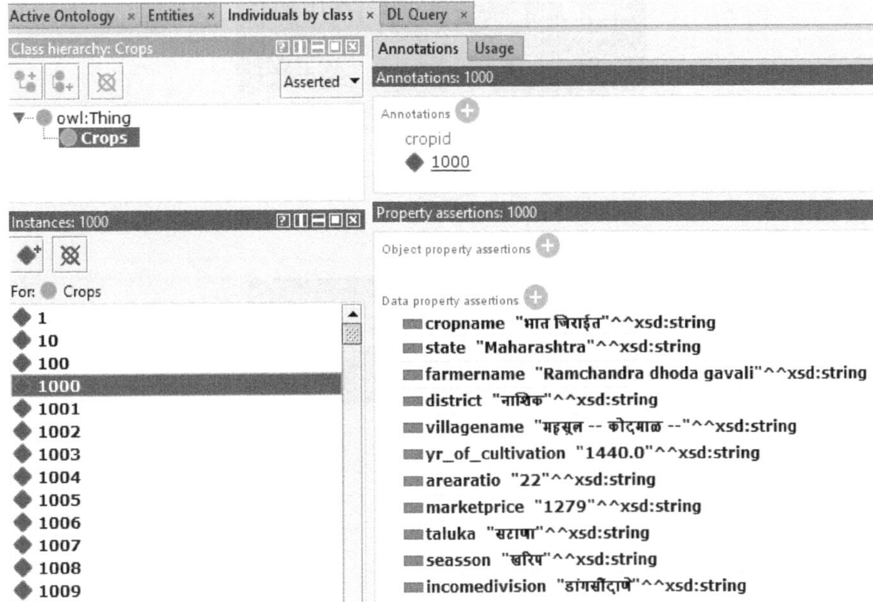


**FIGURE 8.2**
Crop yield history stored in ontology.

In OWL file, data properties about the crops are stored, which represent the relationship between the crop and their attributes. As shown in Figure 8.2, cropid, cropname, district, taluka, season, etc., are the data properties of the OWL class called Crop. All records received from government in excel sheets are converted to ontology data property values using APIs available for data conversion in ontology form.

System applies random forest algorithm using knowledge base in ontology as training set for crop recommendation. Random forest algorithm is used as the accuracy of it is found to be higher than ID3 algorithm for a given dataset. This is because ID3 algorithm constructs only a single tree. If one node/crop is not included into the tree accurately, the entire prediction may be wrong. A random number of trees are constructed by random forest algorithm and outputs of random trees are calculated. Final output of random forest algorithm is aggregation of output random trees. Decision criteria for crop recommendation are based on production quantity of the crop and market price of the crop in specific area.

District, state, season are the input parameters for random forest. Random forest generates many number of decision trees by extracting training data stored in ontology, each tree predicts a crop for given test data. Final output is calculated as the probability of a particular crop predicted by random trees. Figure 8.4 shows example of predicted probabilities for crops suitability.

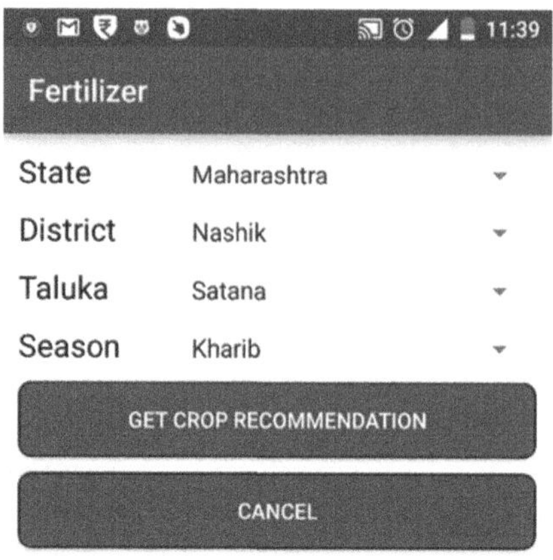

**FIGURE 8.3**
Input form for crop recommendation.

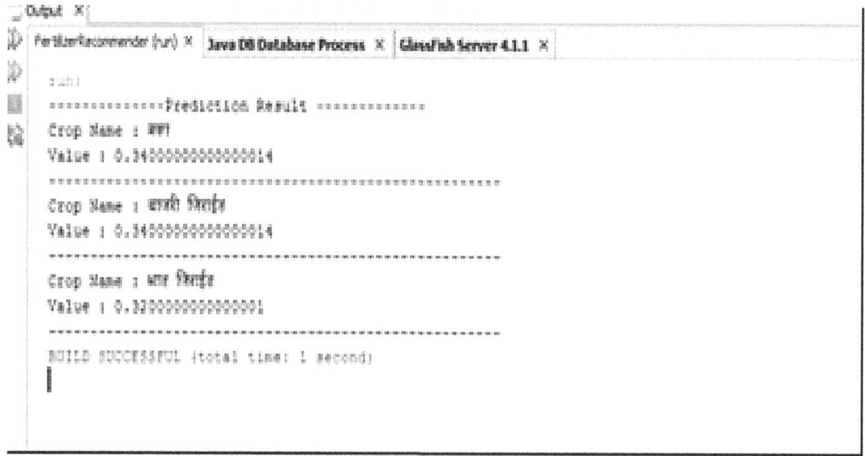


**FIGURE 8.4**
Output of random forest algorithm for suitable crop recommendation.

Probability of a particular crop is calculated as:

$$P_a = n_a / n_t$$

where:

$P_a$ = Probability of a particular crop (a)
$n_a$ = Number of predicted trees of crop (a)
$n_t$ = Total number of trees

#### 8.2.1.1 Fertilizer Recommendation

Recommendation of fertilizers is based on nitrogen, phosphorous and potassium measurements from soil. Nitrogen in the soil is responsible for color of leaves. If low quantity of nitrogen is found in the soil, then plants will have slight yellowish leaves and if quantity is moderate or high, it will have greener leaves. The phosphorous content in soil is responsible for the

**FIGURE 8.5**
Fertilizers recommendation for the selected crop.

reproductive system of the plant. Its value will predict the growth of fruits and flowers of plants. The potassium content of soil is responsible for its overall growth. Its value predicts how stronger the plant roots are and also determines the overall growth process of the plant.

For recommending fertilizer to the farmer, K-means clustering algorithm is used here. It is an unsupervised learning algorithm used to find out fertilizers with NPK contents nearest to requirements for the specified crop. Crop name and soil contents: nitrogen (N), phosphorous (P) and potassium (K) are given as input to the clustering algorithm.

There are two main steps in the algorithm implementation. Algorithm first calculates the required amount of fertilizer as follows:

$$R_a = S_a - M_a \tag{8.1}$$

where:

$R_a$ = Required NPK for crop 'a'
$S_a$ = Standard NPK for crop 'a'
$M_a$ = Measured NPK for crop 'a'

In the second step, algorithm forms clusters of nearby fertilizers with the help of Euclidean distance. It is the difference between NPK values. Fertilizers in clusters with minimum distance are recommended to farmers.

## 8.3 Performance Evaluation

Implemented algorithms are checked for performance and accuracy with the help of farmers. Standard precision measure is used for calculating accuracy. Precision is a fraction of the retrieved information that is relevant. It is marked for evaluation of accuracy and exactness. Here accuracy of predicted crops and fertilizers is compared against actual values given by experts for those fields and set of crops for each farmer. If the crops recommended by the system belong to the expert's recommendations, then those crops are relevant crops. Considering these relevant crops, precision of the recommendation system is calculated. The graphical representation of precision versus number of users is shown in Figure 8.6.

$$\text{Precision} = A/T \tag{8.2}$$

where:
A = Number of users who got relevant predictions
T = Number of users

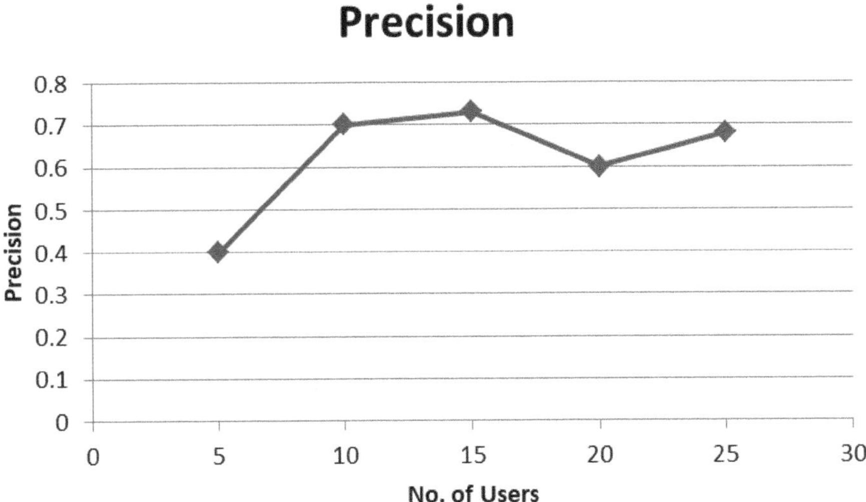


**FIGURE 8.6**
Performance evaluation of crop suitability recommendation system.

## 8.4 Conclusions

The chapter proposes the use of data mining techniques to provide recommendations of suitable crop in the field and fertilizers for crops to farmers with the help of data stored in ontology. Proposed system provides crop recommendation based on region, type of crop and fertilizer recommendation based on NPK content of soil. Thus, the aim of this system is to increase the production of farmers by recommending correct crop and fertilizer. An Android application is provided to access the developed system. The performance evaluation shows that the accuracy of developed system is reasonably high.

# Part 2

# Automated Negotiation

# 9

# *Negotiation*

Negotiation is ubiquitous, clearly an important activity in our lives as well in the global economy and is worthy of academic study. However, according to Fatima et al. (Shaheen et al., 2014), negotiation is central to our lives; it does not imply that we are good at it. Negotiation is usually a better and dynamic stand to other related approaches of reaching to an agreement like social choice, arguments and fair division. The very purpose of negotiation as a life process is to reach an agreement, in the presence of conflicting goals and preferences. Usually in the real world, preferences, goals, aspirations of individuals do not match, there negotiation can be utilized. The analysis of this deep psychological phenomenon and a question of how computers can be useful in implementing it virtually, to give inherent benefits of negotiation in trading, buying, selling, auctioning, bidding and bargaining, raise many interesting scientific problems.

## 9.1 Need of Negotiation Automation

With the advancements and proliferation of web technologies, it is becoming more important to make the traditional negotiation pricing mechanism automated, intelligent and efficient. The behavior of software agents which negotiate on behalf of humans can be determined by their tactics in the form of decision functions. Prediction of partner's behavior in negotiation has been an active research direction in recent years as it will improve the utility gain for the adaptive negotiation agent and also achieve the agreement much quicker or look after much higher benefits. Although negotiation is practically very complex activity to automate without human intervention, this is an attempt to propose an architecture for predicting the opponent's behavior and various factors which affect the process of negotiation. The concept is such that the information about negotiators, their individual actions and dynamics can be used by software agents which are equipped with adaptive capabilities to learn from past negotiations and assist in selecting appropriate negotiation tactics. While engaged in complex negotiations, people become irritated, tired, confused and sometimes emotional also making inconsistent, rash decisions. They fall prey to personal prejudices, misapprehensions and

DOI: 10.1201/9781003408253-11

fallacies. Many times, it can be a profoundly stressful activity. So ultimately this is an era where we have to have computer programs/software agents/ agents to negotiate on our behalf. These agents should be capable of overall activities ( not all but few) like recognition of social conflict/problem where negation can be an approach, gathering and structuring private information, deciding participants/ stakeholders, opponent analysis, protocol/rules selection, all exchange of offers and the feedback, argumentation/justifications/promises, learning, dynamic strategy selection, resolution in case of failure, renegotiation. Figure 9.1 shows the classification.

The main focus in this research is on how effectively and optimally few of the existing negotiation mechanisms (Bargaining-bilateral/multilateral, Bidding and Auctioning) can be suitably implemented with techniques like decision support systems, linear programming and form a consolidated research material on various strategies with set of rules/protocols with few assumptions.

## 9.2 History of Electronic Negotiation

Negotiations, according to Bala et al. (2015) and Vij et al. (2019b), have a long history in human society, and they currently play a prominent role in such areas as distributed artificial intelligence, sociopolitical decision making and electronic commerce and business activities particularly rely on them. According to Cao et al. (2009) as well as Mukun (Mukun, 2010), negotiation is a dialogue intended to resolve disputes, to produce an agreement upon courses of action, to bargain for individual or collective advantage, or to craft outcomes to satisfy various interests. They also say that it is a kind of decision making where two or more parties jointly search a space of solutions with the goal of reaching a consensus. Electronic negotiations have gained heightened importance due to the advance of the web and e-Commerce. The tremendous successes of online auctions show that the dynamic trade based on e-negotiation will gradually become the core of e-Commerce. According to Bala et al. (2015), it is becoming more and more important to make the traditional negotiation pricing mechanism automated and intelligent. The automation saves human negotiation time and computational agents are sometimes better at finding deals in strategically complex settings (Vij et al.) (2015a). Traditionally, e-negotiation processes have been carried out by humans, registering at certain web pages, placing bids, making offers and receiving counter offers from other participants (Bala et al. (2013a) and Cao et al. (2009) as well as Mukun (2010). One of the major challenges these systems face is that the parties conducting the negotiation have very less knowledge of each other. So humans were replaced by negotiation agents in the process

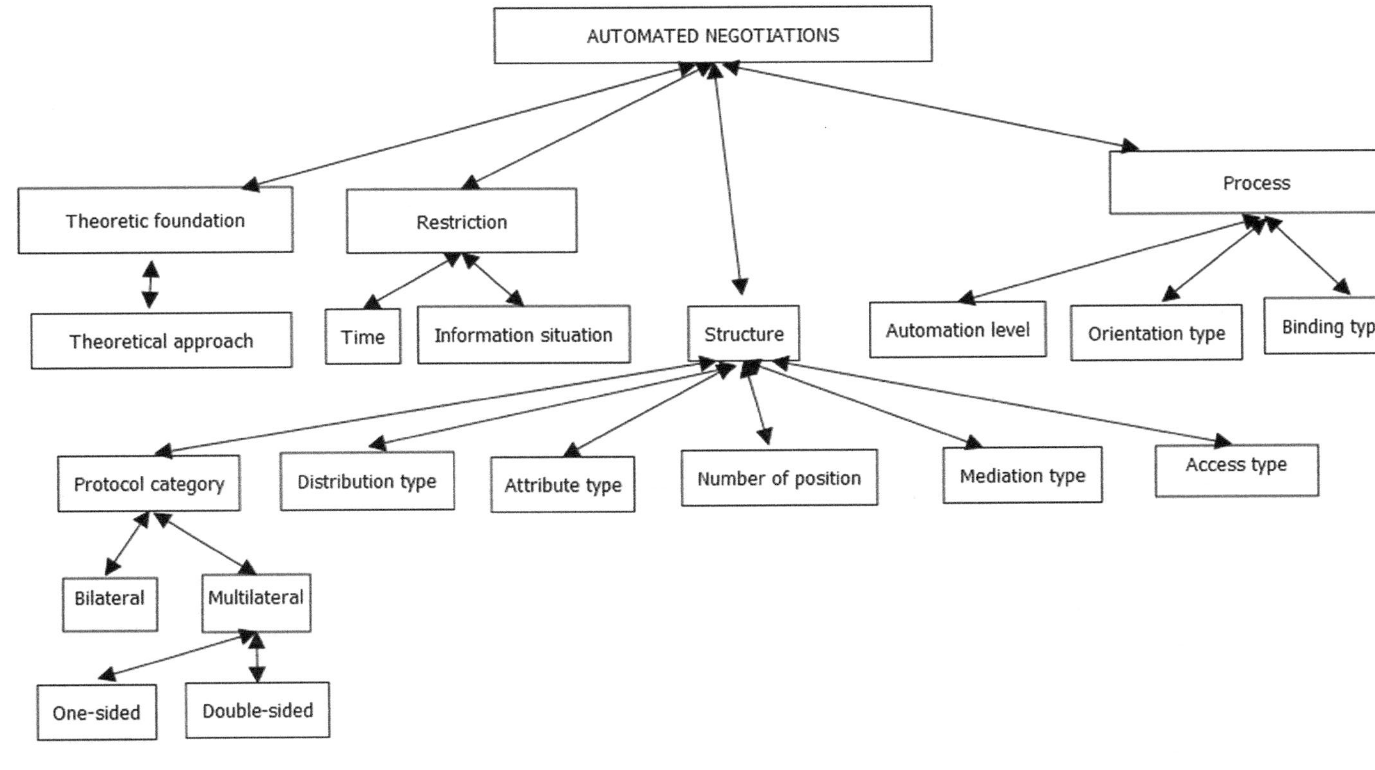


**FIGURE 9.1**
Classification of automated negotiation.

of negotiation. However, various problems are faced by the negotiation agents such as limited and uncertain knowledge and conflicting preferences. Also agents may have inconsistent deadline and partial overlaps of zones of acceptance. Moreover, multilateral negotiations are more complicated and time consuming than bilateral negotiations (Bala et al.) (2013b). These factors make it difficult to reach consensus. So decision-making mechanism is required to overcome this problem. Since the mid-90s last century, the research on automated negotiation system has been given high priority by researchers (Cao et al.) (2009). The need is that the agents should be equipped with a decision-making mechanism which allows them to adapt to the behavior of the negotiation partner. Intelligent systems for negotiation aim at increasing the negotiator's abilities to understand the opponent's needs and limitations. This ability helps to predict the opponent's moves which can be a valuable tool in negotiation tasks. Various negotiation strategies have been proposed which are capable of predicting the opponent's behavior. The research presented here also focuses on the online prediction of the other agent's tactic in order to reach better deals in negotiation. While the extensive coverage of all the prediction methods employed in negotiation is beyond the scope of the current work, it is useful to mention several key studies.

## 9.3 Negotiation and Latest Technologies

E-Negotiation, according to Mukhopadhyay et al. (2015), is basically a type of interaction in which a group of agents, with conflicting interests and a desire to cooperate, try to come to a mutually acceptable agreement on the division of scarce resources. These resources do not only refer to money but also include other parameters like product quality features, guaranty features, mode of payment, etc. Electronic negotiations have gained heightened importance due to the development of the web and e-Commerce. The rapid success of online auctions clearly shows that e-negotiation will eventually become the basis of e-Commerce. Whether it is a case of B to B purchase or a case of online shopping, it is required to make the traditional negotiation pricing mechanism automated and intelligent. The automation saves human negotiation time and computational negotiators are better at finding deals in combination and strategically complex settings. Mukun (2010) said Cloud Computing is technology for next generation Information and Software enabled work that is capable of changing the software working environment. It is an interconnection between the large-scale computing resources to effectively integrate and to computing resources as a service to users. Cloud computing allows users to use applications without installation of any application and easier access to their personal files and application at any system with internet or intranet access. Cloud computing is effectively the actual separation of physical and virtual services, a number of business services reduced costs, improved utilization of network resources. Cloud computing is a technology that uses the internet or intranet and central remote servers to maintain the data and applications. This technology allows for efficient computing by centralizing storage, memory, processing and bandwidth given by Singh, Kumar and Khatn (2012). Cloud Computing is an innovation that uses advanced computational power and improved storage capabilities. Cloud computing is a new processing scheme in which computer processing is performed in the network. This means that users need not concern themselves with the processing details. Although Cloud computing enables more flexible, easier and faster computing. It is evident in today's era that Amazon, Microsoft, OpenStack and Google are all cloud providers. Google Apps, Google Driver are the examples of cloud. Case-based reasoning (CBR) is a problem solving paradigm where solution of new problem is based on solution of similar past problem. According to Mukhopadhyay et al. (2015), we can use rule-based reasoning (RBR) concept, where there are some rules such as discount, festival offers, etc. In one of their papers, they have introduced an E-negotiation agent-based system using rule-based reasoning and case-based reasoning. Due to the use of rule-based reasoning and case-based reasoning, system should improve the efficiency and success rate of the negotiation process. For making system faster and secure cloud computing concept can be used. The product details, Agent details, rule-based data, case-based data would be stored on the cloud. Seller and buyer select their respective agents through the cloud for negotiation. In this E-negotiation system, agent acts as a negotiator. Agent has user's (seller and buyer) details and their requirements for a particular product. For making successful negotiation, there are three ways to do with latest technologies. The first way is rule based. In this way, agent checks users' requirement with rule-based data which is stored on the cloud. If any rule is matched with users, then seller's agent and buyer's agent start negotiation through rule-based data. The second way is case based. In this way, agent checks users' requirement with case-based data which is stored on the cloud. If any similar case is matched with user's requirement, then seller's agent and buyer's agent start negotiation through case-based data. The third way is bilateral negotiation. According to Mukhopadhyay et al. (2015), if both rule-based and case-based data are not matched with users' requirements then both parties' agents will start negotiation with each other using bilateral negotiation model. After completing negotiation process, both parties' agents will give feedback to their respective user whether negotiation is successful or not. If negotiation is successful, then agent will give bid price of particular product to their respective user. This negotiation process will be stopped when both parties will come to final decision. Web services can also be used to make the process dynamic.

## 9.4 Multilateral Negotiations and Related Issues

Nowadays, the view of organizations toward negotiation has changed. E-commerce changed the way of business interaction, no matter whether it's a B2B or B2C trading or online shopping. E-procurement leads to enhanced business relationship and cost saving. Software agents are assigned the job of negotiation and should be able to simulate the human behavior and be able to learn from the past experience of negotiation and improve their respective negotiation strategies. In automated multi-attribute negotiation, time-based, resource-based and behavior-based strategies are used. Heuristic method can be used to attain private information about agents. In the process of negotiation, additional information about user or offer can be exchanged by using argumentation-based negotiation method by Raz Lin (Lin & Kraus, 2010). Attributes of negotiation can be dependent or independent. For example, a buyer agent and a seller agent are buying a product with several attributes, in the situation where attributes are dependent on value of another attribute, if one of the value of attribute is increased from buyer or seller then other attribute's value is decreased automatically. Total number of issues, dependency between them, representation of utility, negotiation rules or protocol, form of negotiation and time constraints are main factors in any negotiation process. This takes place when two or more people, with differing viewpoints, come together to attempt to reach an agreement on an issue. It is known as persuasive communication or bargaining. Attributes of negotiation can be dependent or independent. Negotiation is conducted in various ways such as bidding, bargaining or by using auctions. In bilateral negotiation, two agents are involved in negotiation with single issue or multiple issues. According to Vij et al. (2015a), when more than two agents are involved with multiple issues then this complex phenomenon is known as multilateral automated negotiation. Multilateral automated negotiation is possible in one-to-many, many-to-one or many-to-many ways. Summary of forms of automated negotiations is shown in Table 9.1.

In bilateral automated negotiation, Vij et al. (2015a) say that maximum utility for a single agent can become minimum utility for opponent agent; therefore, the chance of agreement is low. This problem is avoided by multilateral

**TABLE 9.1**

Forms of Negotiation

| Sr. No. | Bidding | Auctions | Bargaining |
|---|---|---|---|
| 1. | Buyer starts | Seller starts | Buyer starts |
| 2. | Bilateral/Multilateral | Multilateral | Bilateral/Multilateral |
| 3. | Simplest negotiation | Medium negotiation | Complex negotiation |

automated negotiation. A major challenge in the negotiation using the bilateral protocol is that the agents hide their preferences. So agent does not know which preferences the opponent will prefer.

## 9.5 Negotiations and Multiple Strategies

According to Vij et al. (2019b), an E-negotiation facilitates electronic interaction between two or more parties having disagreement over some issues of negotiating object. This disagreement can be resolved through persuading the opponent by exchanging offer and counter offer which are generated using certain negotiation strategies. Every strategy has certain characteristic which decides its applicability and will yield accordingly against the kind of opponent. Negotiation system based on single strategy, chosen by individual at pre-negotiation stage, limits its applicability to known negotiation scenario, which does not relate to real-world situation where opponent and its preferences are unknown. There is a need to develop system which can adapt to the kind of opponent we are negotiating with. Negotiation strategy is an umbrella term which defines the bidding, opponent profiling and acceptance criteria of a party. Every party can define and develop its negotiation strategy. Traditionally, the negotiation system comes with some assumptions; for example, a particular strategy works well for single negotiation scenario (Patrikar et al. (2015); Bala et al. (2015); Deochake et al. (2012)). According to Vij et al. (2019b), only one type of strategy is sufficient for negotiating with a particular opponent (Cao et al.) (2015). But in real-life scenario, negotiating scenario is not known in advance (Cao et al.) (2015). A single strategy against any type of scenario cannot guarantee optimal result (utility) and is considered as poor choice (Baarslag et al.) (Tim et al., 2013). So, there is a need to have a system which can cope up with a high number of negotiation scenarios and can handle dynamic negotiation environment. For that, we need to establish the applicability of strategies, i.e., to say a rule-base for selecting them during the negotiation. Each strategy will yield accordingly against a type of opponent.

Selection of strategy is a multifaceted problem: (1) the bid should be made in such a way that it maximizes its own utility and have high acceptance probability; (2) the behavior of opponent is difficult to predict and profile; (3) establishing and validating the applicability (selection) rule-base.

Apart from conceptual challenges, the inherent implementation challenges are as follows: (1) unavailability of reliable dataset and test bed, (2) negotiation strategy module, (3) simulator, (4) performance matrices. One major challenge with e-negotiation is to support inter-operable environment. The objective of research can be to automate the negotiation process effectively with higher success rate. The sub-objectives are: (1) to develop and design the decision-making model to support strategy selection during the course of Automated Negotiation (AN); (2) to establish the applicability of negotiation strategies against a class of particular opponent, preference and agenda; (3) to construct and validate strategy selection algorithm; (4) to construct a web-service-based framework for AN. Every negotiation process requires an active collaboration of buyer and seller negotiating software entity (also called as negotiating agent) by Mukhopadhyay et al. (2012a) and Ito et al. (Ito et al., 2009). This drives a need for a negotiation framework which is flexible in terms of platform, implementation and place. According to Vij et al. (2019b), there can be also a web-service; multi-strategy selection-based Decision Support System (DSS) which can select strategies during the course of negotiation in a more informative way and can deal with a range of negotiation scenarios. The advantage of using multi-strategy is high success rate, i.e., successful negotiation; fast response because of profiling; high number of scenarios because of strategy pool. The contribution of this research work is to maximize the success rate of negotiation process, i.e., convergence into successful contracts and eventually maximizing the efficiency and effectiveness of the system.

## 9.6 Organization of Part 2

Part 2 of this book contains some results and detailed analysis on a working of bilateral negotiation protocol using behavior prediction in decision support system given by Bala, Vij and Mukhopadhyay (2013); multilateral negotiation protocol using linear programming given by Vij et al. (2015a, 2015b); negotiation analysis using RBR and CBR by More, Vij and Mukhopadhyay (2013); few strategies selected by Vij, Agrawal, Mukhopadhyay (2019a) and overall protocol relevance by Vij, Agrawal, Mukhopadhyay (2019b).

**Chapter 10** presents extensive Literature survey.

**Chapter 11** is about problem statement, scope, purpose and SRS, timeline schedule.

**Chapter 12** presents the methodology, design aspects and working model.

**Chapter 13** discusses results and analysis.

**Chapter 14** includes conclusions and future scope. It also includes the contributions of this research, overview, experimental work and result analysis, limitations of research and contribution.

# 10

# *Literature Survey*

## 10.1 Motivation for the Survey

According to internet sources www.computingscience.nl, Leo Baekeland sold the rights to his invention, Velox photographic printing paper, to Eastman Kodak in 1899. It was the first commercially successful photographic paper and he sold it to Eastman Kodak for $1 million. Baekeland had planned to ask $50,000 and to go down to $25,000 if necessary, but fortunately for him, Eastman spoke first.

It has been nearly a century since Baekeland's negotiation with Eastman Kodak and the business world has changed substantially. The internet is rapidly connecting businesses across the globe, and electronic commerce technologies and processes have introduced new ways of doing business. The infrastructure for a completely new business paradigm of electronic commerce is being laid. However, the infrastructure is not yet complete. Negotiation is an important part of the procurement process, and yet most corporate negotiation today is conducted in much the same manner as Baekeland's was nearly a century ago. In order to support current business practices as well as new ones on the internet, electronic commerce systems need the ability to negotiate.

According to Brzostowski and Kowalczyk (2006), negotiation is the process of exchanging information among interested parties in order to find an agreement satisfying requirements of these parties. Different fields such as decision and game theory, management and social sciences, artificial intelligence and agent technology study the problem of negotiation from different perspectives. The negotiation agents face various problems such as limited and uncertain knowledge and conflicting preferences. In addition, in the case of positional bargaining used commonly in agent-based negotiations, the agents may not have consistent deadlines and partial overlaps of zones of acceptance. These factors may make reaching an agreement very difficult and there is a need to develop new decision-making mechanisms that can overcome such problems. The agent has to learn and adapt to the behavior of its negotiation opponent in order to be successful. In the approach proposed

DOI: 10.1201/9781003408253-12

by Faratin (2000) the agents are equipped in a decision-making mechanism allowing for limited adaptation to the behavior of negotiation partner. The adaptation is realized by the use of so-called behavior-dependent tactic that imitates the partner's behavior. This decision-making mechanism allows agents to mix time-dependent tactics with the behavior-dependent tactics using weights that can result in quite complex negotiation behavior. However, such a negotiation strategy has a large number of parameters that have to be set up by the user, and sometimes it is difficult to decide how to set these parameters. Therefore, some approaches based on learning from previous interactions have been proposed.

Most of the work devoted to learning approaches supporting the negotiation focuses on learning from previous encounters, i.e. off-line learning. The approaches include: Bayesian learning, Q-learning, case-based reasoning and evolutionary computation by Beheshti and Mozayani (2009) and Brzostowski and Kowalczyk (2006). According to Brzostowski and Kowalczyk (2006), these approaches require usually history of repeated interactions and such data may not always be available. Therefore, it is important to learn from the history of offers of the current encounter and adapt to the negotiation opponent behavior, i.e. online learning. The online learning approaches supporting the negotiation are quite rare. Hou (2004) proposes such an approach based on the non-linear regression analysis. In that work the history of partner's concessions is used to predict its future offers and for deciding which negotiation strategy to use in order to adapt to the forecast. However, the predicting mechanism is applied only for pure tactics, i.e. either time-dependent or behavior-dependent.

According to Buttner (2006), one of the most important criteria is the protocol category. It describes the number of negotiating partners. There bilateral and multilateral are separated. One-sided and double-sided are two types of multilateral automated negotiations.

## 10.2 Auctions versus Negotiations

According to the internet sources opus4.kobv.de, online auctions have recently gained a lot of importance, leading to the assumption that auctions are the only class of negotiation protocols. However, auctions are not the only one group but just one possible group of negotiation protocols. This section will briefly compare these two concepts.

Hudert (2006) says that 'traditional auctions are resource allocation mechanisms based on competitive bidding over a single issue (i.e. price) of a single, well-defined object'. Auction rules 'specify how the winner is determined and how much he has to pay' and therefore govern the auction as a whole.

Auction participants post bids indicating their willingness to pay and on termination of an auction a clear is created which assigns the negotiated object to the winning participant, following a 'set of rules determining resource allocation and prices on the basis of the bids from the market agents', above stated as auction rules. Thus, the main goal of an auction is to establish certain value through a bidding process. Initially, the value of an object is unknown. During the auction process the value of an object is determined by the bids received and finally the clear reached. On the other hand, according to Lau (2007), 'traditional negotiations are based on bilateral, multilateral or multi bilateral negotiation processes over a single or multiple issue/s of one or more well-, partly, or ill-defined objects and involve cooperation and/or competition among the negotiating agents'. According to the internet sources opus4.kobv.de, negotiations can therefore also produce win-win situations. This can be defined by using utility as a measure of offers. This concept allows for scenarios with multiple negotiated issues to produce simultaneous improvements for all negotiating parties (integrative negotiating).

The emergence of new electronically conducted forms for decision-making processes, like multidimensional auctions, more and more show that the traditional auctions are just a subclass of the negotiation protocols possible. Negotiation protocols do not only include single issue negotiation in some form of bidding process (i.e. auctions) but also protocols like bilateral bargaining or multi-bilateral negotiations, where the participants engage in multiple bilateral negotiations with many other parties. Therefore, for the rest of this thesis auctions are assumed to be a subclass of all possible negotiation protocols. The following section will therefore list some of the traditional auction protocols as examples for negotiation protocols, but also multidimensional negotiations or one-on-one bargaining will presented to give a more comprehensive overview on what protocols are possible to conduct negotiations.

## 10.3 Negotiation Types

Like it or not, everybody is a negotiator. Everyday people are negotiating using different negotiation techniques. When kids, everybody negotiated trading sports cards or toys and we still do it while we negotiate for salary rise with the organizations, also while shopping on streets. We use negotiation in our personnel lives also. Everyone has some of friends, family, significant other, or kids and at some time we negotiate with them in subconscious mind, body language, without even knowing about it. Many people don't like to negotiate because they view it as a hassle. Even though we might consciously think we're avoiding the blatant negotiation process, we end up doing it without realizing that's exactly what's happening. According to web sources mcmba.blogspot.com and the theory of human psyche, there are two distinct types of negotiations, known as distributive negotiations and integrative negotiations.

### 10.3.1 Distributive Negotiations – The Fixed Pie

The term distributive means according to web sources www.oppapers.com; there is a giving out or the scattering of things. By nature, there is a limit or finite amount in the thing being distributed or divided among the people involved. Hence, this type of negotiation is often referred to as *'The Fixed Pie'*. According to the web source www.sunshineglobaleducation.net, there is only so much to go around, but the proportion to be distributed is not only limited but also variable. In the real world of negotiations, two parties face off with the goal of getting as much as possible. The seller wants to go after the best price they can obtain, while the buyer wants to pay the lowest price to achieve the best bargain. It's really just good old plain haggling, which is not all that much different from playing a tug of war.

A distributive negotiation involves people who have never had a previous interactive relationship, nor are they likely to do so again in the near future. Simple everyday examples would be when we're buying a car or a house. Purchasing products or services are simple business examples where distributive bargaining is often employed. Remember, even friends or business acquaintances can drive a hard bargain just as well as any stranger. Secondly, when we are dealing with someone unknown to us, and it's a onetime only occurrence, we really have no particular interest in forming a relationship with them, except for the purpose of the deal itself. We are generally less concerned with how they perceive us, or how they might regard our reputation. Ours and their interests are usually self-serving.

### 10.3.2 Integrative Negotiations – Everybody Wins Something (Usually)

The word integrative means to join several parts into a whole. Conceptually, this implies some cooperation, or a joining of forces to achieve something together. It usually involves a higher degree of trust and a forming of a relationship. Both parties want to walk away feeling they've achieved something which has value by getting what each wants. Ideally, it is a twofold process. In the real world of business, the results often tilt in favor of one party over the other because it's unlikely that both parties will come to the table at even strength, when they begin the talks.

Nonetheless, reference www.oppapers.com says that there are many advantages to be gained by both parties, when a cooperative approach is taken by them for mutual solution to a problem. Generally, this form of negotiation is looking down the road, to them forming a long-term relationship to create mutual gain. It is often described as the win-win scenario.

## 10.4 Negotiation Tactics

According to the negotiation theory given in web source www.negotiation tactics.net, there are many different tactics that are commonly used in the negotiation process. All of them have their place, and many of the methods that have been popularized are specialized for specific types of negotiation. The level of detail the best negotiators put into understanding the human mind and how to use certain tones of voice coupled with specific tactics to lead the other party in the direction that they would like them to head is, to say the least, quite impressive. Just knowing the tactics is only half the battle, but putting them into effective use can be tricky if you do not know how to properly propose them. A few of the more common tactics that are used in negotiations include:

- **Nibbling**

  Nibbling is among the most popular of negotiation tactics. The actual strategy is to continue the negotiations after the deal is supposedly done. This tactic is most effective when a great deal of time has been spent finalizing the negotiation and the other party has invested a great deal of time into it. For instance, if you are buying a piece of property, after the deal is finalized you may ask for other accommodations that were not originally part of the plan for the property that you purchased. This can be a fairly risky tactic; although, a large majority of individuals will not renege on the deal after so much time has been put into it. If you choose to try the nibbling technique, you may not want to ask for too much as this can break down the entire process.
- **Outright Refusal**

  One popular negotiation tactic that has yielded a great deal of success is the outright refusal method. This method works by outright refusing the original offer made to you and asking them to do better. Oftentimes the individuals who are making the offer will actually negotiate with themselves and provide you with an offer that is much higher than the offer that was originally made. While this tactic might be simplistic in nature, it is a well-documented method that has provided many negotiators with positive results for many years.
- **Conditioning**

  Conditioning calls for you to place a starting point in their mind prior to beginning the negotiation. For instance, if someone started to discuss a negotiation for the purchase of a boat with you, and you initially responded by saying 'You'll be wasting your time unless you are willing to offer $10,000 and haul it after the sale.' This allows you to give them a starting figure that is much closer to the end result you are looking for than you would have been otherwise. This is an age-old method that has always been an effective negotiation tactic. Keep in mind that this tactic can also cause the individual you use it on to not make an offer on the item at all.

- **Calling Bluffs**

  Calling the opposing party's bluff is a negotiation tactic that can really be to your advantage. For instance, if you have a house that is for sale for $200,000, and they claim that their bank will only qualify them for a $175,000 loan, you can call their bluff by saying that you cannot let it go for less than $190,000. If you would like, you can also make up an excuse as to why you cannot go any lower than that amount in order to make it seem as if you too have your limits. For instance, you could say that the money is going to cover your child's college education and that is as low as you are willing to go. By taking their financing problem and responding with an explanation of why that won't work, you will be able to make them come out of their shell if they are truly interested in the product that you are selling.

There are two environment forms of automated negotiations typically in bargaining:

1. **Bilateral Automated Negotiations**: Bilateral negotiations are done between only two parties. Bilateral negotiations can be done using single issues or multiple issues. In that two agents are negotiated on behalf of their respective owners. It is a simple environment form.
2. **Multilateral Automated Negotiations**: In multilateral automated negotiation, more than two agents are involved with multiple issues. One-to-many, many-to-one and many-to-many are three forms of multilateral negotiation. According to Bala et al. (2013a), in one-to-many negotiation, buyer is represented by a combination of one coordinating agent and multiple sub-buyer agents and each supplier is represented by a seller agent.

## 10.5 Existing Systems and Issues

According to Lau (2007), the Kasbah e-marketplace is one of the early attempts at exploiting agent technology for automated negotiations in e-Commerce. A group of buyer agents and seller agents meet at the centralized Kasbah e-marketplace. These agents proactively seek out potential buyers or sellers and negotiate with each other on behalf of their owners. The objective of each agent is to complete an acceptable deal based on the user-specified constraints such as initial asking (or bidding) price, a reservation price, a date by which to complete the transaction, and restrictions on which parties to negotiate with and how to change the price over time. A Kasbah agent is restricted to exercising one of the three negotiation strategies: anxious, cool-headed, and frugal, corresponding to a linear, quadratic, and exponential function, respectively, for increasing (decreasing) its bid for a product over time. Unfortunately, the Kasbah agents can only negotiate over the single issue of price. However, B2B negotiations often involve multiple issues. Moreover, the Kasbah agents can only act according to one of the three pre-defined negotiation strategies which may not lead to the optimal negotiation results.

According to Lau (2007), the Michigan AuctionBot is a general purposed internet-based auction server hosted by the University of Michigan. Sellers can create new auctions on AuctionBot by choosing from a set of pre-defined auction types and then enter their specific auction parameters such as clearing time, minimum bid increment and whether proxy bids are allowed. In general, a seller will set a reservation price after creating an auction and let AuctionBot manage the bidders and enforce the bidding rules according to the chosen auction protocol. Although e-markets or auction houses are popular in B2C e-Commerce, they are not effective for B2B e-Commerce where there are multiple negotiation issues to deal with.

According to Lau (2007), MAGNET is a secure multi-agent marketplace which supports a variety of types of transactions, from simple buying and selling of goods and services to complex multi-agent negotiation of contracts with temporal and precedence constraints. The MAGNET agents are self-interested which attempt to gain the greatest possible profits from their endeavors. In this sense, MAGNET is more suitable for B2C e-Commerce rather than B2B e-Commerce where cooperative negotiation behavior is possible. To trade in the market, a customer agent generates a plan which is a collection of tasks with time and precedence constraints and then submits one or more Requests for Quotes (RFQs) to suppliers via the MAGNET market. Any supplier agent who wants to bid will respond. After receiving the bids, the customer agent decides which bids to accept. Finally, the winning supplier agents execute the tasks included in their winning bids. The MAGNET market administrator mediates all communication among agents, and its trust model is somewhat different from other online auction system. Three standard cryptographic techniques are used for security purpose. As a whole, MAGNET is only an e-Auction mechanism with enhanced security facilities.

According to Lau (2007), Montano et al. have reported a Genetic Algorithm (GA)-based negotiation mechanism for searching optimal solutions for multi-party multi-objective negotiations. Basically, a negotiation problem is treated as a multi-objective optimization problem. Apart from the standard genetic operators such as selection, crossover and mutation, the GA is enhanced with a new operator called trade. The trade operator simulates a concession-making mechanism which is often used in negotiation systems. However, the main problem of their particular GA-based negotiation mechanism is that the preferences (i.e., the utility functions) of all the negotiation parties are assumed available to a central negotiation mechanism. Such an assumption does not correspond to the reality often found in B2B e-Commerce.

According to the web source www.negotiationtactics.net, Onsale (www.onsale.com) is a 24-hour-a-day auction house, founded by Silicon Valley entrepreneur Jerry Kaplan in June 1995. It sells refurbished and 'end of life' computer and high-technology goods by auction, usually a hybrid English/sealed-bid auction of 1–10 identical items, over the internet. The auctions close three times a week, and bidding is continuous. Onsale claims weekly revenues of $700,000, profit margins of 13–20%, and a growth rate of 15–20% per year.

JEM Computers (www.jemcomp.com) also operates in the refurbished computer market, but using slightly different mechanisms. Founded in 1992 in Cambridge, Massachusetts, JEM Computers specializes in direct sales of PC manufacturers' inventories. They offer both straight-sale discounted computer items and JEM's Basement, a descending (Dutch) auction in which the price of an item is progressively lowered until all items are sold, negotiating the price by that type of auction mechanism.

Koll-Dove (www.koll-dove.com) was an established auction house long before the internet began, and today on the internet provides a wide variety of auction services. Of special interest are their sealed-bid auctions run over the internet; a recent example was the sale of four multi-million dollar institutional quality real estate projects in Texas and Louisiana by sealed bid. Bidders could submit either paper or electronic mail bids.

According to Lau (2007), genetic algorithm has also been applied to learn effective rules to support the negotiation processes. A chromosome represents a negotiation (classification) rule rather than an offer. The fitness of a chromosome (a rule) is measured in terms of how many times the rule has contributed to reach an agreement. In order for the system to determine if an agreement is possible, each negotiator's preferences including the reservation values of the negotiation attributes are assumed known or hypothesized. Therefore, this approach also suffers from the same common problem found in the other negotiation models which assume complete information about negotiation spaces. The future negotiation mechanism does not assume the availability of the opponents' negotiation preferences, and therefore it is more suitable for the development of an automated negotiation service for real-world B2B applications.

According to Lau (2007), defeasible logic has been used to model negotiation strategies based on argumentation semantics. Different classes of arguments are identified based on the notions of strict arguments, defeasible arguments and supportive arguments. According to these notions, a negotiation agent can evaluate incoming arguments or generate new arguments with different strength with respect to the requirements of a particular negotiation situation. Defeasible rules are not only suitable for specifying negotiation strategies but they are also useful for expressing offers and counter-offers exchanged among agents during a negotiation session. It is believed that by enabling agents to exchange rules, instead of just exchanging simple communication, the flexibility of the negotiation protocol can be improved considerably. Nevertheless, how multi-agent multi-issue negotiation is supported by the defeasible logic-based negotiation system is not clearly defined. Moreover, the computational complexity of the defeasible negotiation system will be a major obstacle for its application to real-world B2B e-Commerce applications.

According to Lau (2007), other negotiation models such as case-based reasoning (CBR), fuzzy constraint-based negotiation, belief revision and argumentative logic have also been explored to develop automated negotiation systems. However, these models either suffer from the lack of operational semantics to conduct multi-party multi-issue negotiations, computationally inefficient, or the lack of a concrete system design and implementation.

According to Cao Mukun (2010), at present, one severe problem for the research of automated negotiation is how to take the theoretical results into practical applications. For more than 10 years, compared with the fruitful results of theoretical research, the application of automated negotiation has lagged far behind. So far there is scarcely any practical automated negotiation system that can be applied in e-Commerce. The realization of system remains at experimental stage as most prototype systems were developed in university laboratories and automated negotiation technology is still under investigation in research labs. It could take some time before practical B2B e-Commerce systems to adopt a negotiation tool. That has been a barrier for the research of automated negotiation. The fact that many good theories, models and algorithms cannot be verified without a practical application platform constrains the further development of automated negotiation research. This situation is widespread in the entire e-Commerce-oriented automated trading applications. As mentioned in a web source www.computingscience.nl, while some systems have been widely cited in literatures, strictly speaking, they are not automated negotiation systems. Because software agent technology in these systems is mainly used to achieve automated trading functions, such as product selection, price comparison and so on. Even some applications involved in negotiation are mainly for auction. This situation can be mainly attributed to the following: First, the theory of automated negotiation is still under development; new theories and methods appear one after another. The industry and academia have not yet reached a consensus for some basic questions and have not formed a unified standard. Second, the research of automated negotiation has close relationship with the disciplines of artificial intelligence, multi-agent systems theory and software agent technology. These disciplines are not mature and constrain the actual application of automated negotiation system. Automated negotiation system is essentially a multi-agent system, whose development is inseparable from the software agent technology. Therefore, the development of automated negotiation system has no technology roadmap to follow nowadays. Third, the basic rules of software engineering tell that the creation, development and application of a new technology is a time-consuming process. Human's psychological acceptance of this new technology is also a time-consuming process. Finally, the automated negotiation system does not have a suitable application model for its own development. This is one of the most important reasons. The first three are common reasons for most new technologies and are likely to be encountered during the process of development. However, under the circumstances of the rapid development of e-Commerce applications and network technology, nowadays, researchers cannot ignore the fact that the automated negotiation system has developed too slowly. This problem should be solved first to pave the way for future automated negotiation research.

### 10.5.1 Survey on Prediction Part in E-Negotiation

According to internet source www.inderscience.com, predicting the agent's behavior and using those prediction results to maximize agents own benefits is one of the crucial issues in the negotiation process. It is necessary for an agent to produce offers based on his own criteria because an agent has limited computational power and incomplete knowledge about opponents. Various approaches have been proposed according to internet source www.ijert.org for predicting the opponent's negotiation behavior. We reviewed some of the approaches to come up with certain conclusions regarding the efficiency of each approach and their shortcomings.

**Paper 1**. Initially game theory was used in the negotiation process. It treats negotiation as a game and the negotiation agents are treated as players of the game. Zeng and Sycara (1998) used game-theoretic approach with Bayesian belief revision to model a negotiation counterpart. However, game theory has two main drawbacks which make it unsuitable for use in the negotiation process. First is that it assumes the agent has infinite computational power and secondly it assumes all the agents have common knowledge. These limitations of the game theory were overcome by the decision functions.

**Paper 2**. Faratin (2000) and Faratin et al. (2000) proposed a bilateral negotiation model in which the two parties negotiate on an issue like price, delivery time, quality, etc. The two parties adopt opposite roles (buyer and seller) and use one of the three families of negotiation tactics, namely time-dependent tactics, resource-dependent tactics and behavior-dependent tactics. The offers exchanged between the agents are represented as $x^{t_n}_{a\leftrightarrow b}$. This is the offer generated by agent 'a' for agent 'b' at time 'tn'. All the offers are restricted in between mina and maxa which specifies the range of all possible offers of 'a'. Each agent has a scoring function Va which assigns a score to each offer produced. A sequence of alternating offers and counter offers by the agents is called negotiation thread. An agent may respond to the offer by any of the three ways: withdraw, accept or offer, according to the internet source www.inderscience.com,

$$R^a\left(t^n, x^{t_{n-1}}_{b\to a}\right) = \begin{cases} \text{withdraw}\,(a,b) & \text{if } t^n > t^a_{max} \\ \text{accept}\left(a,b,x^{t_{n-1}}_{b\to a}\right) & \text{if } V^a\left(x^{t_{n-1}}_{b\to a}\right) \geq V^a\left(x^{t_n}_{a\to b}\right) \\ \text{offer}\left(a,b,x^{t_n}_{a\to b}\right) & \text{otherwise} \end{cases}$$

$x^{t_n}_{a\to b}$ is the counter offer A generates to B when offer $x^{t_{n-1}}_{b\to a}$ is according to the internet source kmi.open.ac.uk, not accepted by A. $t^a_{max}$ is A's deadline by which A must have completed the negotiation.

According to the internet source link.springer.com, offers generated use one of the three families of tactics. In time-dependent tactics time is the predominant factor and each offer generated depends on the amount of time remaining and amount of time already consumed. In resource-dependent

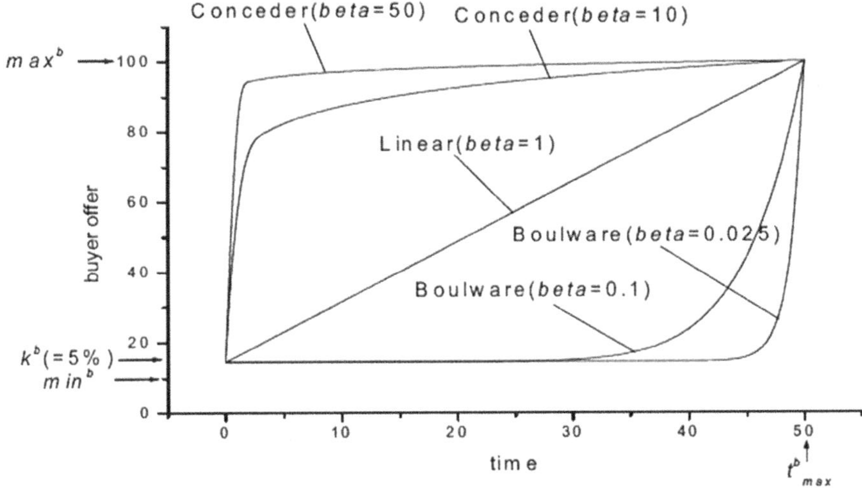


**FIGURE 10.1**
Concession curves, kmi.open.ac.uk in time-dependent family of tactics.

family of tactics offers depend on how a resource is being consumed. Offers become more and more cooperative as the quantity of the resource diminishes. In behavior-dependent family of tactics, agent imitates the behavior of the opponent. These tactics differ depending on the behavior of the opponent they imitate and to what degree.

According to the internet source link.springer.com, time-dependent tactics are further divided into three types depending on how quickly the agent starts to concede to the opponent's demands. In Boulware, an agent does not concede until near the deadline. In Conceder an agent starts giving ground fairly quickly and in linear an agent concedes same amount in each round. Similarly behavior-dependent family of tactics is also divided into three types: relative tit-for-tat, relative absolute tit-for-tat and average tit-for-tat. In relative tit-for-tat offers produced imitate the opponent's behavior in previous offers in terms of percentage. Random absolute tit-for-tat is similar to relative tit-for-tat except that the behavior is imitated in absolute terms. In average tit-for-tat, concession offered is averaged over the previous offers of the opponent. The above-given figure shows the various curves where each curve represents different tactics of time-dependent family.

**Paper 3**. According to the internet source link.springer.com, author Chongming Hou (Hou, 2004) proposed to use non-linear regression approach for the prediction of the opponent's tactics. It could predict the approximate value of opponent's deadline and reservation values. The performance of the agent improved by using this approach as it reduced the number of negotiation breakdowns and caused early termination of unprofitable negotiations. But this approach is restricted for bilateral negotiations only and can be used only when the agent is sure that the opponent is using one of the abovementioned families of tactics for negotiation.

Many other prediction approaches have been proposed which are based on machine learning mechanism. Most of the work devoted to the learning approach is focused on learning from previous offers, i.e. offline learning. They require training data and such agents need to be trained in advance. However, this approach may not always work well for the agents whose behavior has been excluded from the training data. Also such data may not be always available.

**Paper 4**. Brzostowski and Kowalczyk (2006) presented a way to estimate partners' behaviors by employing a classification method. They used a decision-making mechanism which allows agents to mix time-dependent tactics with behavior-dependent tactics using weights which can result in quite complex negotiation behavior. However this approach only works for the time-dependent agent and the behavior-dependent agent, which limits its application domains.

**Paper 5**. Gal and Pfeffer (2008) presented a machine learning approach based on a statistical method. The limitation of this approach is the difficulty of training the system perfectly. Therefore, for some unknown kind of agents whose behaviors are excluded in the training data, the prediction result may not reach the acceptable accuracy requirements.

**Paper 6**. I. Roussaki et al. (2006) and Bala and Chishti (2017) proposed an approach based on learning technique which has been employed by Client Agents and uses a feed-forward back-propagation neural network with a single output linear neuron and three hidden layer's neurons, Li and Ma (2005). According to internet source www.inderscience.com, these neural networks require minimal computational and storage resources making it ideal for mobile agents. The agents use a fair relative tit-for-tat negotiation strategy and the results obtained were evaluated via numerous experiments under various conditions. The experiments indicated an average increase of 34% in reaching agreements. This approach has excellent performance when the acceptable interval of the negotiation issue overlaps irrespective of the concession rate. On the other hand if the acceptable intervals' overlap is limited and deadline is quite high, this approach is likely to fail.

### 10.5.2 Survey on Multilateral Negotiations and Issues

There are many methods for multilateral automated negotiation. The commonly used methods are utility theory, heuristic-based algorithm, argumentation-based negotiation, fuzzy-based negotiation and game theory.

**Paper 7**. Lijuan Wang and Jun Shen (2014) mixed integer programming algorithm provides optimal solutions, but the scalability and computation time would increase if the number of agents are increased. Lijuan et al. are inspired by bio-inspired algorithm. Bio-inspired algorithm based on the genetic theory. Lijuan et al. proposed ant-inspired negotiation. Autonomy, scalability and adaptability are features of ant-inspired automated negotiation algorithm. They need to improve technical strategies to improve offer (Cao et al., 2015). Mukhopadhyay, Vij, More and Agrawal have given comparative studies in bilateral negotiations (Mukhopadhyay et al., 2015; More et al., 2013; Vij et al., 2019a, 2019b).

**Paper 8**. According to the web source www.ijert.org and Buttner (2006) automated negotiation is classified mainly as structure, theoretic foundation and restriction. We are going to focus on the protocol for the structure. The Protocols can be classified into bilateral, one-sided and double-sided protocols. One-sided and double-sided negotiations are also called multilateral automated negotiation. The Kasbah model was built on only a single issue as price. The system was built on multiple issues with two agents, but it has not given good results to buyers and sellers.

**Paper 9**. Mentioned by Patrikar et al. (2015), discovered by Susanne Klau et al. (2001), gave an overview of game theory based negotiation, multi-attribute utility theory based negotiation and auction-based negotiation as mentioned in internet source www.ijert.org. As per these papers, there is scoring function problem and user dependent problem in many-to-many multilateral negotiation. For linear scoring function, optimal solution can be found but for non-linear scoring function, the mathematical analysis is very difficult. How to construct the negotiation strategy is not cleared in this paper. As Klau et al., multilateral negotiation using game theory is very difficult to use. Utility theory can give better results than the game theory.

**Paper 10**. Sanghyun Park and Sung-Bong Yang (2006a, 2006b) have proposed a negotiation agent system based on the incremental learning in order to increase the efficiency of bilateral negotiations and to improve the applicability toward multilateral negotiations. For the system, they also have introduced a framework for multilateral negotiations in an e-marketplace in which the components can dynamically join and disjoin. They proposed an automated negotiation system that can efficiently carry out multilateral negotiations with multi-attributes in pervasive computing environments. The effects of learning ability are investigated with focusing on the reciprocity of participants and on the execution time of negotiation. The issues in relation to the improvement in the incremental learning and the development of delicate protocols for agent interoperability are not included in this system. Also they developed linear programming based automated negotiation system. They used concept of mediator agent and two bilateral automated negotiation schemes based on linear programming. The experimental results show that the proposed system produces higher joint profits and is faster in reaching agreements on an average under the condition of agreement for reciprocity than a negotiation system based on the trade-off mechanism given by Vahidov (Carbonneau et al., 2008).

**Paper 11**. According to Patrikar et al. (2015), the multi-issue negotiation model with distributed problem-solving was presented by P Faratin, C Sierra, N R Jennings and P Buckle (2000). In this, they developed fully autonomous agent who coordinates both agents' interaction and handles individual agent also.

**Paper 12**. Monotonic Concession Protocol for Multilateral Negotiation has been described by Ulle Endriss (2006). It is a deadlock free protocol in which they restricted on the utility function. It is not applicable for all the cases of negotiation. When the participant does not share his preference in the negotiation, the agent needs to analyze the behavior of the opponent. Performance of negotiation can be measured in two ways: using agent's performance as a benchmark for the model's quality and directly evaluating its accuracy by using similarity measures.

**Paper 13**. As per Tim Baarslag (Lin et al., 2012; Li et al., 2013; Baarslag et al., 2017) and as mentioned by Patrikar et al. (2015), there is an almost linear correspondence between accuracy and performance of the system. They measure accuracy of system over timing but do not consider system based on resource dependent. Dong proposed multi-attribute negotiation model based on internal factors argumentation, the system can achieve Pareto efficiency solution and promotes the cooperation between agents and then reach a win-win result. In multilateral multi-issue negotiation protocol, MAS (multi-agents system) is used for decision making by Liu et al. (2008).

According to internet source www.ijert.org and considering these papers, we can say multilateral automated negotiation gives better result to buyers and sellers. In multilateral negotiation, we can use desperate or patient coordination strategies. In desperate strategy, if one of the sub agent successes then process is stopped. In that, agent wants negotiation process to be completed as early as possible and in patient strategy, if one of the sub agents gets success then process will be continued till all agents get success. After completing the process, the score of each agent is checked and among them, the agent who gives more profit is selected. Negotiation protocol is a general rule which can be used by anybody in the negotiations. The protocol determines the flow of messages between the negotiating parties. Request-based negotiation protocol and sequential bilateral negotiation protocol are used for bilateral negotiation. Automated mediation, baseline mediation, multiple bilateral, feedback-based mediation and contract net protocol are used for multilateral negotiation. Win-win strategy gives better outcomes to buyer and seller. Intelligent techniques such as neural networks, genetic programming, fuzzy logic theory and Bayesian theory are used to learn opponent's behavior, decision making and generating offers and fuzzy system, multithreading, game theory, genetic algorithms and linear programming are some of the methods which can be used for multilateral automated negotiations by Lin and Krauss (2001).

### 10.5.3 Survey on Latest Technologies in E-Negotiation

**Paper 14**. According to the web source file.scirp.org, Liu Xiaowen and Yu Jin (2012) introduced automated negotiation model for tourism industry. To improve the negotiation efficiency and success rate, this system proposed RBR and CBR. The model employs CBR method to support an automated negotiation by past successful negotiation cases used for those negotiation partners who have no contract rule existing with each other. This system does not support multi-party multi-issue negotiation.

**Paper 15**. Mohammad Irfan Bala, Sheetal Vij and Debajyoti Mukhopadhyay (2015) introduced E-negotiation system with behavior prediction. This work reviews the various methods used for predicting the opponent's behavior and then proposes architecture for behavior prediction using artificial neural networks. It proposes the use of database for storing the results and suggests various issues that can be taken into consideration while predicting the opponent's behavior.

**Paper 16**. Mira Vrbaski and Dorina Petriu (2012) proposed Context-aware systems which use rule-based reasoning engines for decision making without involving explicit interaction with the user. It is difficult to rank suitable solutions based on unclear, qualitative criteria with a rule- based approach, while rule-based systems excel in filtering out unsuitable solutions based on clear criteria.

**Paper 17**. Leen-Kiat Soh and Costas Tsatsoulis (2001) used case-based reasoning (CBR) and utility to learn, select and apply negotiation strategies. Agent uses case-based reasoning (CBR) approach to solve new problem of negotiation strategy which is based on previous similar past problem. Agent also learns from its previous negotiation experience.

**Paper 18**. P. Maes, R. Guttman, A. Moukas (1999) introduced a Kasbah negotiation model. In this system, agents can only negotiate over the single issue of price. However, B2B negotiations often involve multiple issues. Moreover, the Kasbah agents can only act according to one of their pre-defined negotiation strategies which may not lead to the optimal negotiation results.

**Paper 19**. P. Wurman, M. Wellman, W. Walsh (1998) introduced the Michigan AuctionBot that is a general purposed internet- based auction server hosted by the University of Michigan. Sellers can create new auctions on AuctionBot by choosing from a set of pre-defined auction types and then enter their specific auction parameters such as clearing time, minimum bid increment and whether proxy bids are allowed. E-bay is the example of AuctionBot negotiation system.

Some of above papers support multi-party multi-issue negotiation rule-based reasoning and case-based reasoning. Our negotiation system is a bilateral, multi-party, multi-issue negotiation model. In this system, buyer and seller negotiate on multiple issues at a time and when both buyer and seller come to final decision, then only negotiation process will be stopped.

**Paper 20**. Debajyoti Mukhopadhyay, Suresh Sarode, Subhadip Chakraborty, Shashank Kanth and Saurabh Deochake (2012b) proposed a system that allows multi-party multi-issue negotiation as mentioned by More et al. (Mukhopadhyay et al., 2015). This system focuses on the negotiation protocol to be observed. It also provides a platform for concurrent and independent negotiation on individual issues using the concept of multi-threading.

**Paper 21**. Debajyoti Mukhopadhyay, Sheetal Vij and Suyog Tasare (2012a) present a new combinatory framework and architecture, NAAS. The feature of this framework is a component for prediction or probabilistic behavior pattern identification of a buyer, along with the other classical approaches of negotiation frameworks and architectures. Practically, negotiation is very complex activity to automate without human intervention. Therefore, in the future they also intend to develop a new protocol. This protocol will facilitate automation of all the types of negotiation strategies like bidding, bargaining and auctions, under NAAS framework.

**Paper 22**. As mentioned in internet source link.springer.com, Amir Vahid Dastjerdi and Rajkumar Buyya (2012) described SLA negotiation challenges in cloud computing environment. This system also proposed time-dependent negotiation which solves negotiation challenges. To increase the dependability of negotiation process, their system has reliability assessment. Cloud providers can accommodate more requests and thus increase their profit by discriminating regarding the pattern of concession.

**Paper 23**. As mentioned in the internet source link.springer.com, Li Pan (2011) introduced a framework for automated service negotiation in cloud computing environments. In this framework, software agents negotiate with each other on behalf of service consumer and provider. This system is also used a bilateral multi-step monotonic concession negotiation protocol for service negotiation in cloud computing environments. Service provider and consumer agents interact with each other due to negotiation process, and they make decisions according negotiation protocol.

**Paper 24**. Miguel A. Lopez-Carmona, Ivan Marsa-Maestre and Mark Klein (2011) say that consensus policy-based mediation framework is used to perform multi-agent negotiation. This paper also proposed a mediation mechanism which is used to perform the exploration of negotiation space in the multi-party negotiation setting. The performance of mediator mechanism is under guidance of aggregation of agent performance and on the set of alternatives the mediator proposes in each negotiation round.

**Paper 25**. Mikoto Okumura, Katsuhide Fujita, 2011 proposed (2011) a collaborative park-design support system which is an example of collective collaboration support systems based on multi-agent systems. In this system, agents collect user information, many alternatives and reach optimal decision using automated negotiation protocol. Especially, in this paper, the attribute space and utility space of user in real world is decided. At the end of the system user gives feedback. According to users' feedback, if most of the users agree on some alternative, then this alternative is final or optimal alternative.

**Paper 26**. As mentioned in the internet source arxiv.org, Ivan Marsa-Maestre, Miguel A. Lopez-Carmona and Mark Klein (2011) presented a framework for characterization and generation of negotiation process. Considering both the structural properties of the agent utility functions, and the complexity due to the relationships between the utility functions of the different agents, a set of metrics to measure high-level scenario parameters is provided. Then a framework is presented to generate scenarios in a parametric and reproducible way. The basis of generator is the aggregation of hyper volumes which is used to generate utility functions. Generator is also based on the use of shared hyper volumes and non-linear regression which is used to generate negotiation scenarios.

**Paper 27**. Bo An, Victor Lesser, David Irwin, Michael Zink (2010) designed a system for dynamic resource allocation problem and implemented a negotiation system. In negotiation model, multiple sellers and buyers are allowed to negotiate with each other concurrently. At the same time, an agent is allowed to decommit from an agreement at the cost of paying a penalty. This system also presents negotiation strategies for both seller and buyer.

**Paper 28**. Moustapha Tahir Ateib (2010) presented a fuzzy logic-based negotiation modeling that can be used to overcome the complexity of automation negotiation processes. This system uses a fuzzy logic to deal with ambiguity and uncertainties.

**Paper 29**. As mentioned in the internet source link.springer.com, Hsin Rau, Chao-Wen Chen and Wei-Jung Shiang (2008) developed a negotiation model which is used for a supply chain with one supplier and one buyer. This model is useful to achieve coordination under incomplete information environment. To find an optimal solution, an objective programming approach is applied.

**Paper 30**. As mentioned in the internet source file.scirp.org, Leen-Kiat Soh and Costas Tsatsoulis (2001) use case-based reasoning (CBR) and utility to learn, select and apply negotiation strategies. Agent uses case-based reasoning (CBR) approach to solve new problem of negotiation strategy which is based on previous similar problem. Agent also learns from its previous negotiation experience.

## 10.6 Survey on Multiple Strategies

According to the internet source www.inderscienceonline.com, literature survey on strategy selection, deployment model and acceptance model is presented in the following sections.

### 10.6.1 Literature Survey on Strategy Selection

**Paper 31**. As mentioned in the internet source www.inderscienceonline.com, Nguyen et al. (Jennings et al., 2002; Luo et al., 2003; Nguyen & Jennings, 2004) proposed a novel heuristic model for coordinating multiple bilateral one-to-many negotiations in service-oriented contexts. The bilateral concurrent model comprises of coordinator and number of negotiation thread (one per seller) for a coordinating manager. The coordinator selects strategy for each thread on the basis of probability distribution, success matrix and payoff matrix. The significant shortfall of the model is suitable for the situations where the number of sellers are more than one, for every seller different strategy is chosen, but our proposed system will be selecting among the strategies for a single thread, i.e.; one seller one buy dynamically; second shortfall in the model is designed based on the buyer's view point. Third shortfall is that the architecture lacks the corresponding functional components required in the generic agent model defined in paper by Brazier et al. (2000), mentioned in web source www.jucs.org, such as The World Interaction Management, The Agent Interaction Management, The Maintenance of World Information and The Maintenance of Agent Information.

**Paper 32**. Mentioned by Awasthi et al. (2016b); Crawford and Veloso (2005) has proposed a reward- and regret- based strategy algorithm (Crawford & Veloso, 2005) inspired by the book of Kraus et al. (Shaheen et al., 2014) who use a Soccer Play approach for learning the best strategy. In this model, a pool of strategies is chosen by experts where every strategy has a weight associated with it, implying the applicability for a negotiating situation. The effectiveness of this method can be verified if weight of a strategy is chosen or adjusted against a negotiating situation in such a way that it minimizes the regret associated with the selection of strategy. Compared to Goal deliberated model in (Shaheen et al., 2014), this model needs more computational time for finding the best strategy and also needs an expert to choose the strategies to be included into the pool of strategies.

**Paper 33**. As mentioned in the web source www.inderscienceonline.com; Mukun Cao (Mukun, 2010) has proposed goal deliberated architecture (Mukun, 2010) which is based on BDI theory using Faratin's time-dependent and behavior-dependent tactics. It uses Boulware or Conceder and concession rate to predict the behavior and to select the appropriate strategy. This system is faster than the earlier ones.

**Paper 34**. Kostas Kolomvatsos et al. (2015), as mentioned in the web source www.inderscienceonline.com, has proposed a method which can handle imprecise and incomplete knowledge about the negotiating environment; it uses fuzzy logic and a system member function to represent the updates related to the Fuzzy Logic rule base. Drawback is in Buyer point of view; the strategy employed is time-dependent ignoring the resource- and behavior-dependent aspect.

### 10.6.2 Literature Survey on Deployment Techniques

**Paper 35**. As mentioned in the web source www.inderscienceonline.com, Generic Agent Model (GAM) is a universal model for agent architecture, proposed by Brazier et al. (2000). Its aim is to provide a unified formal definition of a model for weak agent hood. It can be reused as a template or pattern for a large number of agents, variety of agent types and application domain types. GAM has been later refined to obtain a formal design description of the BDI agent (Jazayeriy et al., 2011; Haim et al., 2010; Rau et al., 2009; Shojaiemehr & Rafsanjani, 2014). According to www.inderscienceonline.com, precisely, the beliefs on the environment (the world and the other agents) are preserved by the maintenance of the world information and the agent information components while the desires and intentions are represented through a refinement of the Own Process Control component.

**Paper 36**. Huang and Liang (Huang et al., 2010) designed an Intelligent Negotiation Agent Architecture which includes Negotiator, Manager, Searcher and Agent Interface. The Negotiator optimizes product utility based on customer's requirements and constraints.

The Manager delivers status messages of active services between the negotiators and the clients; an agent and its agency; and between the peer agents. The Searcher searches the products located in other distributed databases and performs the role of managing, querying or collating product information from many distributed sources. The Agent Interface communicates between the customer and the other agents. The architecture can be considered as a multi-agent system that includes several functional agents. All the agents work together to perform autonomous negotiation. This represents a type of method to design the negotiation system based on agent theory.

### 10.6.3 Literature Survey on Acceptance Model

All existing negotiation agent implementations deal with the problem of whether to accept and when to accept. In many cases, the agent accepts a proposal when the value of the offered contract is higher than the offer in papers (Awasthi et al., 2016a, 2016b).

**Paper 37**. As mentioned in the web source www.inderscienceonline.com Agent K in paper by Minje Zang et al. (Ren & Zhang, 2007; Ito et al., 2012) employs the most sophisticated method to decide when to accept. Its acceptance mechanism is based on the mean and variance of all received offers. It then tries to determine the best offer it might receive in the future and sets its proposal target accordingly. Shortcoming of this acceptance model is that it's not fully decoupled from the bidding strategy as it directly influences its bid target. Furthermore, it does not restrict its scope to the remaining or previous time window. The Acceptance model of this paper takes into account the offer it is ready to send out at that moment in time as history of offers are not considered. Moreover, the focus of the work is not on comparing acceptance conditions as only one specific instance is studied.

## 10.7 Comparison of Different Methods with their Strengths and Limitations

**Paper 38**. Mukun Cao et al. (2015), as mentioned in the web source www.inderscienceonline.com, the goal-liberated agent architecture for multi-strategy selection (Thomas, 2000; Xue-Jie et al., 2013; Kurbel et al., 2004; Bala & Chishti, 2017; Lopes et al., 2008; Zhang et al., 2004; Luo et al., 2006; Holmes, 1992; Alsrheed et al., 2014; Lee & Chang, 2008) a time-dependent concession-based strategy is given but no provision for resource-dependent tactics as well as no opponent profiling and guidance for acceptance model is given.

**Paper 39**. As mentioned in the web source (Aydogan et al., 2014), Tim Baarslag et al. gave an agent which is decoupled into three components. Here, selecting and evaluating best component match is time-consuming and there is no provision for adaptation as well an optimum solution cannot be guaranteed.

**Paper 40**. Whereas an adaptive fuzzy logic system for automated negotiation by Kostas et al. (Kolomvatsos et al., 2015) can be used with imprecise and uncompleted knowledge, but it gives only time-dependent strategy ignoring resource and behavior-dependent strategies. Also many generic algorithms based on discrete surrogate approaches are slow and not suitable for real-time online systems in e-Commerce.

# 11

# *Problem Statement and Scope*

## 11.1 Problem Definition

The project is to develop a system capable of automated negotiation and also predict the behavior of the opponent which can be later used by the agent to improve its own utility. To automate a bilateral bargaining negotiation system which has got capacity to predict opponents' behavior to enhance rate of successful negotiations and to study various technological solutions to make the negotiation process better and efficient one. Also to construct and validate, a decision-making model to support multi-strategy selection during a course of automated negotiation in e-Commerce.

## 11.2 Scope and Purpose

The research as mentioned by Bala and Chishti (2017) in the field of automated negotiation has been going on for the last two decades, but still no such system is available which can be used for automated negotiation. I have developed a system which can negotiate of its own although with limited ability. I have refined the equations which will handle the behavior of the agents during negotiation. And finally, I have developed one algorithm to predict the preferences of the opponent.

The most prominent issues, according to the web source eprints.qut.edu that must be addressed in a negotiation mechanism are:

1. How to represent negotiators' preferences and offers?
2. How to evaluate an incoming offer?
3. How to compute concession and generate an offer? eprints.qut.edu
4. How to predict the opponents' preferences?

DOI: 10.1201/9781003408253-13

Patrikar et al. (2015) mention, in bilateral negotiation, maximum utility of one agent becomes minimum utility for another agent and both have limited space to take their decision.

**To make faster and efficient negotiation process**, a research on RBR-CBR on cloud, multilateral environment, multiple strategies and also a thought on web service based E- Negotiation has been conducted. Every strategy has certain applicability, and its selection impacts the utility and final outcome of negotiation.

1. No existing E-negotiation system is available which are a multi issues (B2B), multiparty and also commercially available. The existing systems such as Kasbah (MIT Media Lab), Michigan AuctionBot (University of Michigan), Magnet (University of Minnesota), Inspire (InterNeg Group at Carleton University), Bazaar (University of Copenhagen), Henry, etc., are only developed for training and research purpose. Some of these universities are doing research on various techniques like rule-based expert system, decision function, case-based reasoning, fuzzy logic, defeasible logic, game theory and soft computing technique. So More et al. (Mukhopadhyay et al., 2015) give us idea of working on a new approach toward automated negotiation system which will be based on rule-based and case-based reasoning and using the cloud. This would be an attempt toward making a faster (higher success rate of negotiation process), flexible E-negotiation process.
2. Flexible using cloud computing. In this E-negotiation agent system, cloud can be used to store the organizations product details so that maintenance of organizing data is reduced. Due to the use of cloud computing, the system will be flexible and easily available.
3. Faster using case-based and rule-based reasoning.
4. Faster using multiple strategy selection. According to web source citeseerx.ist.psu.edu, to construct and validate a decision-making model to support multi-strategy selection during a course of automated negotiation in e-Commerce.

The scope of this project work is limited to the designing and analysis of a Decision Support System (DSS) and its deployment model for a bilateral, multi-issue automated negotiation system. This work does not investigate any aspects related to different negotiation type, negotiation protocol and environment. This system can be multi-issue, multi-strategy-based bilateral automated negotiation system, with bid generating capability for a particular opponent and changing it dynamically when required. Its discount off the acceptance model or criteria for stopping or concluding the negotiation and adopts acceptance weight for evaluating bid acceptance.

The most prominent issues that must be addressed in a multi-strategy selection-based negotiation system are:

How to design a decision-making model to support the multi-strategy selection?

- Generic model of negotiation for autonomous agents which need to persuade one another to act in a particular manner.
- Assigning applicability to each strategy.
- Finding criteria for changing the strategy.
- Finding the threshold value for each criterion.
- How to design a framework or platform for the decision-making mode?
- Architecture which have a clear link with specification and their implementation.

According to internet sources www.inderscienceonline.com, the contribution of this research work is to maximize the success rate of negotiation process, i.e. convergence into successful contracts and eventually maximizing the efficiency and effectiveness of the system.

> *Hypothesis I:* Negotiation with multi-strategy approach will be better than that of single strategy in term of Utility of bid generated, acceptance weight and high success rate.
>
> *Hypothesis II:* The win-win case of negotiation using multi-strategy approach will yield into higher acceptance weight of bid generated than that of win-loss case of negotiation.
>
> *Hypothesis III:* The win-loss case of negotiation using multi-strategy approach will yield into overall higher utility of bid generated than that of win-win case of negotiation.

One of the important phases of any business deal is negotiation where the parties try to resolve their conflicting demands. Automating this negotiation process will not only save time of the negotiation parties but will also find better solutions improving the benefits of all parties involved in the negotiation. User is required only at the beginning of the process for assigning preferences and selecting agents, rest of the process will be automatic, producing one mutually acceptable offer. The benefit of each party may be further increased by predicting the opponent preferences and later using those predicted results to find the optimal offer from the domain space.

Participants should present at same place, and at the same time till the end of the process is a requirement in the traditional negotiation. E-negotiation has solved the problem of absence of the participants.

To develop negotiation model, we require the following:

Knowledge and information are required from intelligent and expert persons in the negotiation.

How to take preferences from participants?

How to generate offers?

Which technique is used to generate offer and evaluate best offer?

Behavior of opponents.

According to web source www.ijert.org, E-Negotiation design is currently more of a trial-and-error game because of lack of a coherent resource that indicates which negotiation technique is the best suited to a given type of domain. Also due to wide variety of possibilities, it should be clear that there is no universally best approach or technique for automated negotiation. Researchers are researching on electronic negotiation to find the best solution.

In bilateral negotiation, Patrikar et al. (Mukhopadhyay et al., 2015) mention that the maximum utility of one agent becomes minimum utility for another agent, and both have limited space to take their decision. This problem is solved by multilateral negotiation.

## 11.3 Constraints

According to the web source www.ijert.org, the fact that many good theories, models and algorithms cannot be verified without a practical application platform constrains the development of automated negotiation research. This situation is widespread in the entire e-Commerce-oriented automated trading applications. The proposed solution has a few more constraints; most important being that the system will not be able to negotiate in all possible situations. It will be able to negotiate only in some specific and predefined situations. Human intervention in not required throughout the negotiation process, but they have to specify the requirements at the start of the negotiation. Assigning the numbers to each issue to represent the preferences of the user may not be always easy. Also we have a time limit for the negotiation process to complete and we assume that there is no network delay which would otherwise reduce the number of offers exchanged.

According to web source, the fact that many good theories, models and algorithms cannot be verified without a practical application platform constraints the further development of automated negotiation research. This situation is widespread in the entire e-Commerce-oriented automated trading applications. The proposed solution has a few more constraints; most important being that the system will not be able to do negotiation in all possible situations. According to web source www.ijert.org, it will be able to identify all possible strategies of the negotiation. Human intervention is not required throughout the negotiation process, but they have to specify the requirements at the start of the negotiation. Here, we consider three buyer's agents and three seller's agents. Equal number of agents is required on both sides.

## 11.4 Feasibility Study

According to web source, a lot of negotiation systems produced in an academic environment is usually experimental systems developed to verify a particular model or theory. In those systems, issues such as usability, scalability and security need to be resolved. There is a long way to use them in the practical commercial application. At the same time, researchers find that it is difficult to meet completely such requirements of industrial development. Consequently, these systems only stay in the early stage of system's development and application. Moreover, many such systems were abandoned later, which is a great waste. According to web source www.ijert.org, E-Negotiation design is currently more of a trial and error game because of lack of a coherent resource that indicates which negotiation technique is best suited to a given type of domain. Also due to wide variety of possibilities, it should be clear that there is no universally best approach or technique for automated negotiation. The automated negotiation is still in its infant stage, because there are still some difficulties in this field. The first is the ontology issue; the second is agent's strategies and third is Communication protocol.

## 11.5 The Gap and Analysis

Looking at the research papers, we can positively say that an automation of negotiation as an intrinsic tactic in business (trading) systems, we need to use decision support systems:

Game theory (common knowledge is required)

Decision Functions (behavior, resource and time dependent)

Linear/nonlinear Regression (too complex and restricted for bilateral systems)

Machine learning and classification (too complex for negotiations)

ANN (likely to fail when time deadline is high and acceptable interval overlap is limited)

HMM and Bayesian learning (good for big datasets, our dataset is small and time is crucial)

Soft computing (Fuzzy, Genetic algorithms, Probabilistic reasoning)

Here are few points on existing E- Negotiation systems still in research phase, which can be consolidated:

No practical platform to verify the model, cannot predict in all situations.

Cannot identify all the strategies – where, strategy is a method (mathematical function), in the form of contending or conceding.

Network delay could reduce the performance.

Best strategy is to concede when negotiating with competitive agent and be hard headed when negotiating with cooperative agent.

There is no universally best approach or technique for automated negotiation, ref.

Prediction results are used to improve the performance of agents.

Huge scope for improvement in E-Negotiation systems.

Bilateral negotiation to multilateral negotiation.

Using web service-based systems and cloud to store data.

## 11.6 Mathematical Modeling

According to web source www.ijert.org, the given mathematical model is for bilateral negotiations where an agent can negotiate about multiple issues. It also supports learning from the previous negotiation rounds. Let M be the system used for automated negotiation

$$M = \{A, S, T, D, P\}$$

A: The set of agents that will participate in the negotiation.

A= {a1, a2 … an} represents n agents. Each agent will follow a distinct strategy during negotiation. The strategies followed by the agents are given by the following equations (See Table 11.1):

**TABLE 11.1**
Equations of Agent Behavior

| Agent Name | Equations |
|---|---|
| Conceder | $y=\begin{cases}7.518x^3-10.229x^2+5.05x & \text{if } x\le 0.5\\ 0.185x+0.815 & \text{if } x>0.5\end{cases}$ |
| Moderate Conceder | $y = -\ 0.8162x^3 + 2.266x^2 - 2.459x + 1.013$ |
| Linear | $y = 1 - x$ |
| Moderate Hardheaded | $y=\begin{cases}-8.33x^3+15x^2-9.417x+2.85 & \textit{if } x>0.6\\ 1-0.333x & \textit{if } x\le 0.6\end{cases}$ |
| Hardheaded | $y=\begin{cases}-101.3x^3+246.6x^2-200.8x+55.6 & \textit{if } x\ge 0.8\\ 1-0.102x & \textit{if } x<0.8\end{cases}$ |

S: According to web source www.ijert.org, the set of scenarios in which the agents can negotiate. Each scenario will have some predefined issues associated with it. Each issue is assigned some weight to indicate its importance.

For all Si ϵ S, Si = {I1, I2 … In}, where I represents the issue in the given scenario and is given by:

$$\mathrm{I} = \{\mathrm{R1W1}, \mathrm{R2W2}, \ldots \mathrm{RnWn}\}$$

R is the range of values an issue can take, and W is the weight assigned to each issue.

T: The time limit for the negotiation. Whole process of negotiation should be completed before the time limit.

D: It is a log file containing the offers received from the opponent. These offers, according to web source www.ijert.org are used to predict the preference of the opponent.

P: The vector set of the forecasted values.

The output may be successful or unsuccessful negotiation. The output will be some offer which is acceptable to both the agents when the negotiation is successful. Utility function will be used to evaluate the utility of each offer.

### 11.6.1 Mathematical Model for Multiple Strategies

A mathematical model is a description of a system using mathematical concepts and language. The process of developing a mathematical model is termed mathematical modeling. In this chapter, a mathematical model is presented using set theory. The subsequent section and subsection discuss mathematical model of system. Strategies and performance metrics, already mentioned by authors in earlier publication are referred to in the web source www.sppu.edu.in.

Mathematical model of multi-strategy-based automated negotiation system is denoted by ANS as follows:

$$\text{ANS} = \{\text{I}, \text{NE}, \text{NP}, \text{SB}, \text{P}, \text{O}\}$$

where,

I – The set of possible inputs (items, issues, preferences); NE – Is the negotiation environment; NP – Negotiation Process; SB – Set of strategies; P – Performance parameter; O – Output

NEGOTIATION ENVIRONMENT

$$\text{NE} = \{\text{A}, \text{P}, \text{TP}, \text{V}, \text{O}, \text{SA}, \text{Message}, \text{T}, \text{Thread}\}$$

$$\text{A} = \{1, 2, \ldots, n\}\, \text{TP}\{\text{tp1, tp2}, \ldots, \text{tpn}\}$$
$$\text{OG} = \{\text{o1, o2}, \ldots., \text{on}\}\, \text{SA}\{\alpha 1, \alpha 2, \ldots., \alpha n\}$$
$$\text{Message} = \text{TP} \times \text{OG} \times \text{V} \times \text{SA}\, \text{T} = \{\text{t1, t2}, \ldots., \text{tn}\}$$

where,

A – Negotiation agent code name; P – the Negotiation protocol; OG – the set of ontology; V – the set of effective value of topics; Agent – the set of all negotiating agents participating in the negotiation; SA – the finite set of executable speech-acts; T – A time point

$$\text{Threadijk} = \left(\text{OGk}\left(\text{tpk}, \left(\text{message}(\text{i}, \text{j}, \text{t1}), \text{message}(\text{j}, \text{i}, \text{t2}), \text{message}(\text{i}, \text{j}, \text{t3} \ldots)\right)\right)\right)$$
$$\text{i}, \text{j} \in \text{A}\, \text{ok} \in \text{OG}\, \text{tpk} \in \text{TP}\, \text{tk} \in \text{T}$$

where,

Threadijk is negotiation thread between Agenti and Agentj on T opick.

NEGOTIATION PROCESS

$$\text{NP} = \{\text{GS}, \text{Si}, \text{LS}, \text{trans}, \text{gen}, \text{gs0}, \text{ls0}\}\, \text{GS} = \{\text{gs0}, \text{gs1}, \ldots \text{gsn}\}\, \text{Si} = \{\text{si0}, \text{si1}, \ldots, \text{sin}\}$$
$$\text{LS} = \{\{\text{s10}, \text{s20}, \ldots, \text{sn0}\}, \{\text{s10}, \text{s21}, \ldots, \text{sn1}\}, \{\text{s1m}, \text{s2m}, \ldots, \text{snm}\}\}$$
$$\text{trans: } \wp(\text{LS}) \times (\{1, 2, .., \text{n}\} \times \text{Message})\text{n} \rightarrow \text{LS}\, \text{gen: GS} \times \text{LS} \rightarrow \text{GS}$$

where,

GS is global state. Negotiating; Agent's instant negotiation state; Negotiating agent's instant negotiation state; trans: Transformation function; gen: Global negotiation transformation function; gs0 ∈ GS is system's initial global negotiation state; gs0 ∈ GS is system's initial local negotiation state

NEGOTIATION SPACE

$$Xi = \{x1, x2, x3.....xn\} \text{ where } U(xi) > U(xi+1)$$

STRATEGY BASE

According to web source www.inderscienceonline.com

$$SB = \{C, B, NTT, RTT, UB, BRAM\}$$

where,

C: Conceder; B: Boulware; NTT: NiceTitforTat; RTT: RelativeTitforTat; UB: UtilityBased; BRAM: BRAM (author defined name)

INPUT

$$I \in \{A, TP, OG, B, N, V, R, T, S\}$$

where,

M, N, X, P, R, T, S are sub set of IN. According to web source www.sppu.edu.in

N – Number of issues; V – Value of issue; S – Scoring function; P – Preferences; T – Required time of negotiation; R – Reservation value

Note: Each preference has weight in between (0, 1).

OUTPUT

$$O = \{Accept | Reject | Offer | Counter\ offer\}\ O \in SA$$

# 12

# *Methodology*

## 12.1 Design

This chapter will cover some of the design aspects of my project. The negotiation system is supposed to be an online system where the buyer or seller can negotiate even if they are at different locations. The negotiation system should contain all the e-Commerce functionalities to be used in the business deals. But the system developed has limited functionalities and cannot be used in real life for negotiations. It was developed purely for simulation purpose. So a standalone application is developed. A general architectural design of the online negotiation system is given in Figure 12.1.

**Architectural aspects and working for negotiation automation**

The most prominent issues, mentioned in a web source eprints.qut.edu, generally which must be addressed in a negotiation mechanism are as follows:

1. How to represent negotiators' preferences and offers?
2. How to evaluate an incoming offer?
3. How to compute concession and generate an offer?
4. How to predict the opponents' preferences?

Components of automated negotiation system are; given in an internet source www.csulb.edu, called Nissen's integrated e-Commerce model; Service registration center, Negotiation service requester, Negotiation service provider, Protocol.

Figure 12.1 illustrates a simple negotiation service interaction cycle, which begins with a negotiation service advertising itself through a well-known service registration center. A negotiation requester, who may or may not run as a separate service, queries the service registration center to discover a service that meets its need of negotiation. The service registration center returns a (possibly empty) list of suitable services, and the service requester selects one and passes a request message to it, using any mutually recognized

DOI: 10.1201/9781003408253-14

| Seen by the buyer | Seen by the seller |
|---|---|
| Identify Business Needs | Arrange to Provide Offers |
| Find Source | Find Customer |
| Arrange Terms (Negotiation) | |
| Purchase Goods | Fulfill Order |
| Use, Maintain, and Dispose of Goods | Support Customer |

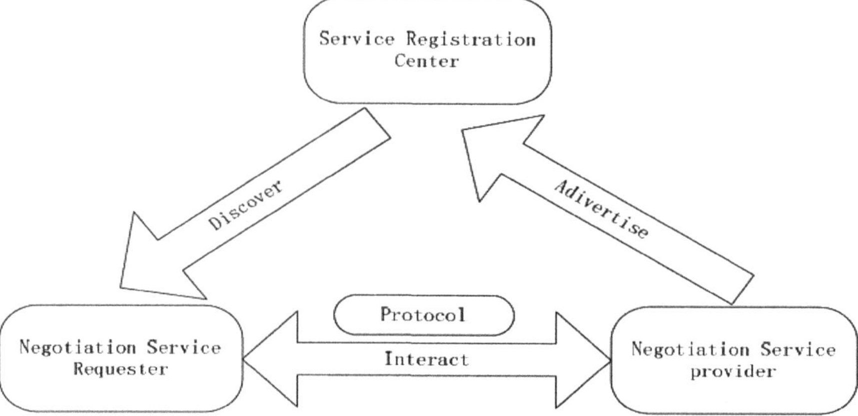


**FIGURE 12.1**
Nissen's integrated commerce model and Components of automated negotiation system, web www.csulb.edu.

protocol. In this example, the negotiation service responds either with the result of the requested operation or with a fault message. Then they interact with each other continuously. The architecture of the proposed system is given in Figure 12.2.

### 12.1.1 System Architecture Bilateral E-Negotiation and Opponent's Behavior Prediction based on Decision Support Systems

In this particular protocol, we are using time-dependent tactics of Decision Functions algorithm. We could analyze our readings of offers and counter offers as noted in our previous research values, and by graphical representations of hardheaded/Conceder and Linear strategies we can say an efficient bilateral negotiation protocol with opponent's behavior prediction and then

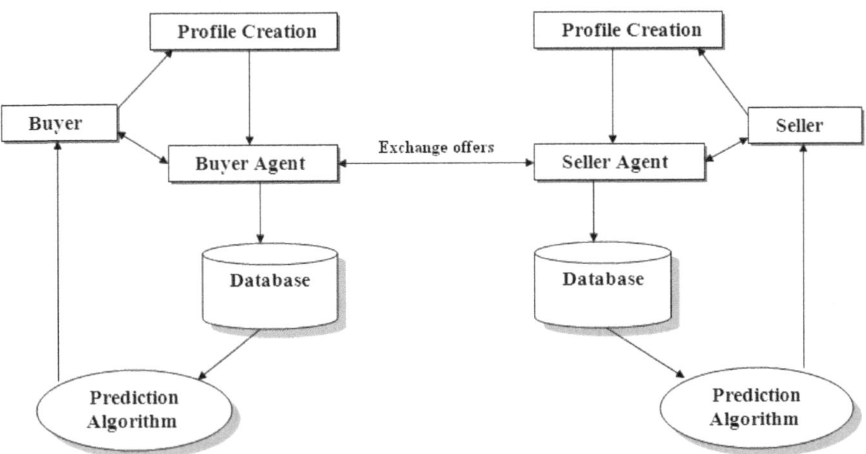


**FIGURE 12.2**
Bilateral system architecture.

counter offer can be established by time-dependent family of decision functions. Although it's a tough task yet to predict in all cases and identify all strategies and also the network delays could be taken care of in exterior environment of the system.

The system as mentioned in one of the earlier papers on this research, as referred by the web source www.inderscience.com, is developed as a standalone system where buyer and seller are the two participants or parties in the negotiation process. Both buyer and seller will create their preference profile assuming that both parties want to negotiate in the same situation. Both parties will be represented by agents of their choice. Issues of conflict may be mutually decided or pre-decided. All the preferences of two parties should be known to their corresponding agents only. Then the agents will start negotiation exchanging a sequence of offers and counter offers. Let $x^{t}_{a\to b}$ be the offer proposed by agent A to agent B for a negotiation issue at time t. Negotiation determines a value of x which is mutually acceptable to both A and B. Each agent has a utility function $V^a : D^a \to [0, 1]$ that assigns a score to value x in each Da. Negotiation is terminated by accept or withdraw. Proposals and counter proposals are evaluated using scoring function or utility function, given clearly on www.inderscience.com.

In General, Agent A's response at time, tn to Agent B's offer $x^{t_{n-1}}_{b\to a}$ sent at time tn-1 is given by:

$$R^a\left(t^n, x^{t_{n-1}}_{b\to a}\right) = \begin{cases} \text{withdraw}\,(a,b) \text{ if } t^n > t^a_{max} \\ \text{accept}\left(a,b,x^{t_{n-1}}_{b\to a}\right) \text{ if } V^a\left(x^{t_{n-1}}_{b\to a}\right) \geq V^a\left(x^{t_n}_{a\to b}\right) \\ \text{offer}\left(a,b,x^{t_n}_{a\to b}\right) \text{ otherwise} \end{cases} \quad (12.1)$$

$x^{t_n}_{a \to b}$ is the counter offer A generates to B when offer $x^{t_{n-1}}_{b \to a}$ is not accepted by A as mentioned on www.inderscience.com. $t^{a}_{max}$ is A's deadline by which A must have completed the negotiation.

All the offers and counter offers generated during negotiation are stored in a database which is accessible to the agent only. This database can be used by the agent to learn about the behavior of opponent and also predict the next offers of the opponent.

### 12.1.2 System Architecture Automated Multilateral Negotiation with Linear Programming

As mentioned in our research paper on the web source www.inderscience.com, in bilateral automated negotiation, maximum utility for a single agent can become minimum utility for opponent agent, and therefore the chance of join decision is low.

Evaluating the profits, the utility function Profits (xi) of a participant are as follows:

$$\text{Profit}(\text{xi}) = \sum_{i=1}^{n} w_{\text{i.E(xi)}}, \sum_{i=1}^{n} w_{\text{i=1}}, \tag{12.2}$$

Given in our earlier research paper www.inderscience.com, where n is the number of attributes, xi is a variable representing the offer value of the ith, attribute, wi is the weight of the ith attribute and finally the evaluation function E(xi) of the ith attribute expressed in terms of the request values (request_valuei) and the allowable values (allowable_valuei) is:

$$E(\text{xi}) = \frac{\text{xi} - \text{alloable value i}}{\text{request\_value i} - \text{allowable value i}} \tag{12.3}$$

According to Patrikar et al. (2015), multilateral negotiations are more complicated and time consuming than bilateral negotiations because in the multilateral automated negotiation, we require to do multiple matching between the participants. According to early stages of this research, published on internet source www.ijert.org, gives better result than bilateral automated negotiation system. The system, in which the technique of finding the behavior of opponents is used, is always better than the system not using it.

### 12.1.3 System Architecture E-Negotiation Using Rule-Based and Case-Based Reasoning (earlier published in www.igi-global.com)

Our research, referred to as More et al. 2013, (Mukhopadhyay et al., 2015), on Automated Negotiation throws light on the aspect of making the protocol

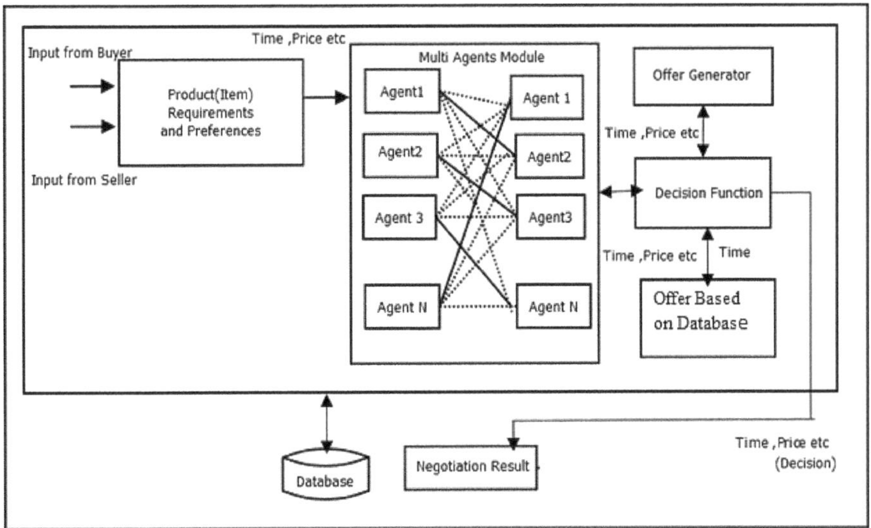


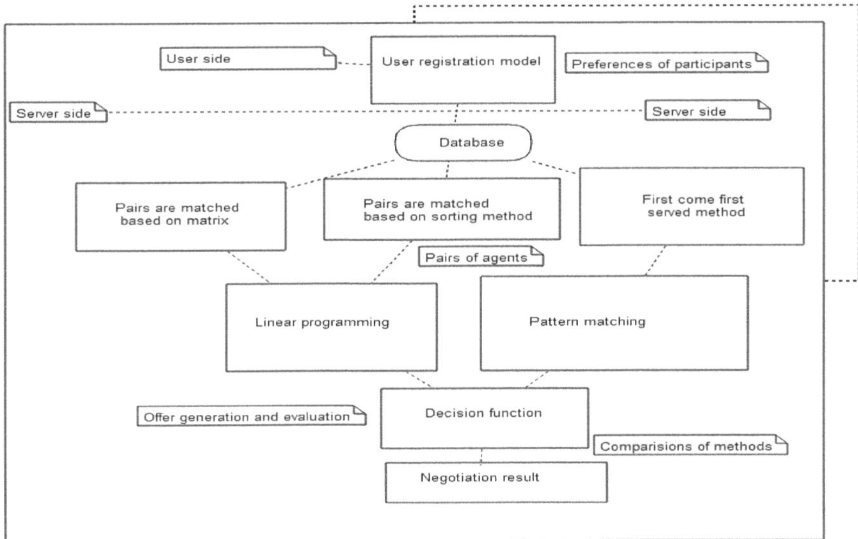


**FIGURE 12.3**
Multilateral system architecture.

efficient; if product data as well as negotiation process data is stored on cloud, we can say the negotiation process becomes easy. In this section, let us see how to make faster negotiation process using rule-based reasoning and case-based reasoning.

According to the web source link.springer.com, there are organizations to maintain data of the negotiation process and product data. But this

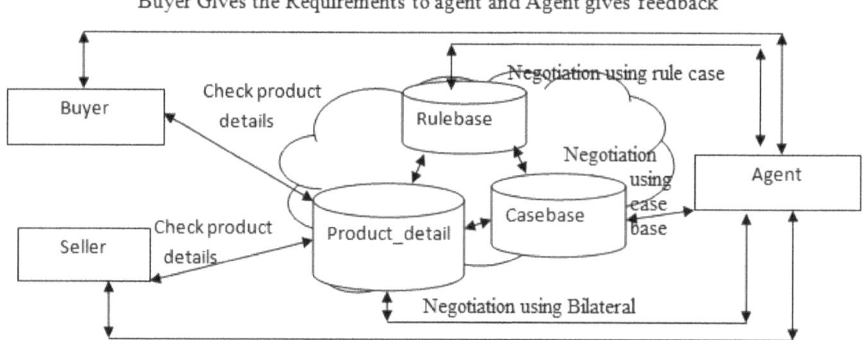


**FIGURE 12.4**
E-negotiation agent system with RBR and CBR.

maintenance is a very tedious job. As mentioned on file.scirp.org, in order to overcome this problem, all organizations' product data is stored on cloud. In order to make faster E-negotiation process, we can use the rule-based and case-based approaches. This system is a bilateral negotiation model, which can be implemented in near future as multilateral negotiation model, behavior prediction and also use the concept of expert system for increasing success rate of negotiation process.

### 12.1.4 System Architecture Multi Strategy Based E-Negotiation

Negotiation strategy, as referred in earlier publication on this research on web source www.inderscienceonline.com, is an umbrella term which defines the bidding, opponent profiling and acceptance criteria of a party. Every party can define and develop its negotiation strategy. Every negotiation process www.inderscienceonline.com requires an active collaboration of buyer and seller negotiating software entity (also called negotiating agent). As mentioned on www.inderscienceonline.com, this drives a need for a negotiation framework which is flexible in terms of platform, implementation and place. We propose a web-service, multi-strategy selection-based decision support system which can select strategies during the course of negotiation in a more informative way and can deal with range of negotiation scenario. The advantage of using multi- strategy is high success rate, i.e., successful negotiation; Fast response because of profiling; High number of scenario because of strategy pool. The contribution of this research work is to maximize the success rate of negotiation process, i.e., convergence into successful contracts and eventually maximizing the efficiency and effectiveness of the system.

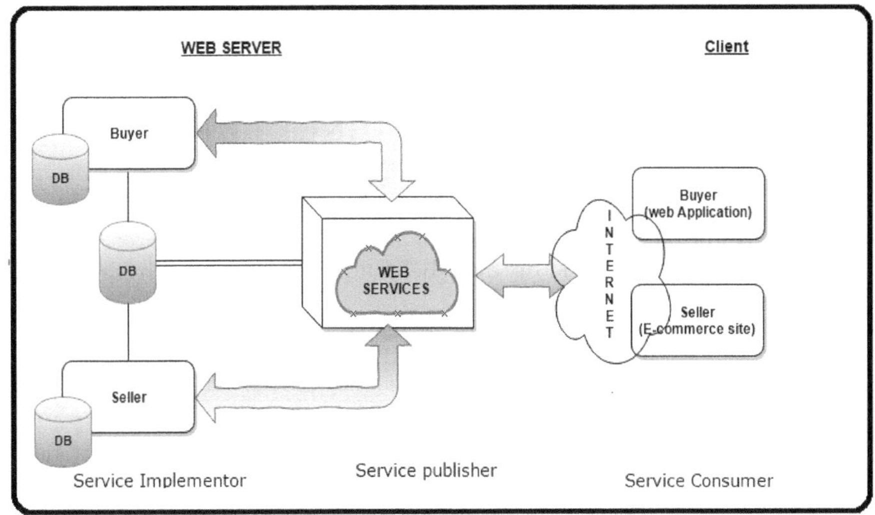


**FIGURE 12.5**
Web-based framework for automated negotiation.

According to www.inderscienceonline.com, as mentioned, negotiation strategy can be broadly classified into time, resource and behavior-dependent strategies. Time-dependent strategies are driven (take certain action) with the tick of time. Behavior-dependent strategies are those which are driven by opponent behavior. And resource-dependent strategy is based on the availability of product. The different strategies can be defined as:

Conceder

Conceder strategy(C) is based on time and exposure to negotiation bids.

$$X_{b\to s}^{t_{n+1}} = \begin{cases} X_{b\to s}\left(i, \frac{\max(i)3}{4}\right) \text{if time (t)>500ms} \\ X_{b\to s}\left(i, \frac{\max(i)}{2}\right) \text{if (t) <500ms and (t)>1000ms} \end{cases} \tag{12.4}$$

where $x_{b\to s}^{t_n+1}$ is the next offer ($t_n$ + 1) {as mentioned on www.inderscience online.com}, from buyer (b) to seller(s) and max (i) is the total number of offer (27 in our case). Total time (t) = 1000ms.

Boulware strategy (as referred from www.inderscienceonline.com)

Boulware strategy (B) is based on time and exposure of bids. Notations are same as above.

$$X_{b\to s}^{t_{n+1}} = \begin{cases} X_{b\to s}\left(i, \frac{\max(i)}{4}\right) \text{if time(t)>500ms} \\ X_{b\to s}\left(\frac{\max(i)}{4+1}\right), \max(i) \text{ if(t)= <700ms and (t)>1000ms} \end{cases} \tag{12.5}$$

Nice tit for tat strategy (NTT)

Nice Tit for Tat strategy is behavioral strategy. Concession $= x^{t}_{s\to b} - x^{t-1}_{s\to b}$

$$X^{t}_{b\to s} = \begin{cases} X^{t-1 \text{ if concession}>0}_{b\to s} \\ X^{t-1}_{b\to s(i) \text{ if concession}=<0} \end{cases} \tag{12.6}$$

Relative tit for tat strategy

Relative Tit for Tat(RTT) is also behavioral strategy with retaliation capability.

$$X^{t}_{b\to s} = \begin{cases} X^{t-1(i+1) \text{ if concession}>0}_{b\to s} \\ X^{t-1}_{b\to s(i-1) \text{ if concession}=<0} \end{cases} \tag{12.7}$$

Utility-based strategy (as referred from www.inderscienceonline.com)

Utility Based (UB) is an opponent-based strategy, it uses average and variance.

$$U_{T=\text{avg}\left[\left(UX^{t0}_{s\to b}\right),\left(UX^{tn}_{s\to b}\right)\right]} + \text{var}\left[\left(UX^{t0}_{s\to b}\right),\left(UX^{tn}_{s\to b}\right)\right] \tag{12.8}$$

$$X^{t}_{b\to s=x_i \text{ where } x_i \in X_i \text{ and } U(x_i)>UT}$$

where UT defines the target utility.

BRAM (author specific name)

$$x^{t}_{b\to x} = x_{i\, t=t_n} \tag{12.9}$$

$$\text{where } n \to (0-10) \text{ and } x_{i(t_n)>x_i(t_{n+1})}$$

$$X^{t_{n+1}}_{b\to s} = \begin{cases} X^{tn \text{ if } X^{t(0-n)}_{s\to b}}_{s\to b} \in X^{t(0-n)}_{b\to s} \\ X^{tn}_{b\to s \text{ if } X^{t(0-n)}_{s\to b}} \text{ does not} \in X^{t(0-n)}_{b\to s}, \text{where } x \to [0-n] \end{cases} \tag{12.10}$$

Every strategy, (as referred from www.inderscienceonline.com) is analyzed against opponent strategy, and the behavior is analyzed. The two main parameters used in our experiments are average utility gain and average acceptance weight. All the six strategies can be categorized into three sub-categories, Conceder and Boulware (hardheaded) are time-dependent, NTT and RTT are behavior-dependent, BRAM and utility based is resource-dependent. The experiment is conducted with two motives: first to prove the concept of multi-strategy, i.e. with the change in opponent strategy the performance of applied strategy varies, and second to gain the insight of the negotiation strategy.

## 12.2 System Details

### 12.2.1 Proposed Negotiation Protocol

According to the web source file.scirp.org, the negotiation protocol determines the overall order of actions during a negotiation and the agents are obliged to stick to this protocol. In the bilateral alternating offers protocol, two parties – agent A and agent B – take turns. Agent A starts the negotiation. On each turn an agent presents one of the three possible actions:

Accept: This action indicates that agent accepts the opponent's last bid.

Offer: This action represents the bid made by an agent.

EndNegotiation: This action indicates that the agent terminates the negotiation.

When it is an agent's turn, it is informed about the opponent's action. Based on the opponent's action the agent comes up with another action, which it presents to the opponent. Sequentially, the opponent presents a counter action. This process goes on until the negotiation finishes in one of the following ways:

Agent accepts the opponent's offer using the action Accept. The utility of the opponent's last bid is determined for both agents according to their preference profiles.

The action returned by an agent is EndNegotiation. In this case, the score of both agents is set to their reservation value.

Finally, according to reference tracinsy.ewi.tudelft.nl, if agent does not follow the protocol – for instance, by sending an action that is not one of the above or by crashing – the agent's utility is set to its reservation value, whereas the opponent is rewarded the utility of the last offer.

### 12.2.2 Reservation Value

A reservation value tracinsy.ewi.tudelft.nl is a real-valued constant that sets a threshold below which a rational agent should not accept any offers. A reservation value is the utility which an agent will obtain if no agreement is reached in a negotiation session. This can happen either if an agent leaves the negotiation or by not realizing an agreement before the deadline. In other words, either the negotiating parties agree on an outcome ω, and both agents receive the associated utility of ω or no agreement is reached, in which case both agents receive their reservation value instead.

1. Time Pressure

   For simplicity, let each negotiation session is allowed to last at most 180 seconds. If no agreement has been reached before the prescribed time, the negotiation will be terminated by ending/killing the negotiation agents, and the utility of both parties is set to their reservation value. The time has been normalized in the negotiation environment, i.e.: time $t \in [0, 1]$, where $t = 0$ represents the start of the negotiation, and $t = 1$ represents the deadline. Agents should not rely on the assumption that the negotiation time window corresponds to 180 seconds in real time but are required only to rely on the normalized time.
2. Negotiation Objects

   Agents participating, according to a web source tracinsy.ewi.tudelft.nl, in a negotiation interact in a scenario. A scenario specifies the possible bids and their preference for both agents. A scenario consists of a domain (also called the outcome space) and two utility spaces (also called preference profiles). The domain describes which issues are the subject of the negotiation and which values an issue can attain. To give a concrete example of a domain: in the laptop domain the issues are 'laptop', 'hard disk' and 'monitor'. In the laptop domain, the issues can only attain discrete values, e.g. the 'hard disk' issue can only have the values '60 Gb', '80 Gb' and '120 Gb'. Combining these concepts, an agent can formulate a Bid: a mapping from each issue to a value. A bid will contain a value for each issue. The Utility Space specifies the preferences of the bids for an agent. Using a utility space, the utility of a bid can be calculated using the evaluator of each issue. As mentioned in tracinsy.ewi.tudelft.nl, given the set of all bids, there is a small subset of bids which are more preferred as outcomes by both agents. Identifying these special bids may lead to a better agreement for both parties. Prediction results can be used to find out such bids which give optimal results for both the agents.
3. Optimality of a Bid

   According to Faisal et al. (Alsrheed et al., 2014), A bid is a set of chosen values V1…Vn for each of the N issues. Each of these values has been assigned an evaluation value eval(vi) in the utility space. The utility is the weighted sum of the normalized evaluation values.

$$U(v_1 \ldots v_n) = \sum_{i=1}^{N} w_i \frac{eval(v_i)}{\max(eval(v_i))} \tag{12.11}$$

As mentioned in tracinsy.ewi.tudelft.nl, for a single agent, the optimal bid is of maximum utility for the agent. Often this bid has a low utility for the opponent, and therefore the chance of agreement is low. A more general notion of optimality of a negotiation involves the utility of both agents.

There are multiple ways to define a more global 'optimum'. One approach to optimality is that a bid is not optimal for both parties if there is another bid that has the higher utility for one party, and at least equal utility for the other party. Thus, the only bid in Figure 12.6 for which there is no other bid at the top right is optimal. This type of optimality is called Pareto optimality and forms an important concept in automated negotiation. The collection of Pareto optimal bids is called the Pareto optimal frontier. Another approach is the Nash optimality. A Nash solution is a bid for which the product of the utilities of both agents is maximal.

As mentioned in www.ijert.org, major challenge in a negotiation using the bilateral alternating offers protocol given in source tracinsy.ewi.tudelft.nl is that agents hide their preferences. This entails that an agent does not know which bid the opponent prefers given a set of bids. This problem can be partly resolved by building a model of the opponent's preferences by analyzing the negotiation trace.

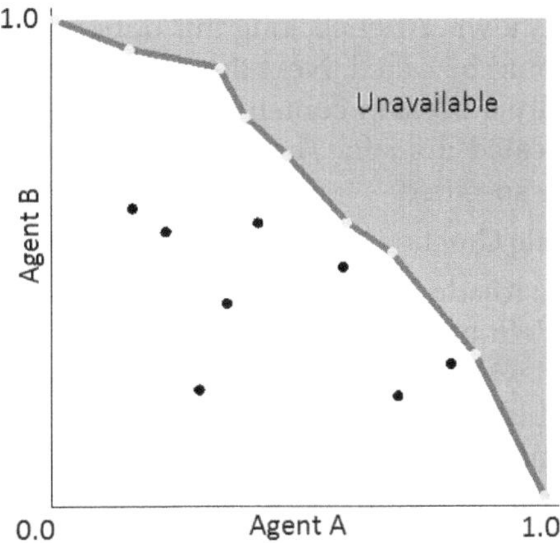


**FIGURE 12.6**
Pareto optimal frontier.

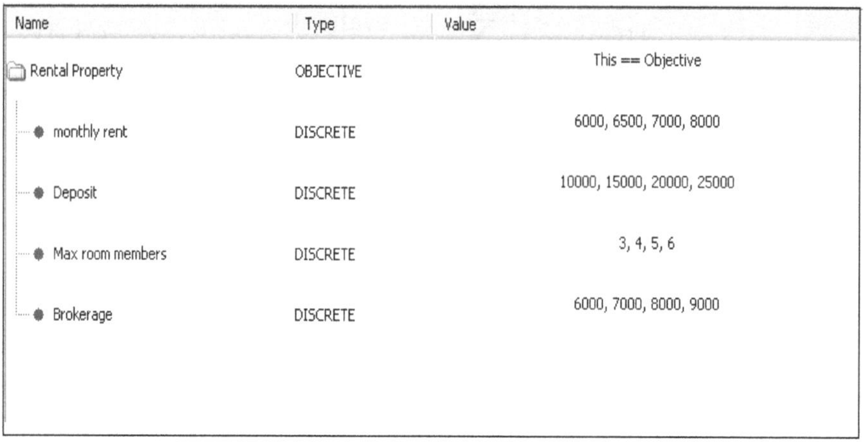

| Name | Type | Value |
|---|---|---|
| Rental Property | OBJECTIVE | This == Objective |
| monthly rent | DISCRETE | 6000, 6500, 7000, 8000 |
| Deposit | DISCRETE | 10000, 15000, 20000, 25000 |
| Max room members | DISCRETE | 3, 4, 5, 6 |
| Brokerage | DISCRETE | 6000, 7000, 8000, 9000 |

**FIGURE 12.7**
'Rental Property' domain creation.

4. Scenario Creation

   Mentioned as in tracinsy.ewi.tudelft.nl, A negotiation can be modeled by creating a scenario. A scenario consists of a domain specifying the possible bids and a set of preference profiles corresponding to the preferences of the bids in the domain. This section discusses how to create a domain and a preference profile.

5. Domain Creation

   By right clicking on the list of available scenarios, as mentioned in tracinsy.ewi.tudelft.nl, a popup menu with the option to create a new domain is shown. After clicking this option, it is requested how the domain should be called. Next the domain is automatically created, but initially a domain contains zero issues. Then we add the issues in the created domain. The list of values each issue can take also needs to be specified.

6. Preference Profile Creation

   The next step is to add a set of preference profiles as mentioned in tracinsy.ewi.tudelft.nl. By right clicking on the domain, a popup menu is opened which has an option to create a new preference profile. Selecting this option results in the opening of a new window which looks similar to Figure 12.8. Each party has to create a preference profile as per its preferences before a negotiation process can be initiated.

   Now to start as given on internet source tracinsy.ewi.tudelft.nl, customizing the preference profile, there are three steps: setting the

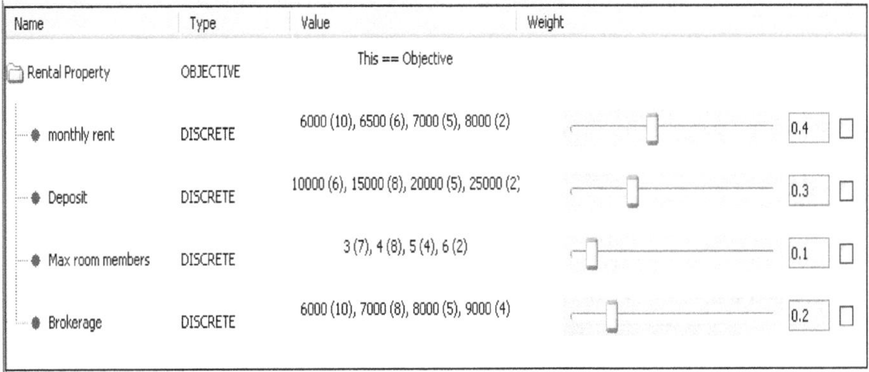


**FIGURE 12.8**
Preference profile of 'Rental property' domain.

importance of the issues, determining the preference of the values of the issues and configuring the reservation value and discount. To start with the first step, adjust the relative weights of the issues by using the sliders next to that issue. When a slider is moved, the weights of the other sliders are automatically updated such that all the weights still sum up to one. The next step is to set the evaluation values of the issues. To specify the evaluation of an issue double click on it to open a new window where a negotiating party can assign ratings to each value that an issue can take. There is no limitation on the values a user can assign. The final step is to set the reservation value and discount of a preference profile. Higher discount value indicates high pressure on the user to complete the negotiation process.

#### *12.2.2.1 Running Negotiation Session*

The following parameters need to be specified to run a negotiation and the window is given in Figure 12.9

Negotiation protocol: The set of available protocols. Normally 'Alternating Offers' is used.

Side A/Side B: The configuration of the agents of both sides.

Preference profile: The preference profile to be used by the agent of that side.

Agent name: The agent participating in the negotiation.

Deadline (seconds): The length of the negotiation in seconds.

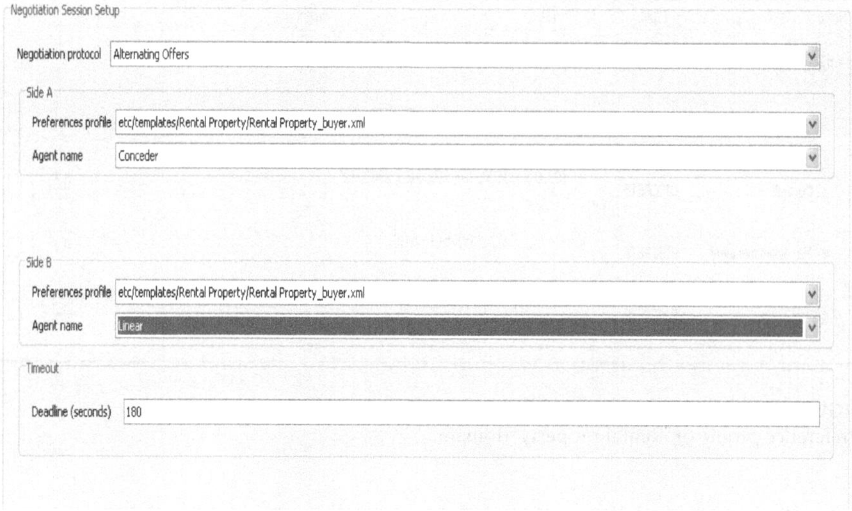

**FIGURE 12.9**
A negotiation session.

#### *12.2.2.2 E-Negotiation Terminologies (in Multi-Strategy Base)*

**Conflict**: According to earlier phase of this research www.sppu.edu.in, negotiation is triggered by real conflict; a conflict is a situation where parties have different concern, sharp disagreement or difference of opinion over issues and items; conflict acts as driving force of negotiation.

**Negotiating Parties**: Let i(i ∈ a, b, c) represents the negotiation agents. Negotiation may involve two parties (bilateral negotiation) or more than two parties (multilateral negotiation). Let j(j ∈ 1, 2, 3, … n) for n issues one issue (single-issue negotiation) or many issues (multi-issue negotiation). According to web source csc.iiv.ac.uk, issues at stake can be derived from a number of sources (e.g. an analysis of the conflict, or past experience in similar situations). Second, every negotiator should assemble all the issues that have been defined into a comprehensive list. The combination of lists from each side in the negotiation determines the negotiating agenda.

**Prioritization**: Is preference of an issue among agenda by a negotiating agent, difference in preference may lead to deadlock or failure in negotiation. According to the web source csc.iiv.ac.uk, prioritization usually involves two steps: (1) determining which issues are most important and which are less important and (2) determining whether the issues are connected or separate. Priorities are often concealed, though in some situations every negotiator can disclose information about its priorities in order to find a mutually acceptable solution.

**Strategy and Tactics**: A strategy, as we understand from earlier research given by www.sppu.edu.in, is a careful plan or method, especially for achieving an end. Negotiation strategy is a set of rules for deciding what time to propose at each point in the process; whereas the use of tactics refers to the skill of using available means to reach that end. According to the web source csc.iiv.ac.uk, the line between strategies and tactics often seems indistinct, but one major difference is that of scope. Tactics are short-term moves designed to enact broad (or high-level) strategies.

**Negotiation Protocol**: The protocol is the set of rules that govern the interaction between the negotiating agents. According to the web source csc.iiv.ac.uk, the protocol specifically defines the negotiation state (e.g. accepting proposals), the valid actions of the agents in particular state (e.g. which messages can be sent by whom, to whom, at what stage) and the events that cause negotiation state to change (e.g. proposal accepted). The strategy accounts for the individual decisions of each agent. While the protocol restricts the possible actions to perform, it often does not specify any particular action instead; it often marks branching points at which every agent has to make decisions according to its strategy.

**Reservation and target**: Let $xj \in [\text{minj } i, \text{max } j\ i]$ be a value for issue j acceptable by agent i. The reservation values, according to Kolomvatsos et al. (Kolomvatsos et al., 2015), are limits that the buyer and the seller do not want to exceed. The buyers have a reservation value, i.e. a valuation, which they are not willing to exceed. The sellers have a production cost and she does not want to sell their product for less than its value. The valuation and the cost defines the agreement zone. This zone indicates whether an agreement is possible.

**Negotiation outcome space**: It Is denoted as $\omega$, according to a web source sdsu-dspace.calstate.edu, which represents all the possible outcomes achievable, i.e. all possible issue value combinations within the domain. The formal definition of a negotiation outcome ($\omega$), also referred to as bid or offer, with n issues can be seen in equation 12.1.1 $\omega = \omega 1 \ldots \omega n$ (1.1), where i denotes a value associated with the i th issue.

**Utility function**: According to web reference www.sppu.edu.in, using the preference profile of a negotiator it is possible to map any offer in the domain to a value (Utility), a rating indicating how well a bid satisfies the negotiator's preferences. The utility of a multi-issue outcome is calculated by means of a linear additive function that evaluates each issue separately. The equation to calculate utility is as follows: $(\omega) = Xn\ i{=}1\ \omega i.ei(\omega i)$ (1.2), where $\omega i$ are the normalized issue weights and $ei(\omega i)$ the evaluation functions for the i th issue.

**TABLE 12.1**

Generic Framework for Automated Negotiation

| Group | Components |
|---|---|
| Preliminaries | Social conflict – detection / exploration, Number of Negotiating Parties |
| Pre-Negotiation | Structuring of personal information, Analysis of the opponent Protocol definition and selection of initial strategy |
| Actual Negotiation | Exchange of offer and feedback information Argumentation Learning Dynamic Strategy |
| Post-Negotiation | Resolution, analysis, improvement of the final agreement |

### 12.2.3 Generic Framework for Automated Negotiation

According to a web source csc.iiv.ac.uk, negotiation, like other forms of social interaction, often proceeds through distinct phases or stages. A phase is a coherent period of interaction characterized by a dominant group of communicative acts that serves a set of related functions in the movement from initiation to a resolution of a dispute (Patrikar et al., 2015). Most models fit into a general structure of three phases: a beginning or initiation phase; a middle or problem-solving phase; and an ending or resolution phase. The initiation phase focuses on the preparation and planning for negotiation; it is marked by each party's efforts to emphasize points of difference and positions. Pre-negotiation processes that are formulation and analysis of the negotiation problem, party's efforts to emphasize points of difference and posture for positions, the incorporation of context of the problem and the access and use knowledge about the participants, problem and context. The problem-solving phase finds a solution for a dispute which is characterized by extensive interpersonal interaction, strategic planning and movement toward a mutually acceptable agreement. Processes include strategies and tactics, context in which the negotiation takes place and the exchange of information, including offers and arguments. The resolution phase implies details on implementation of the final agreement. The parties often demand a gesture of good will and faith commitment to the agreement (close the deal) and determine who needs to do what once the documents are signed (implement the agreement) as in Table 12.1.

## 12.3 UML Diagrams

According to the internet source sdsu-dspace.calstate.edu, the Unified Modeling Language allows the software engineer to express an analysis model using the modeling notation that is governed by a set of syntactic semantic and pragmatic rules. A UML system is represented using five different views that describe the system from distinctly different perspective. Each view is defined by a set of diagram, which is as follows;

### 12.3.1 Use-Case Diagram

As referred to manipal.edu, a use case diagram at its simplest is a representation of a user's interaction with the system, depicting the specifications of a use case. A use case diagram can portray the different types of users of a system and the various ways in which they interact with the system. Figure 12.10 represents the Use Case Diagram of the proposed project concept. The different use cases of the diagrams are opponent matching, profile creation, domain selection, offer generation and offer evaluation and the most important being prediction mechanism.

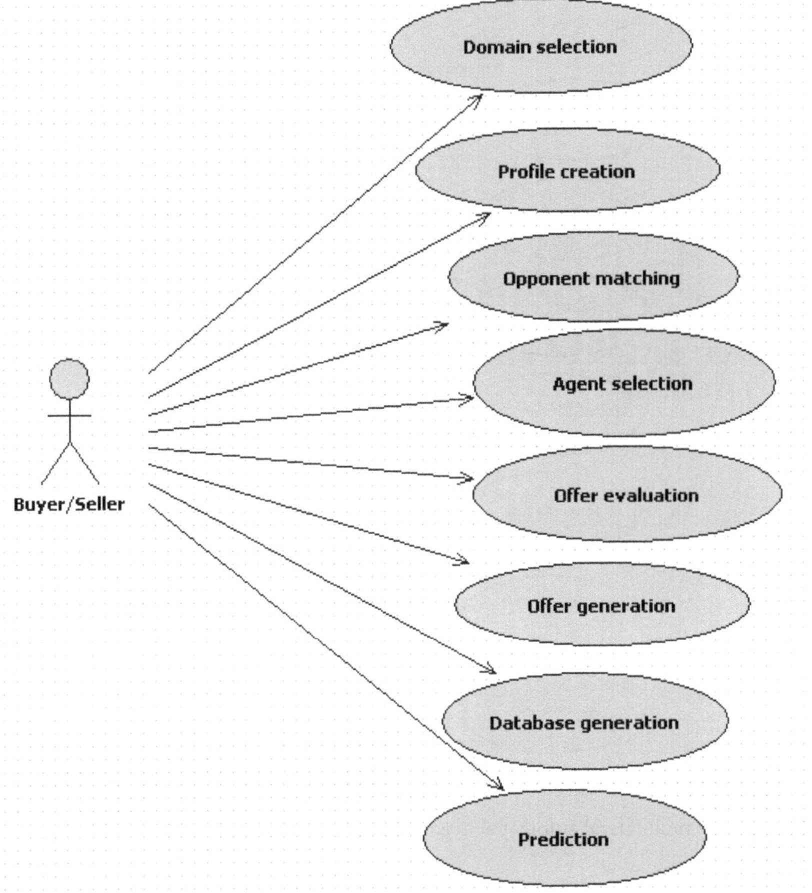


**FIGURE 12.10**
Use case.

### 12.3.2 Class Diagram

According to the reference chicagostateuniversity.edu, the class diagram is the main building block of object-oriented modeling. It is used both for general conceptual modeling of the systematic of the application and for detailed modeling translating the models into programming code. Class diagrams can also be used for data modeling. The classes in a class diagram represent both the main objects, interactions in the application and the classes to be programmed.

A class is with three sections. In the diagram, classes are represented with boxes which contain three parts: • The upper part holds the name of the class. • The middle part contains the attributes of the class. • The bottom part gives the methods or operations the class can take or undertake.

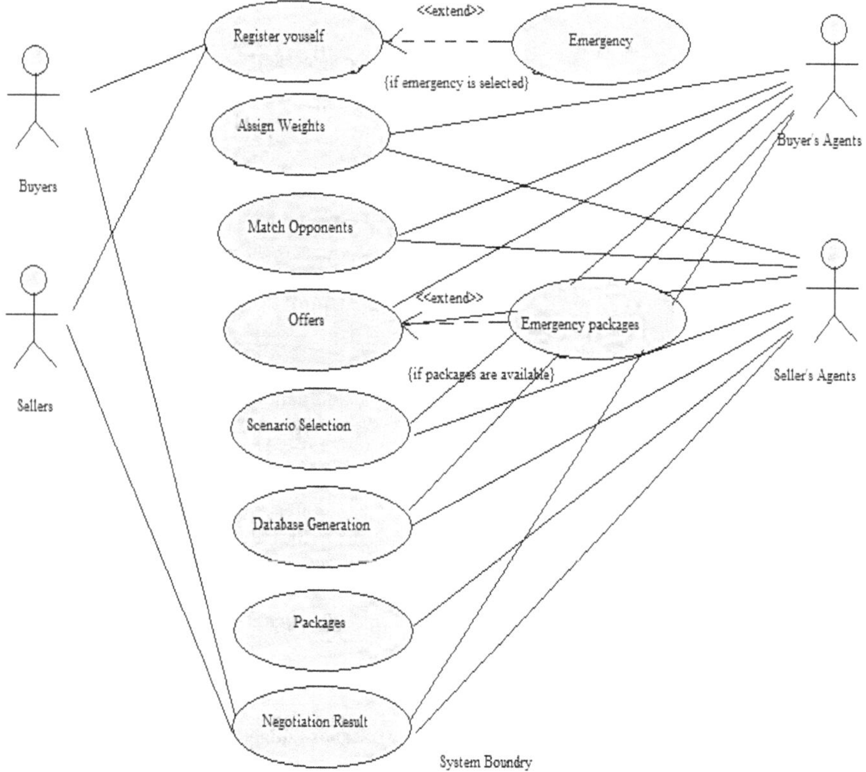


**FIGURE 12.11**
Use case diagram of multilateral automated negotiation.

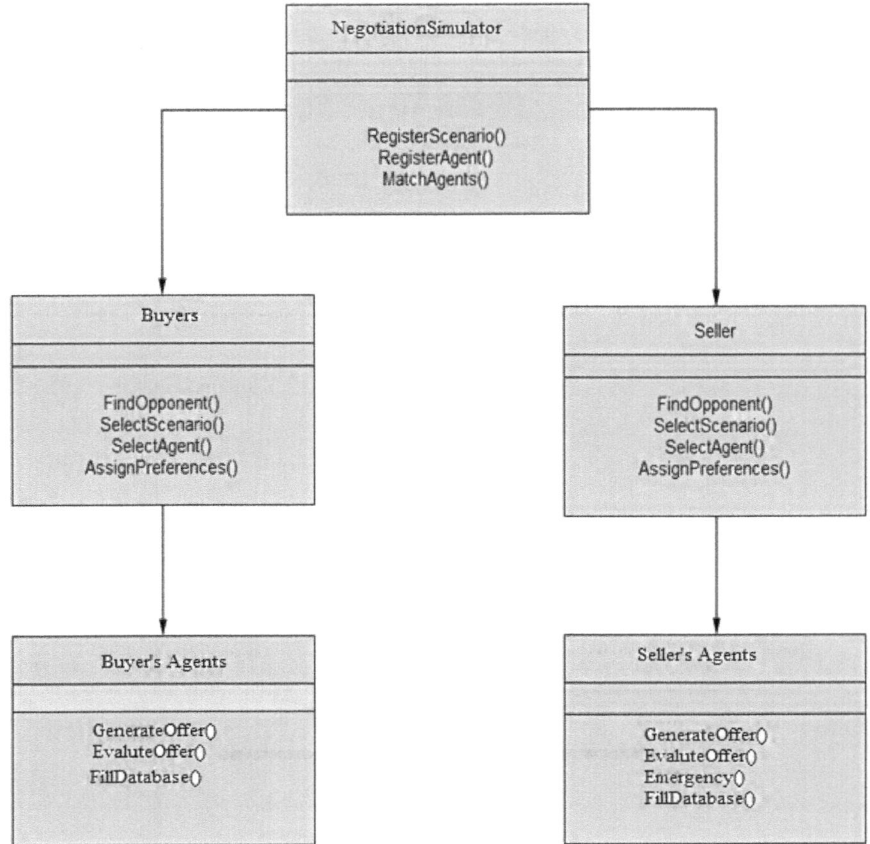


**FIGURE 12.12**
Class diagram of multilateral automated negotiation.

### 12.3.3 Activity Diagram

According to an internet source www.grin.com, ijcsit.com, an activity diagram is another important diagram in UML to describe dynamic aspects of the system. It is basically a flow chart to represent the flow form one activity to another activity. The activity can be described as an operation of the system. So the control flow is drawn from one operation to another. This flow can be sequential, branched or concurrent. The developed negotiation system has different small procedures used for obtaining results that are shown in the following activity diagram.

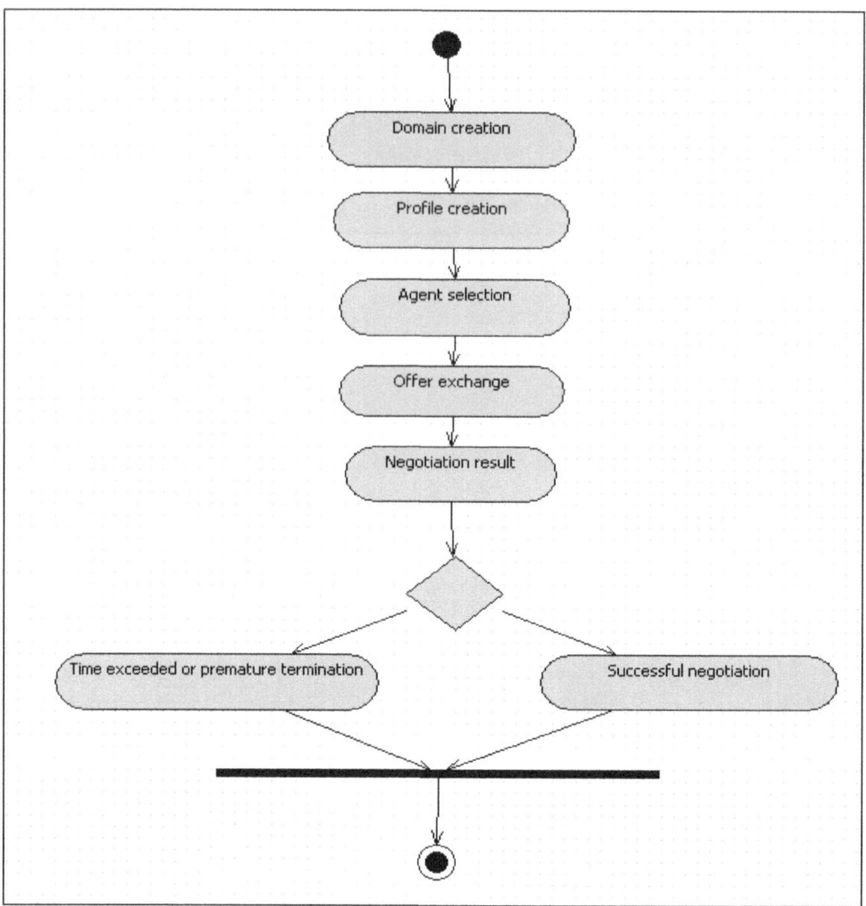


**FIGURE 12.13**
Activity diagram.

### 12.3.4 Sequence Diagram

According to a web reference www.grin.com, ijcsit.com, a sequence diagram is a kind of interaction diagram that shows how processes operate with one another and in what order. It is a construct of a Message Sequence Chart. A sequence diagram shows object interactions arranged in time sequence. It depicts the objects and classes involved in the scenario and the sequence of messages exchanged between the objects needed to carry out the functionality of the scenario. Sequence diagrams are typically associated with use case realizations in the Logical View of the system under development. Sequence diagrams are sometimes called event diagrams, event scenarios, and timing diagrams.

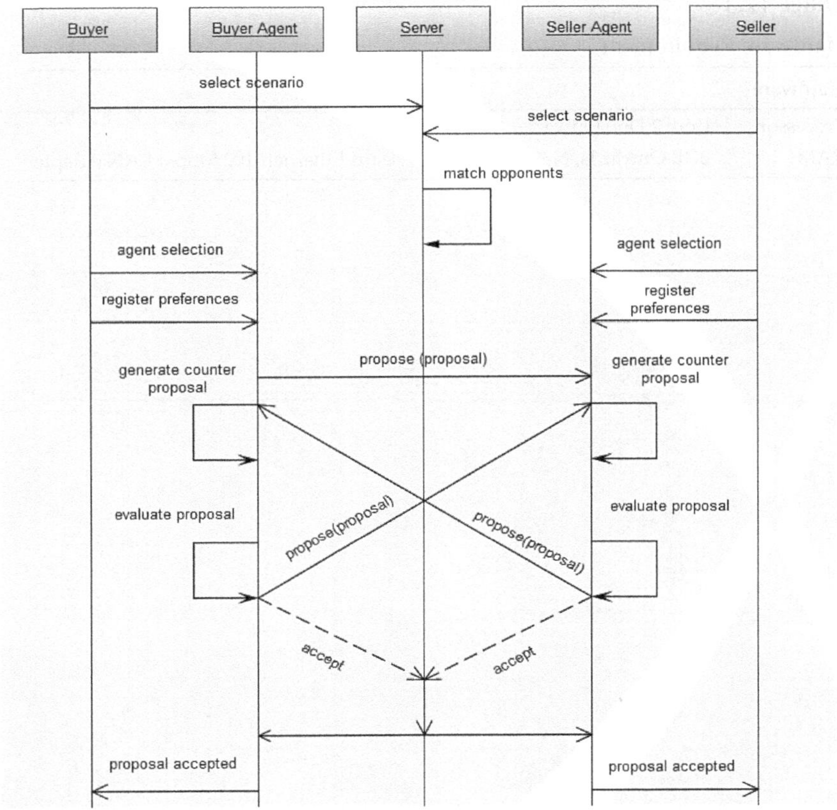


**FIGURE 12.14**
Sequence diagram.

## 12.3.5 Software and Hardware Requirements

**TABLE 12.2**
Software Requirement

| **Software** | **Usage** |
|---|---|
| JDK, Windows 7 64-bit Professional, MySQL | Java development Kit and Java Runtime environment, Internet |
| Eclipse | Platform for code Generation |
| Tomcat Apache | Server, web service platform |
| MatlabR2008a | For preference prediction<br>Internet Environment |

**TABLE 12.3**

Hardware Requirement

| Hardware | Version |
|---|---|
| Processor | Core 2 Duo Onwards |
| RAM | 2GB Onwards, Network Interface Card Ethernet (100 Mbps) LAN Adapter |

# 13

# *Results and Analysis*

## 13.1 Negotiation Scenario

Buyer and seller will represent the two opponent parties who want to negotiate with each other and resolve their conflicting demands. First both the parties have to mutually decide the issues of conflict. Consider a case where buyer and seller have been matched and they are looking to buy and sell the flat, respectively. First they need to decide the issues of conflict. Issues of conflict can be:

1. Monthly rent
2. Deposit
3. Maximum number of room partners
4. Brokerage

For each issue both the parties will have some range of acceptable values. To keep the negotiation process simple, I have allowed only some discrete values for each issue instead of continuous values. This way the number of possible offers that could be generated is greatly reduced. Table 13.1 contains the allowed values for each issue.

Considering the fact that the buyer is a student, monthly rent is the most important issue for him and he will be looking for a flat with minimum rent. He is looking for a flat with rent of 6000 and is willing to pay maximum of 8000. Deposit is also important for him but not as much as monthly rent. He would prefer lesser deposit but his preference for 15,000 is more than 10,000 as that will ensure that none of the roommates breaks the agreement. But preference for 20,000 is less than 10,000. Maximum roommates is the least important issue for him. Also he doesn't want room to be overcrowded. He has the highest preference for four roommates and a little lesser for three roommates. He has the lowest preference for six roommates. Brokerage is not as important as deposit but is more important than maximum roommates.

DOI: 10.1201/9781003408253-15

**TABLE 13.1**
List of Allowed Values for Each Issue

| Issue Name | Allowed Values |
|---|---|
| Monthly rent | 6000,6500,7000,8000 |
| Deposit | 10000,15000,20000,25000 |
| Maximum room mates | 3,4,5,6 |
| Brokerage | 6000,7000,8000,9000 |

In brokerage also the student is trying to save money. So he has highest preference for the least brokerage and least preference for highest brokerage.

Taking the above preferences into consideration, the preference profile of the buyer is given by Figure 13.1.

In the same way seller will create his own profile as per his preferences. The seller profile is given in Figure 13.2.

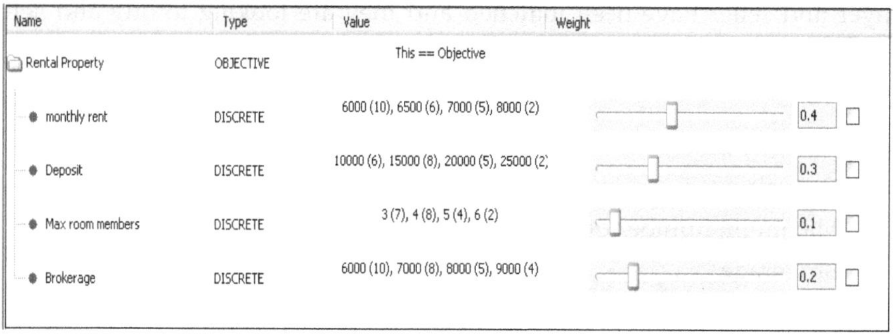

| Name | Type | Value | Weight |
|---|---|---|---|
| Rental Property | OBJECTIVE | This == Objective | |
| monthly rent | DISCRETE | 6000 (10), 6500 (6), 7000 (5), 8000 (2) | 0.4 |
| Deposit | DISCRETE | 10000 (6), 15000 (8), 20000 (5), 25000 (2) | 0.3 |
| Max room members | DISCRETE | 3 (7), 4 (8), 5 (4), 6 (2) | 0.1 |
| Brokerage | DISCRETE | 6000 (10), 7000 (8), 8000 (5), 9000 (4) | 0.2 |

**FIGURE 13.1**
Buyer profile.

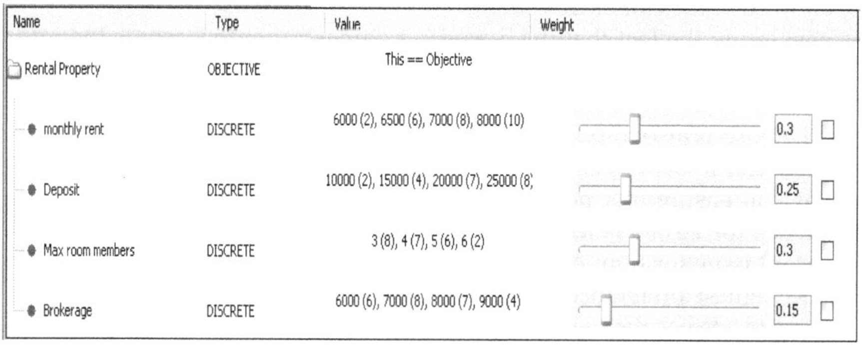

| Name | Type | Value | Weight |
|---|---|---|---|
| Rental Property | OBJECTIVE | This == Objective | |
| monthly rent | DISCRETE | 6000 (2), 6500 (6), 7000 (8), 8000 (10) | 0.3 |
| Deposit | DISCRETE | 10000 (2), 15000 (4), 20000 (7), 25000 (8) | 0.25 |
| Max room members | DISCRETE | 3 (8), 4 (7), 5 (6), 6 (2) | 0.3 |
| Brokerage | DISCRETE | 6000 (6), 7000 (8), 8000 (7), 9000 (4) | 0.15 |

**FIGURE 13.2**
Seller profile.

**TABLE 13.2**

Equations of Agents.

| Agent Name | Equations |
|---|---|
| Conceder | $y=\begin{cases}7.518x^3-10.229x^2+5.05x & \text{if } x\le 0.5\\ 0.185x+0.815 & \text{if } x>0.5\end{cases}$ |
| Moderate Conceder | $y = -0.8162x^3 + 2.266x^2 - 2.459x + 1.013$ |
| Linear | $y = 1 - x$ |
| Moderate Hardheaded | $y=\begin{cases}-8.33x^3+15x^2-9.417 & \text{if } x>0.6\\ 1-0.333x & \text{if } x\le 0.6\end{cases}$ |
| Hardheaded | $y=\begin{cases}-101.3x^3+246.6x^2-200.8x+55.6 & \text{if } x\le 0.8\\ 1-0.102x & \text{if } x<0.8\end{cases}$ |

### 13.1.1 Agent Selection

After the completion of preference profiles, both the parties will select agents who will represent them during negotiation. I have created five agents given by the equation in Table 13.2.

According to Vij et al. (Awasthi et al., 2016a), the graphical representation of the equations given in Table 13.2 is given by Figure 13.3.

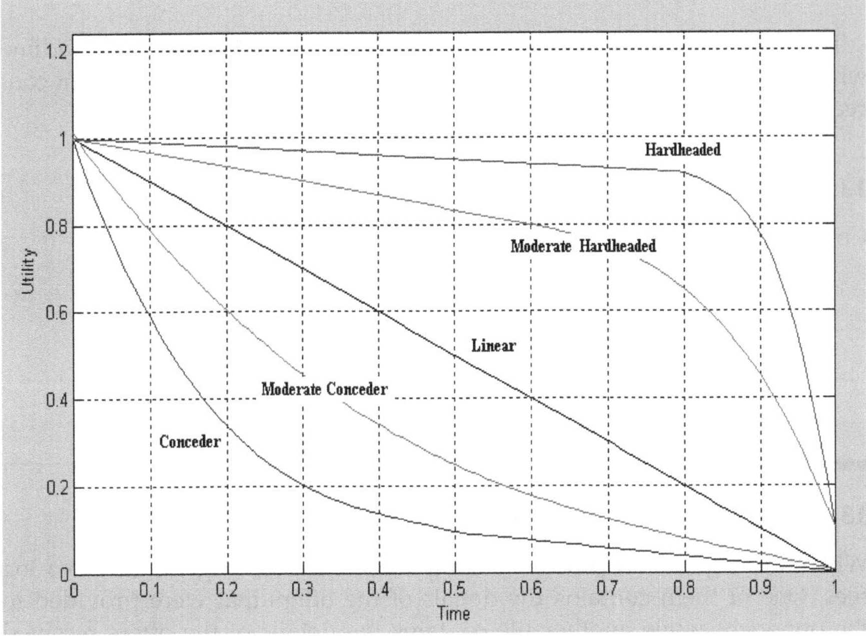


**FIGURE 13.3**
Graphical representation of agent behavior.

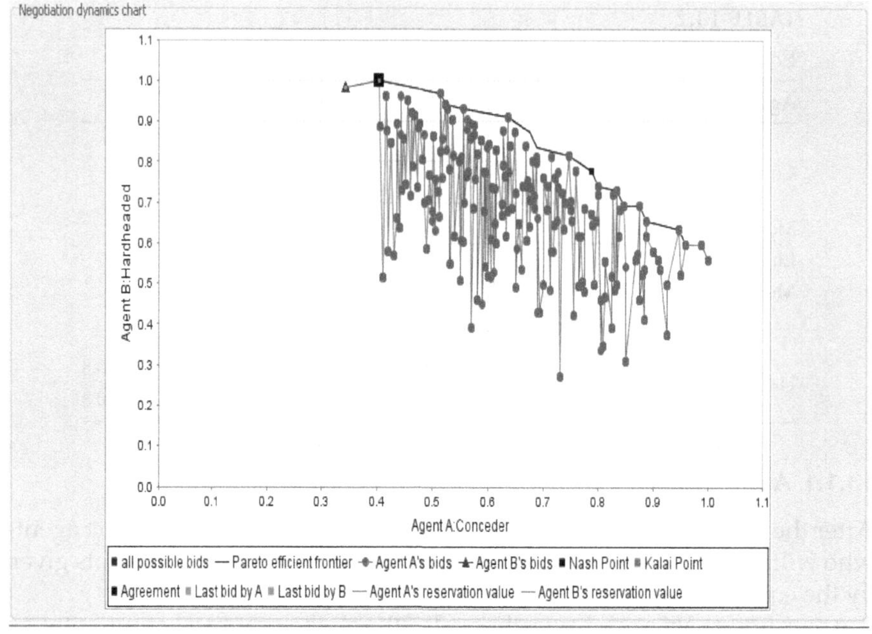


**FIGURE 13.4**
Offer exchange between conceder and hardheaded agent.

The hardheaded agent does not start conceding until near the deadline while conceder will start giving ground fairly quickly. And linear agent concedes the same amount in each round of the negotiation.

### 13.1.2 Negotiations

Conceder versus Hardheaded

1) Conceder versus Linear
2) Conceder versus Conceder

## 13.2 Prediction Algorithm

When the negotiation process is completed, each agent generates two log files. One of them contains the details of the offers that were provided to the opponent while another file contains the details of the offers received from the opponent. According to the earlier publications on web source

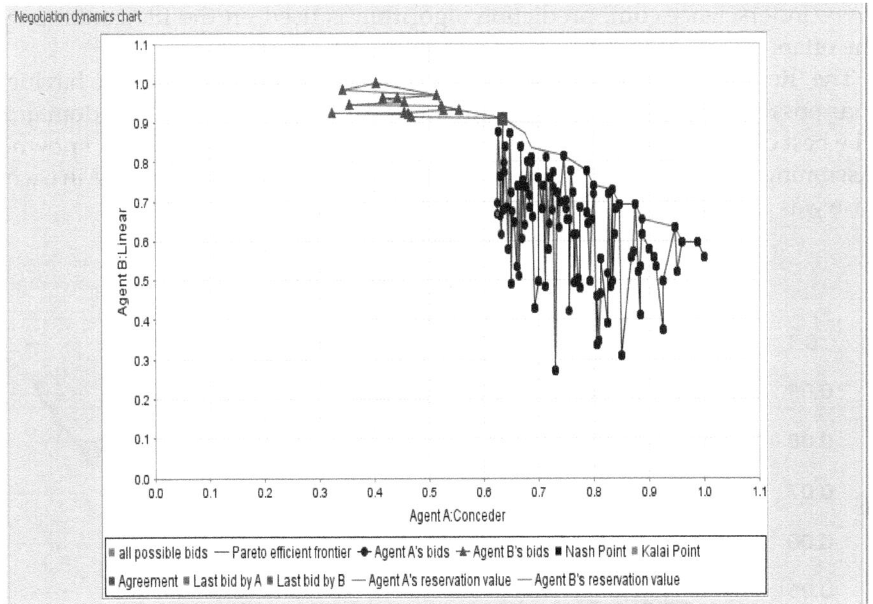


**FIGURE 13.5**
Offer exchange between conceder and linear agent.

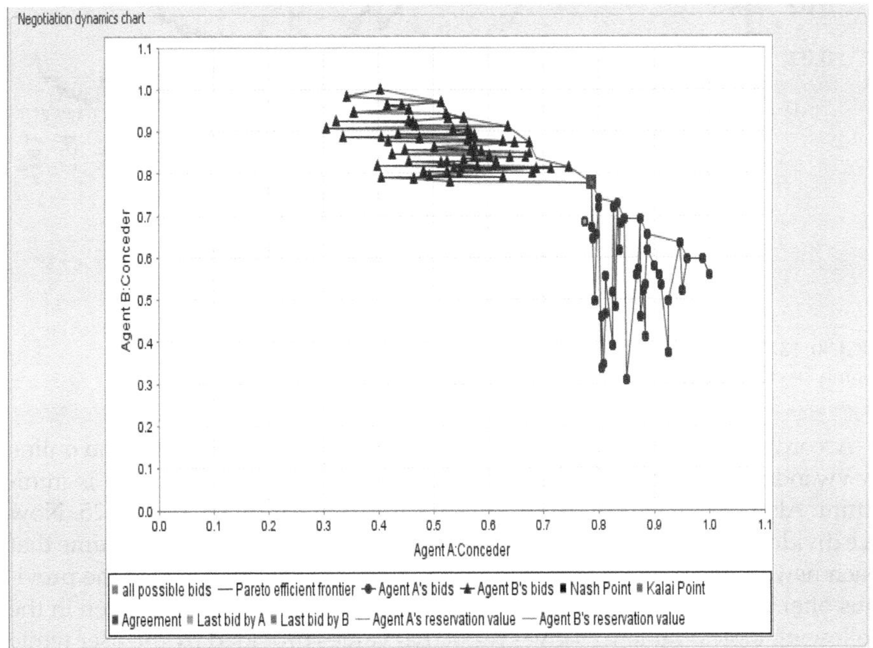


**FIGURE 13.6**
Offer exchange between two conceder agents.

www.inderscience.com, prediction algorithm is used on the file containing the offers that were received from the opponent.

The 'Rental Property' domain contains four issues with each issue having four possible values. So 256 different offers can be generated in this domain. The best offer has a utility of 1 and the utility of the worst offer is not known. Assuming the worst offer has utility of 0.1, 0.15, 0.20 or 0.25, error rate in each case was analyzed and the following results were observed:

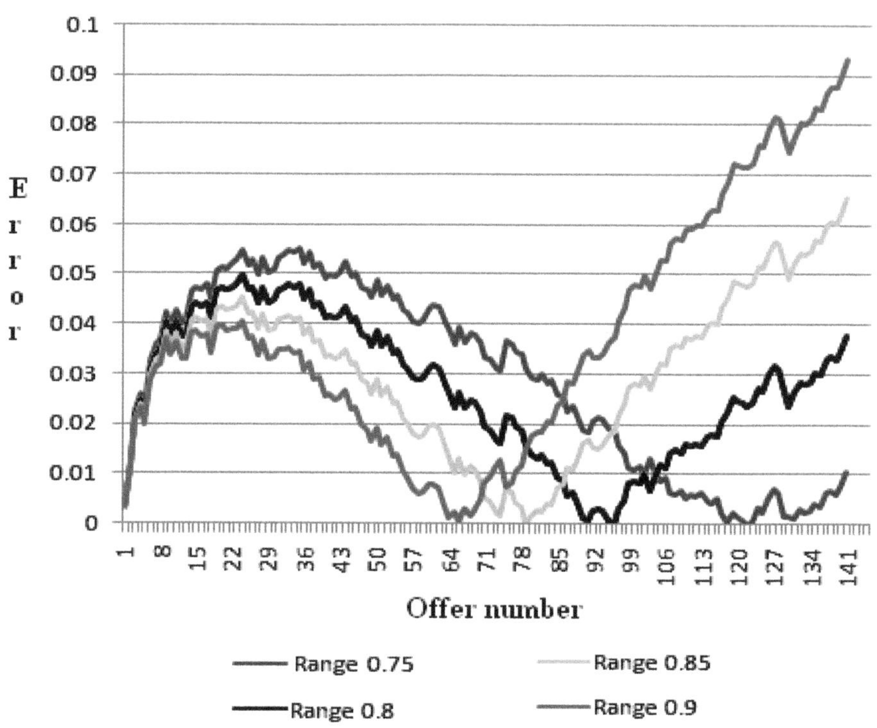


**FIGURE 13.7**
Graph for error comparison.

According to our earlier publication reference by Bala et al. (2015) and online www.inderscience.com, the mean error observed for a range of 0.8 is minimum. Also the maximum error found is 5% only for offer number 25. Now we divide the utility of 0.8 into 256 parts (0.80/256=0.003125) and assume that each new offer will provide a concession of 0.003125 compared to the previous offer. The results obtained from the prediction algorithm are given in the following tables. Table 13.3 gives the actual values provided by the user while Table 13.4 gives the predicted values and the accuracy for each value.

**TABLE 13.3**
Preference Profile of Buyer in 'Rental Property' Domain, Ref (Bala et al., 2015)

| Buyer profile (Rental Property) | | | | | | |
|---|---|---|---|---|---|---|
| **Issue** | **Weight** | **Values of issues** | | | | |
| Rent | 0.4 | 6000(10) | 6500(6) | 7000(5) | 8000(2) | Value(Rating) |
| | | 0.4 | 0.24 | 0.2 | 0.08 | Utility |
| | | 0 | 0.16 | 0.2 | 0.32 | Discount |
| Deposit | 0.3 | 10000(6) | 15000(8) | 20000(5) | 25000(2) | Value(Rating) |
| | | 0.225 | 0.3 | 0.1875 | 0.075 | Utility |
| | | 0.075 | 0 | 0.1125 | 0.225 | Discount |
| Room mates | 0.1 | 3(7) | 4(8) | 5(4) | 6(2) | Value(Rating) |
| | | 0.0875 | 0.1 | 0.05 | 0.025 | Utility |
| | | 0.0125 | 0 | 0.05 | 0.075 | Discount |
| Brokerage | 0.2 | 6000(10) | 7000(8) | 8000(5) | 9000(4) | Value(Rating) |
| | | 0.2 | 0.16 | 0.1 | 0.08 | Utility |
| | | 0 | 0.04 | 0.1 | 0.12 | Discount |

**TABLE 13.4**
Accuracy of the Predicted Values in the Buyer Profile, Ref (Bala et al., 2015)

| Buyer profile (Rental Property) | | | | | | |
|---|---|---|---|---|---|---|
| **Issue** | **Weight** | **Values of issues** | | | | |
| Rent | 0.4 | 6000(10) | 6500(6) | 7000(5) | 8000(2) | Value(Rating) |
| | | 0 | 0.1493 | 0.1996 | 0.3593 | Predicted values |
| | | 0 | 0.16 | 0.2 | 0.32 | Actual values |
| | | | 93.3125 | 99.8 | 87.71875 | Accuracy |
| Deposit | 0.3 | 10000(6) | 15000(8) | 20000(5) | 25000(2) | Value(Rating) |
| | | 0.0455 | 0 | 0.0864 | 0.2239 | Predicted values |
| | | 0.075 | 0 | 0.1125 | 0.225 | Actual values |
| | | 60.66667 | | 76.8 | 99.51111 | Accuracy |
| Room mates | 0.1 | 3(7) | 4(8) | 5(4) | 6(2) | Value(Rating) |
| | | 0.01 | 0 | 0.0335 | 0.054 | Predicted values |
| | | 0.0125 | 0 | 0.05 | 0.075 | Actual values |
| | | 80 | | 67 | 72 | Accuracy |
| Brokerage | 0.2 | 6000(10) | 7000(8) | 8000(5) | 9000(4) | Value(Rating) |
| | | 0 | 0.0203 | 0.0713 | 0.0942 | Predicted values |
| | | 0 | 0.04 | 0.1 | 0.12 | Actual values |
| | | | 50.75 | 71.3 | 78.5 | Accuracy |

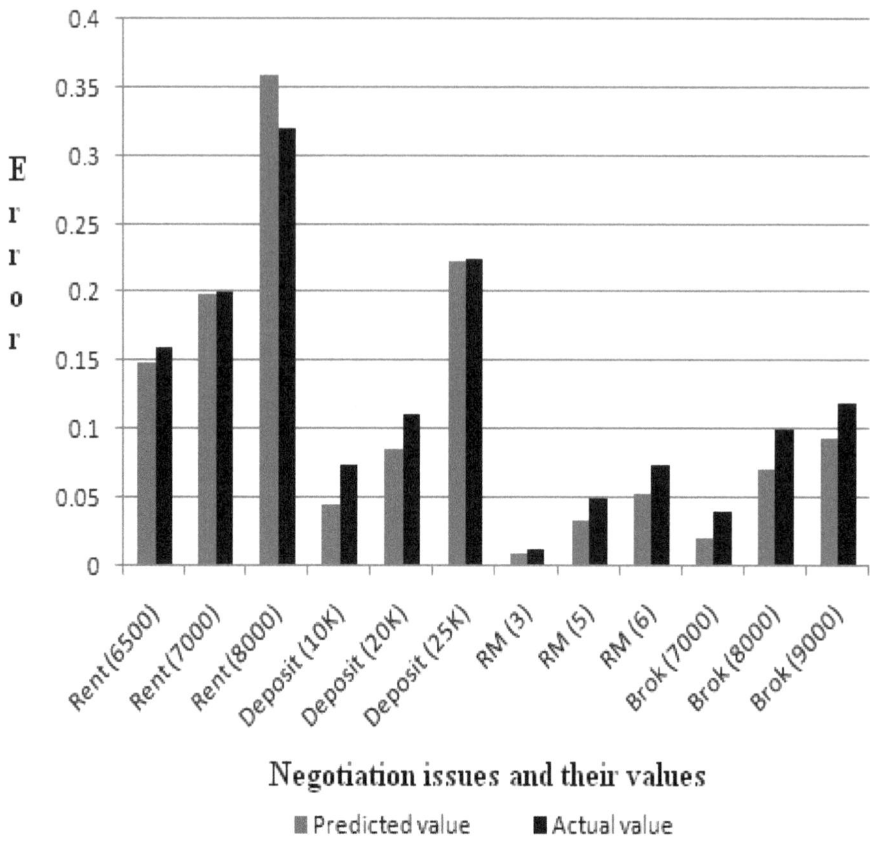


**FIGURE 13.8**
Comparison of predicted and actual values.

The accuracy of the predicted results is 78% for this profile. However, the accuracy will vary for different profiles.

### 13.2.1 Working of Multilateral Model

According to Vij et al. (2015b) and Patrikar et al. (2015), Buyer and Seller register their preferences on registration form of Multilateral Automated Negotiation. Preferences can be taken by using Matlab or XLS. Excel is better than Matlab when you need to keep a table of your data (input, output and descriptions) in front of you at all times, since 'formatted output' is inherent in the tool. MATLAB is best for sophisticated math, especially on large datasets and for things like matrix algebra, differential equation integration, Laplace transforms in the process control, etc. In the perspective of theoretical approach, we conclude that for small dataset use XLS and for large dataset use MATLAB.

AgentMatching: Agent can be selected manually or automatically. For automatic selection of agent gets overhead of computation. Here, we consider manual agent selection process.

$$\begin{pmatrix} \text{UBS1} & \text{UBS2} & \text{UBS3} & \text{UBS4} & \text{UBS5} & \text{--UBSn} \\ \text{UBS1} & \text{UBS2} & \text{UBS3} & \text{UBS4} & \text{UBS5} & \text{--UBSn} \\ \text{UBS1} & \text{UBS2} & \text{UBS3} & \text{UBS4} & \text{UBS5} & \text{--UBSn} \\ \text{UBS1} & \text{UBS2} & \text{UBS3} & \text{UBS4} & \text{UBS5} & \text{--UBSn} \\ \text{UBS1} & \text{UBS2} & \text{UBS3} & \text{UBS4} & \text{UBS5} & \text{--UBSn} \\ | & | & | & | & | & | \\ \text{UBSn} & \text{UBSn} & \text{UBSn} & \text{UBSn} & \text{UBSn} & \text{--UBSn} \end{pmatrix}$$

**MATRIX 13.1**
Final pair selection of agents Ref (Patrikar et al., 2015).

According to Vij et al. (2015b) and Patrikar et al. (2015), here, UBS is the product of buyer and seller utility. Bold letters indicate maximum value of utility of buyer and seller. After matching, if we get more than one maximum value then the pair will be made on the basis of the second maximum value (first come first serve). If one column or row has more than one maximum value then the conflict between agents will take place. This conflict situation is solved by considering the next maximum value of the pair of agents.

Decision function (Preferences, Offer, Round, Time, Emergency): Decision function checks an emergency variable. If emergency=0, then total utility is calculated by using linear programming method on both side of participants such as Total_utility = w1u1 + w2u2+.....wnun, where w is weight and u is the utility of participant, given in Patrikar et al. (2015) and Vij et al. (2015b).

$$\text{Offer} = (\text{min\_utility} + 0.1)\text{UB} + (\text{max\_Utility} - \text{S Discount};)\text{US};$$

Consider an example, if seller gives discount of 20% then discount= 0.2, utility limit of Buyer (0.1, 0.4) and of seller (0.2, 0.8) then we will get offer such as:

First iteration: Offer = 0.2*UB + 0.6*US;

Second iteration: Offer = 0.3UB + 0.4*US;

Third iteration: Offer = 0.4*UB + 0.2*US;

**TABLE 13.5**

Dataset of Multilateral Automated Negotiation

| Product name | Attribute 1 | Attribute 2 | Attribute 3 | Attribute 4 | Attribute 5 | Attribute 6 | Min Utility | Max Utility |
|---|---|---|---|---|---|---|---|---|
| 1. Camera | Maker | Body | Lens | Tripod | Bag | Accessory | 0.07 | 0.33 |
| 2. Laptop | Hard disk | Ram | Headphone | External Speaker | COMPANY | Screen Size | 0.18 | 0.38 |
| 3. Smart Phone | Maker | Screen Size | Color | Carrier | OS | Accessory | 0.2 | 0.9 |
| 4. Flat | Area | Rate | 2 BHK | Garden | School | Market | 0.16 | 0.4 |
| 5. Car | Engine | Company | Color | Cost | Driving | Accessory | 0.2 | 0.5 |
| 6. Hall | Number of People | Lawn | Catering | Rooms | Decoration | Parking | 0.3 | 0.8 |

If UB=US=1 then maximum profit=0.8. Offer will be calculated until minimum and maximum utility limit are attained. On the basis of values, the maximum offer will be generated, so this offer's values will be selected to calculate maximum profit. The following are the constraints: if utility is calculated or increased by more than one then it is rounded to 1 and the value less than zero is rounded to 0. If maximum profit is 0 then negotiation is withdrawn. Maximum profit is calculated by, Maximum profit= profit (UB) + profit (US);

The process will be continued till the specified rounds, time or successful negotiation. Otherwise negotiation will be withdrawn.

*Packages ()*: If emergency=1 then decision function calls package function. Packages are stored in the database using market basket analysis. Frequent dataset or pattern matching are core concepts of data mining for researchers. Consider Table 13.5: frequent dataset of automated negotiation. If buyer and seller are negotiating on product, e.g. Camera and have minimum and maximum utility equal to or between the minimum and maximum utility of Camera's dataset then negotiation on camera will be declared successful. Here the constraints are as follows: the name of product will be same; buyer's and seller's attribute of product will be same; or subset of product's attribute will be matched on Table's attributes and vice-versa. Otherwise negotiation gets to be withdrawn or not successful.

In this phase, we have done agent's matching. Agent's mapping is a basic requirement of our project. Now we work on actual negotiation process and will do analysis on bilateral system and multilateral negotiation systems.

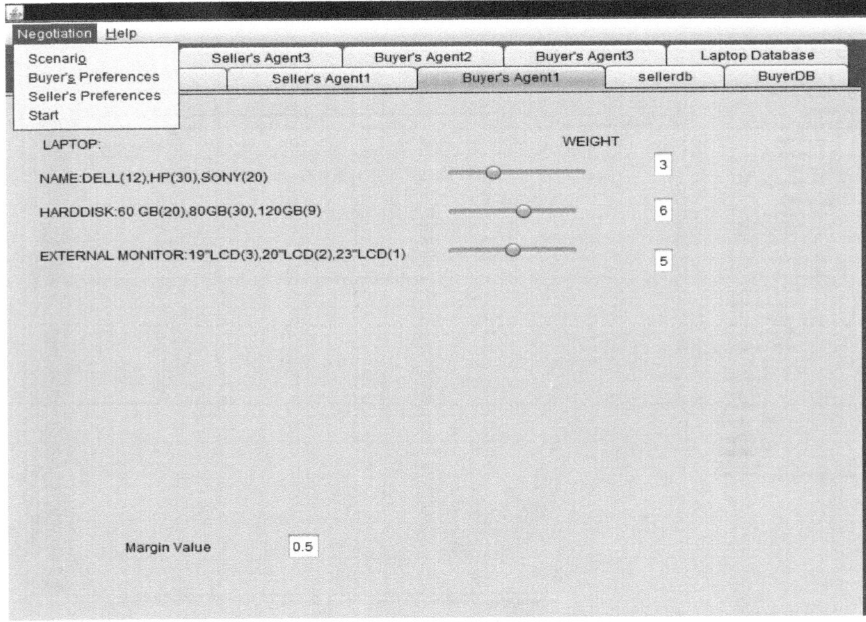


**FIGURE 13.9**
Buyer's form.

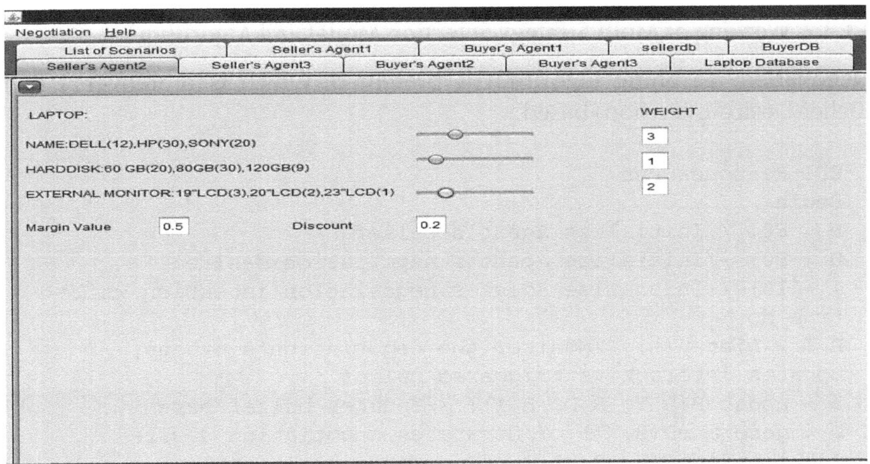


**FIGURE 13.10**
Seller's form.

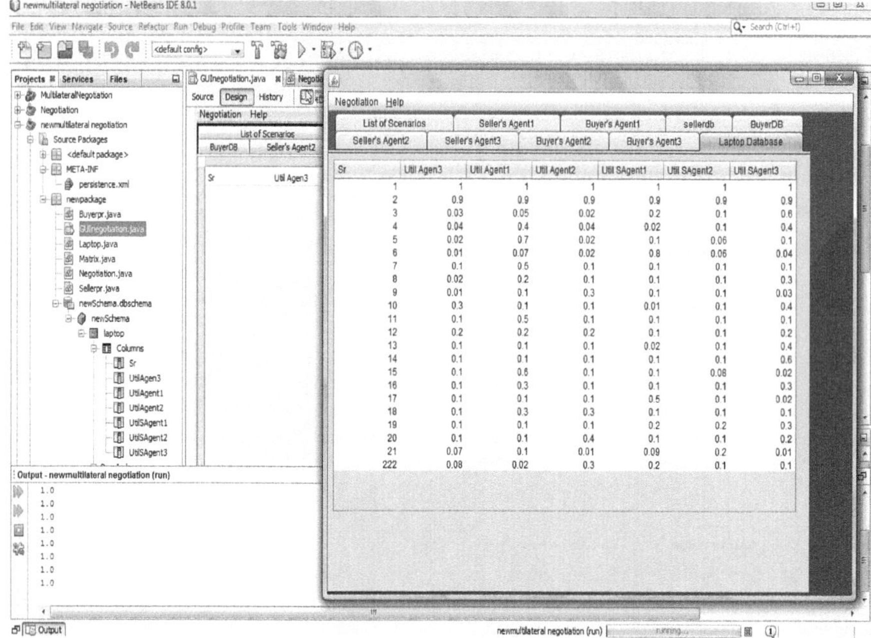


| Sr | Util Agen3 | Util Agent1 | Util Agent2 | Util SAgent1 | Util SAgent2 | Util SAgent3 |
|---|---|---|---|---|---|---|
| 1 | 1 | 1 | 1 | 1 | 1 | 1 |
| 2 | 0.9 | 0.9 | 0.9 | 0.9 | 0.9 | 0.9 |
| 3 | 0.03 | 0.05 | 0.02 | 0.2 | 0.1 | 0.6 |
| 4 | 0.04 | 0.4 | 0.04 | 0.02 | 0.1 | 0.4 |
| 5 | 0.02 | 0.7 | 0.02 | 0.1 | 0.06 | 0.1 |
| 6 | 0.01 | 0.07 | 0.02 | 0.8 | 0.06 | 0.04 |
| 7 | 0.1 | 0.5 | 0.1 | 0.1 | 0.1 | 0.1 |
| 8 | 0.02 | 0.2 | 0.1 | 0.1 | 0.1 | 0.3 |
| 9 | 0.01 | 0.1 | 0.3 | 0.1 | 0.1 | 0.03 |
| 10 | 0.3 | 0.1 | 0.1 | 0.01 | 0.1 | 0.4 |
| 11 | 0.1 | 0.5 | 0.1 | 0.1 | 0.1 | 0.1 |
| 12 | 0.2 | 0.2 | 0.2 | 0.1 | 0.1 | 0.2 |
| 13 | 0.1 | 0.1 | 0.1 | 0.02 | 0.1 | 0.4 |
| 14 | 0.1 | 0.1 | 0.1 | 0.1 | 0.1 | 0.6 |
| 15 | 0.1 | 0.6 | 0.1 | 0.1 | 0.08 | 0.02 |
| 16 | 0.1 | 0.3 | 0.1 | 0.1 | 0.1 | 0.3 |
| 17 | 0.1 | 0.1 | 0.1 | 0.5 | 0.1 | 0.02 |
| 18 | 0.1 | 0.3 | 0.3 | 0.1 | 0.1 | 0.1 |
| 19 | 0.1 | 0.1 | 0.1 | 0.2 | 0.2 | 0.3 |
| 20 | 0.1 | 0.1 | 0.4 | 0.1 | 0.1 | 0.2 |
| 21 | 0.07 | 0.1 | 0.01 | 0.09 | 0.2 | 0.01 |
| 222 | 0.08 | 0.02 | 0.3 | 0.2 | 0.1 | 0.1 |

**FIGURE 13.11**
Database.

### 13.2.2 Working of Multi Strategy Selection Model and Algorithm

Negotiation reasoning algorithm is presented, which is moreover a BDI (Belief-Desire-Intension) based.

```
BDI Reasoner Run
Begin
B = B0; //Initialize Agent's belief
D = D0; //Initialize Agent's negotiation desire
I = I0; //Initialize Agent's negotiation intention while
true do
B T = Listen(); //Monitor the negotiation's status, //
updates interactive triggered belief
B = updateB(B T, B D, B I); //Updates belief base
D = generateD(B, I); //Generates negotiation desire
I = generateI(B, D, I); //Generates negotiation intention
α := plan(B, I, SA); //Execute speech act planning, //
choose speech act from SA if(not(Impossible(I, B)))
```

```
then //If the conditions for //executing intention exit
execute(α); //Execute negotiation speech act
B D = D; //Update runtime belief about negotiation desire
B I = I; //Update runtime belief about negotiation
intention
else quit
end if
end while
End
```

According to our earlier publication's online source www.inderscienceonline.com, it is evident that

1. There are two aspirations of buyer, win–win and win–loss. Win–win aims to maximize the success rate at the cost of relatively low-bid utility but high acceptance weight. Win–loss aims to maximize the utility of bid generated. 2. Buyer using web application decides the aspiration and number of rounds. 3. We have taken 27 as the number of negotiation rounds as total number no of possible bid for the dataset we have taken is 27. 4. Using number of rounds, phase of negotiation will be identified. 5. Every phase has certain agenda, and it acts as a point to evaluate the performance of negotiation and perform appropriate action accordingly. Calculations of strategies are given in section 12.1.4 (Chapter 12) System Architecture Multi Strategy Based E Negotiation.

## 13.3 Analysis

### 13.3.1 For Bilateral System with Opponents Behavior Prediction

Following are some of the project snapshots as well as graphical analysis.

Concession rate of each agent differentiates the various agent strategies. The best strategy is to concede when negotiating with competitive agent and be hardheaded when negotiating with cooperative agent. There does not exist any universally best approach or technique for automated negotiation. Prediction results in general are used to improve the performance of agents. Huge scope for improvement, bilateral negotiation to multilateral negotiation, agent-mediated scenario, also to consider emotional and cultural differences.

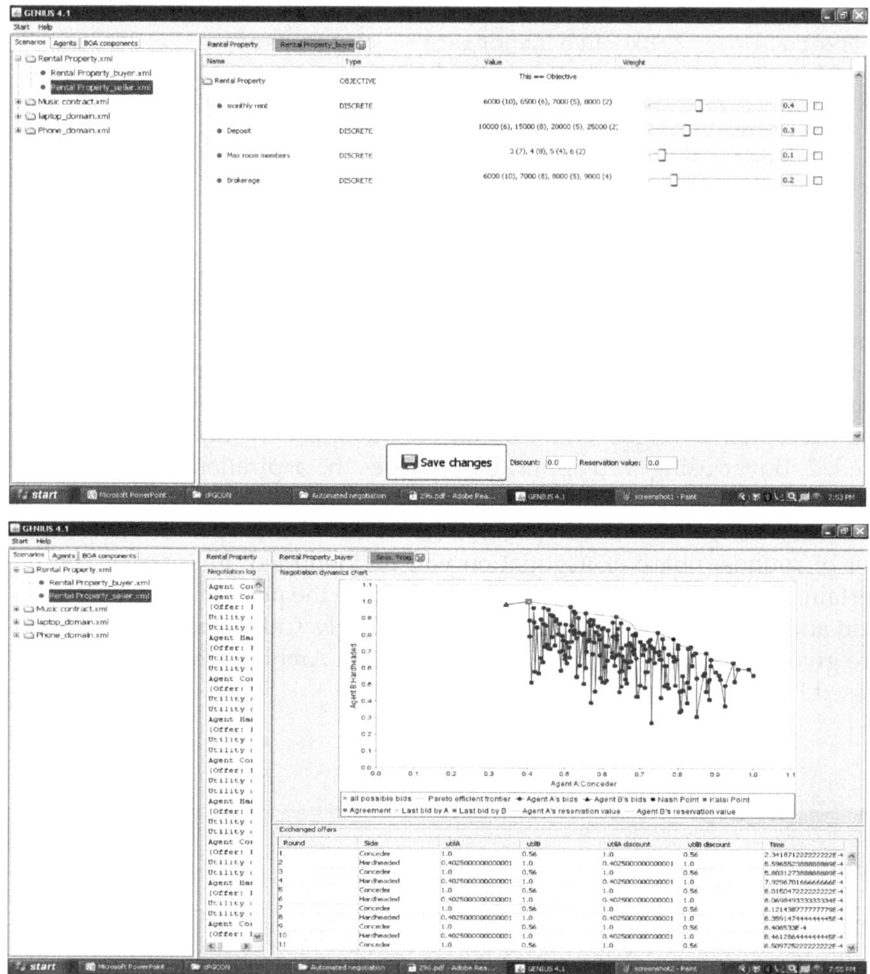


**SNAPSHOT AND GRAPH 1**

Bilateral bargaining with behavior prediction for Automated Negotiation.

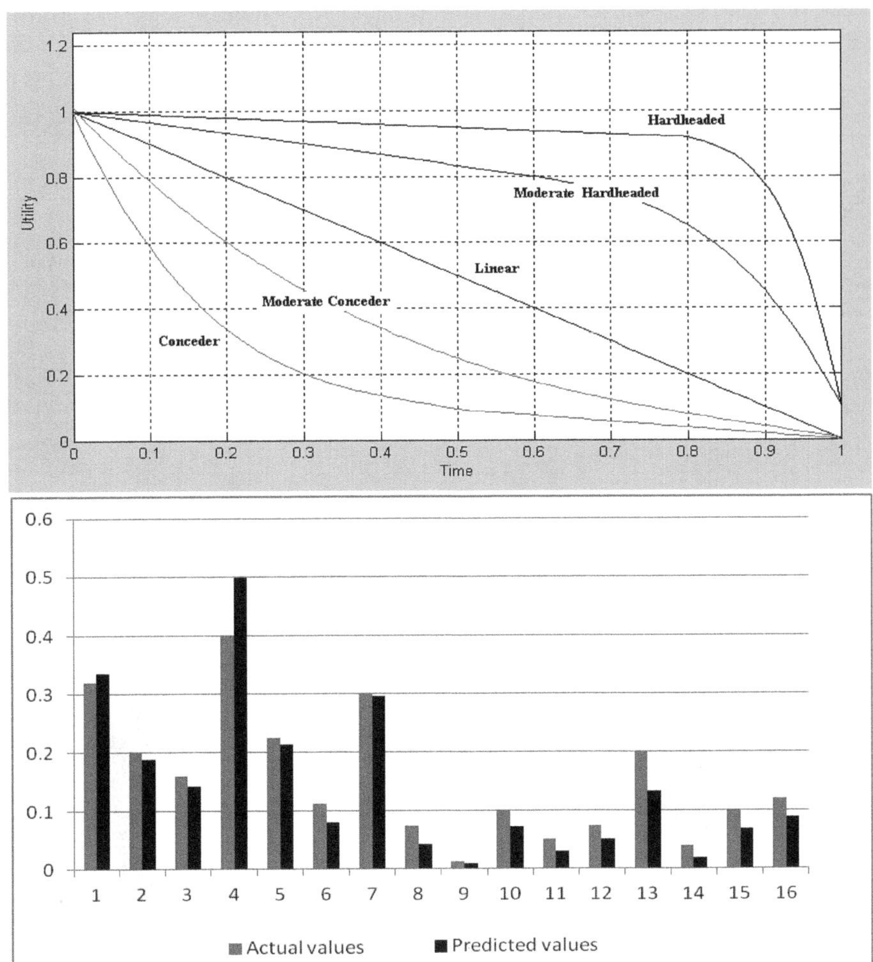


**SNAPSHOT AND GRAPH 1 (Continue)**
Bilateral bargaining with behavior prediction for Automated Negotiation.

### 13.3.2 Multilateral Negotiations

According to our earlier publication reference by Patrikar et al. (2015) and Vij et al. (2015b), multilateral negotiations are more complicated and time-consuming than bilateral negotiations because in the multilateral automated negotiation, we require to do multiple matching between the participants. Multilateral automated negotiation system gives better result than bilateral automated negotiation system. The system, in which the technique of

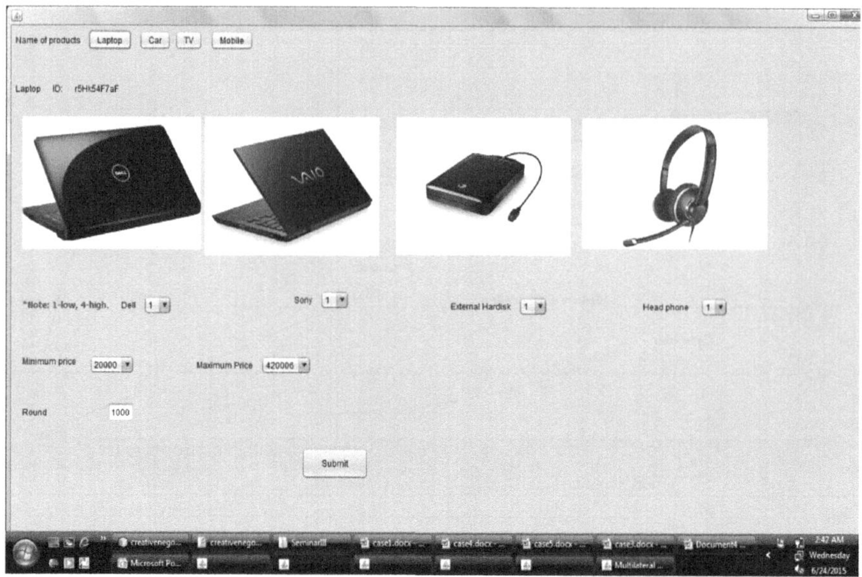


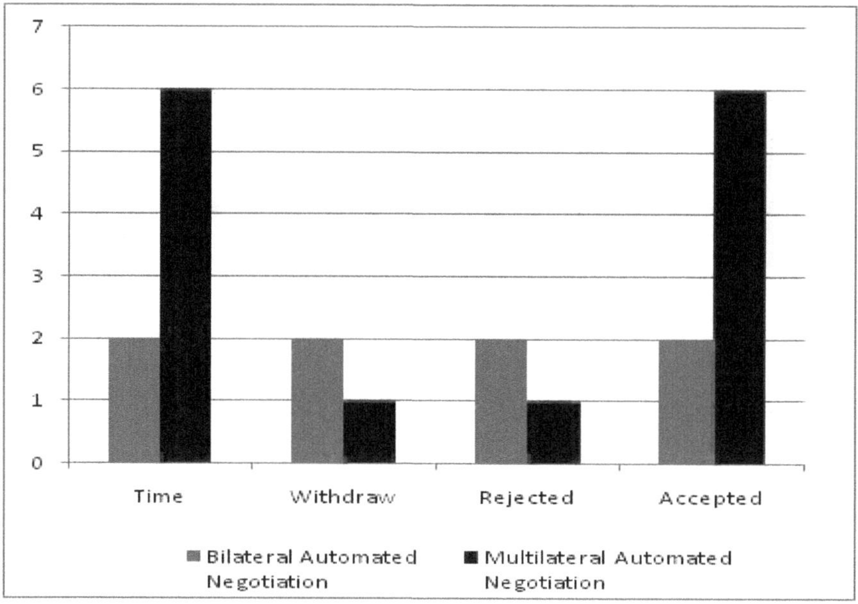


**SNAPSHOT AND GRAPH 2**
Bilateral vs. multilateral automated negotiation.

finding the behavior of opponents is used, is always better than the system not using it.

As given on web source link.springer.com, for real-time multilateral automated negotiation, cloud will be more helpful. Cloud requires low maintenance on data and is more secure, but it is useful for large application because it is costly. Intelligent decision function is required.

### 13.3.3 Negotiation Using RBR and CBR and Improved Memory Utilization and Response Time

There are organizations to maintain data (as given on web source link.springer.com) of the negotiation process and product data. But this maintenance is a very tedious job. In order to overcome this problem, all organizations' product data is stored on cloud. According to Patrikar et al. (2015), in order to make faster E-negotiation process, I can use the rule-based and case-based approaches. This system is a bilateral negotiation model. In future, this system can be implemented as multilateral negotiation model, behavior prediction model and will also use the concept of expert system for increasing success rate of negotiation process.

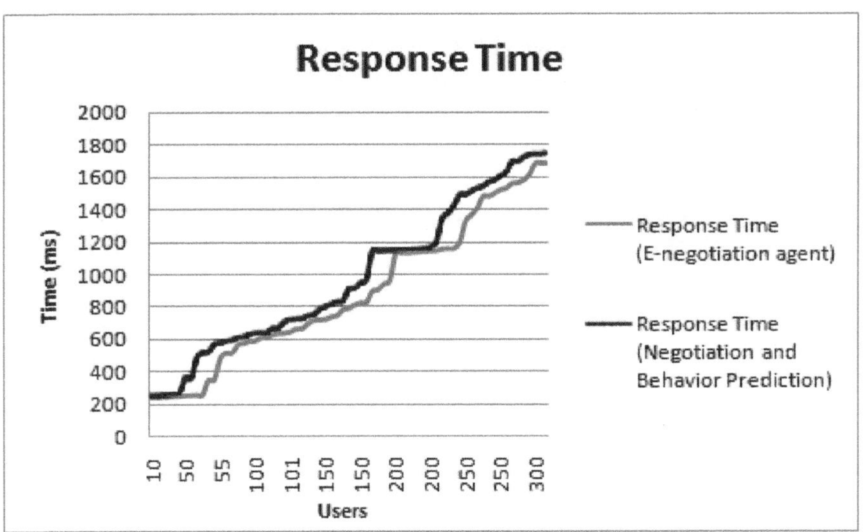


**GRAPH 3**
Response time and memory utilization for automated negotiation.

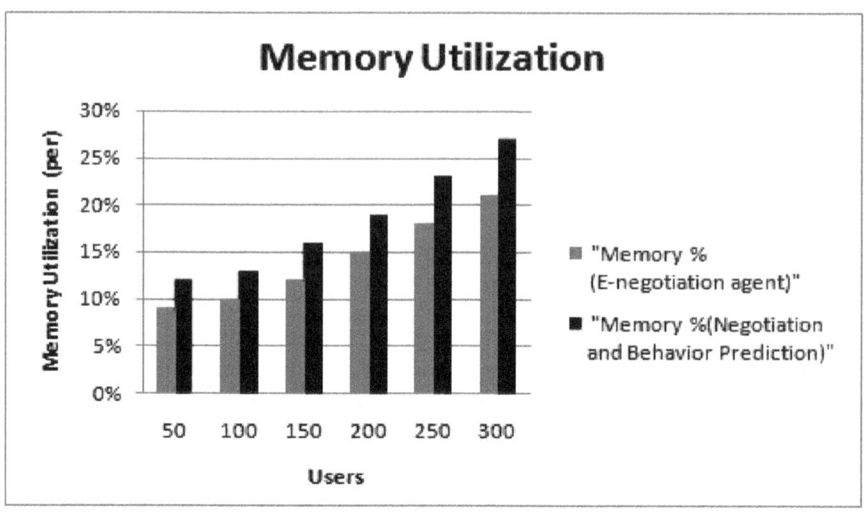


**GRAPH 3 (Continue)**
Response time and memory utilization for automated negotiation.

### 13.3.4 Multi-Strategy Selection

Every Strategy has certain applicability, and its selection impacts the utility and final outcome of negotiation. To resolve the conflict among negotiating parties, hard-bounded strategy is chosen. According to Awasthi et al. (2016a),

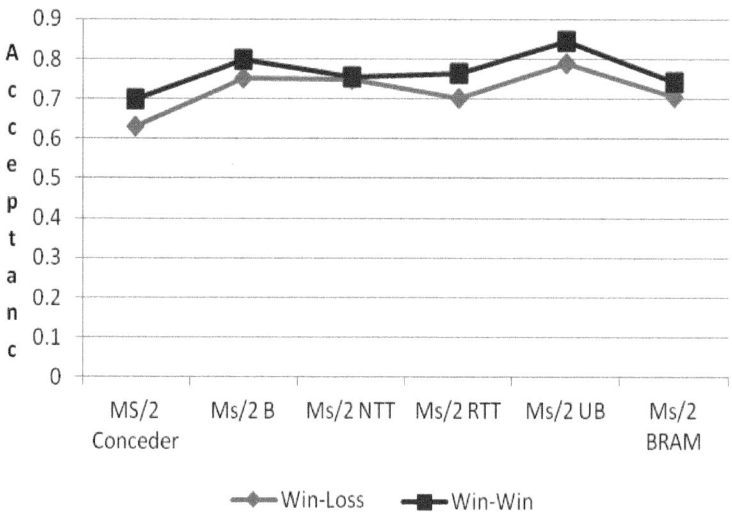


**GRAPH 4**
Multi-strategy-based selection results for automated negotiation.

any selection of strategy has a significant impact on the utilities of agents and final outcome, therefore selecting a strategy is a critical problem since opponents and their behavior are unknown, difficult to model and could be uncooperative. Multi-strategy selection can deal with a high number of negotiation scenarios, can yield into higher success rate and utility gain, further its will be difficult for opponent to predict our strategy.

According to web source www.inderscienceonline.com, selecting strategy for a particular opponent during negotiation for a small dataset is a complex task, as learning, profiling, predicting can't be applied effectively. Web-service-based deployment facilities in-dependency of platform, place, implementation etc. Win–win case of negotiation is best suitable for real-life negotiation. Win–loss goes against the basic; it may incur negotiation failure. The future enhancement can be more number of strategies to enhance the competitiveness of system and the proposed algorithm need to be verified on other negotiation scenario.

# 14

# Conclusion

There is a huge scope for analysis and research on the performance aspect of automated negotiation protocol techniques, mainly in e-Commerce. This book discusses the automated negotiation protocol's relevance in modern times; its dependence on internet-based systems; and improvement techniques in its basic design to improve speed, efficiency and storage, which can be the basis for further interdisciplinary research in E-negotiation and web services, software technology, human psychology in bargaining, bidding and auctions.

## 14.1 Future Work (According to Earlier Published Results on Web Source www.ijert.org)

- The developed system is for bilateral negotiations and can be extended to multilateral negotiations in future to allow multiple parties to negotiate simultaneously.
- Agent strategies can be further improved by taking into consideration prediction results.
- Another direction of future work could be around mediated negotiation scenarios, in which a mediator agent has the task to find the mutually acceptable offer given the requirements of both the parties.
- The system can be extended to work on different scenarios with inconsistent deadlines and partial overlap of zones of acceptance of the negotiation parties.

## 14.2 Limitations of Research

According to earlier published results on web source arxiv.org, the following limitations and challenges have been experienced during the process of this study:

- Agent-mediated scenario is very complex to introduce.
- Consideration of inherent negotiation process aspects which are interdisciplinary as human psychology, emotional and cultural differences, which are difficult to implement in actual system without human intervention.

DOI: 10.1201/9781003408253-16

- To convert the system into practically viable expert system for any B2B or B2C e-Commerce site is difficult.
- More number of strategies to identify, to enhance the competitiveness of system, is very difficult. All these limitations can be considered as future scope of automated negotiations.

## 14.3 Concluding Remarks

The main objective of the research project was to make automated negotiation possible which has been achieved though with some limitations. The system is capable of automated negotiation in some predefined situations. According to the publication on the internet source link.springer.com, user interaction is only required at the beginning of negotiation process to specify its requirements which are given as input to the agents saving the precious time of user. Prediction of partner's behaviors in negotiation has been an active research direction in recent years, and this project presents an online learning approach about other agents' preferences with only the history of offers of current negotiation encounter. This prediction mechanism will further improve the efficiency of the negotiation system. However, both the fields of automated negotiation and behavior prediction are in their initial stages of development and no such software or application is available for the simulation of these processes.

Mentioned in the publication on the internet source kmi.open.ac.uk, multilateral negotiations are more complicated and time-consuming than bilateral negotiations because in the multilateral automated negotiation, we require to do multiple matching between the participants. Multilateral automated negotiation system gives better result than bilateral automated negotiation system. Participants can take joint decision about their number of issues. If web service is used in the multilateral automated negotiation system then it can give faster results to the participants. The system, in which the technique of finding the behavior of opponents is used, is always better than the system not using it. Pattern-matching technique will give fast result and will reduce the overhead of calculations.

As given by Awasthi et al. (Awasthi et al., 2016a), multi-strategy selection can deal with high number of negotiation scenario, can yield into higher success rate and utility gain, further it will be difficult for opponent to predict our strategy.

- As given in www.sppu.edu.in earlier, selecting strategy for a particular opponent during negotiation for a small dataset is a complex task, as learning, profiling, predicting can't be applied effectively.

- Every strategy exhibits certain characteristic, which decides its applicability.
- Web-service-based deployment facilities – dependency of platform, place, implementation etc.
- Win–win case of negotiation is best suitable for real life negotiation.
- Win–loss goes against the basic; it may incur negotiation failure.

# Bibliography

Muhammad Anu Abbas, Giuseppe Berio (2014) Ontology Merging: Compatible and Incompatible Ontology Mapping. In: *Ninth International Conference on Semantics, Knowledge and Grids*. IEEEXplore. pp. 129–134.

H. Abbes, S. Boukettaya, F. Gargouri (2015) 'Learning Ontology from Big Data through MongoDB Database', In the *12th ACS/IEEE International Conference on Computer Systems and Applications (AICCSA)*, 2015 pp. 1–7

AGROVOC Thesaurus: http://aims.fao.org/agrovoc#.VF29AvmUc2U

AGROVOC Retrieved February 3, 2016, from http://aims.fao.org/vest-registry/vocabularies/agrovoc-multilingual-agricultural-thesaurus

E. Alfonseca, S. Manandhar (2002) Extending a Lexical Ontology by a Combination of Distributional Semantics Signatures; A. Gómez-Pérez, R. V. Benjamins (eds) *Knowledge Engineering and Knowledge Management: Ontologies and the Semantic Web. EKAW 2002*; Lecture Notes in Computer Science, vol. 2473, Springer, Berlin, Heidelberg.

R. Alfred, O. K. Chin, P. Anthony, W. P. San, L. T. Im, C. L. Leong, K. G. Soon (2014) 'Ontology-based query expansion for supporting information retrieval in agriculture', *Proceedings of the 8th International conference on Knowledge Management in Organizations*. pp. 299–311.

A. Alka, K.S. Linkon, M. Sudeep, J. Rajni and K.J. Amrender (2015) 'Online system for integrated pest management on Tomato in Agridaksh', in *2nd International Conference on Computing for Sustainable Global Development (INDIACom)*, e-ISBN: 978-9-3805-4416-8. pp. 1125–1129.

Faisal Alsrheed, Abdennour El Rhalibi, Martin Randles, Madjid Merabti (2014) Intelligent agents for automated cloud computing negotiation, *International Conference on Multimedia Computing and Systems (ICMCS)*, Press, Philadelphia.

Bo An, Victor Lesser, David Irwin, Michael Zink (2010) Automated Negotiation with Decommitment for Dynamic Resource Allocation in Cloud Computing, *Proceedings of 9th International Conference on Autonomous Agents and Multi agent Systems AAMAS 2010*, pp. 981–988.

R. S. Z. Aqeel-ur (2011) 'ONTAgri: scalable service oriented agriculture ontology for precision farming', *2011 international conference on agricultural and biosystems engineering vols*. pp. 1–2.

C. Archana, V.K. Jha, D. Mukhopadhyay (2016a) 'Adaptive ontology construction method for crop pest management', in *Proceedings of the International Conference on Data Engineering and Communication Technology*, vol. 468, of the series Advances in Intelligent Systems and Computing, pp. 665–674.

C. Archana, V.K. Jha, D. Mukhopadhyay (2016b) 'Ontology based system for pests and disease management of grapes in India', in *Proceedings of IEEE 6th International Conference on Advanced Computing*, DOI: 10.1109/IACC.2016.34, pp. 133–138.

Moustapha Tahir Ateib (2010) Agent Based Negotiation In E-commerce, International Symposium on Information Technology (ITSim 2010) ©2010 IEEE, vol. 2 Engineering Technology, Piscataway. 978-1-4244-6716-7/101, pp. 861–868.

G. Atemezing, O. Corcho, D. Garijo, J. Mora, M. Proveda-Villalon, P. Rozas, D. Vila-Suero, B. Villazon-Terrazas (2011) Transforming Meteorological Data into Linked Data; Semantic Web – Interoperability, Usability, *Applicability; an IOS Press Journal*; pp. 1–6.

S. Awasthi, S. Vij, D. Mukhopadhyay, A. Agrawal (2016a) Multi strategy selection in e-negotiation: A proposed architecture. *International Conference on Information and Communication Technology for Competitive Strategies, ICTCS'16*, March 04-05, 2016, Udaipur, India (ACM), http://dx.doi.org/10.1145/2905055.2905138, vol. C, no. 79.

S. Awasthi, S. Vij, D. Mukhopadhyay, A. Agrawal (2016b) Multi-strategy based automated negotiation: BGP based architecture, *International Conference on Computing, Communication and Automation*, pp. 588–593, IEEEXplore, Galgotia University, Noida, 27–18 April 2016.

Reyhan Aydogan, Tim Baarslag, Koen V. Hindriks, Catholijin M. Jonker, Pinar Yolum (2014) *Heuristics for using CP-nets in utility-based negotiation without knowing utilities*, Springer-Verlag, London, DOI: 10.1007/s10115-014-0798-z.

Tim Baarslag, Alexander Dirkzwager, Koen V. Hindriks, Catholijn M. Jonker (2017) The Significance of Bidding, *Accepting and Opponent Modeling in Auto-mated Negotiation*, DOI: 10.3233/978-1-61499-419-0-27. Conference: 21st European Conference on Artificial Intelligence, At Prague, vol. 263.

M. Bala, S. Vij, D. Mukhopadhyay (2015) Automated negotiation with behavior prediction. *International Journal of Internet Protocol Technology*, Inderscience publishers, vol. 9, no. 1, pp. 44–50.

Mohammad Irfan Bala, Sheetal Vij (2013) Automated Negotiation And Behavior Prediction, *International Journal of Engineering Research & Technology (IJERT)*, vol. 2, no. 6.

Mohammad Irfan Bala, Mohammad Ahsan Chishti (2017) A model to incorporate automated negotiation in IoT, *2017 IEEE International Conference on Advanced Networks and Telecommunications Systems (ANTS)*.

Mohammad Irfan Bala, Sheetal Vij, Debajyoti Mukhopadhyay (2013a) Intelligent Agent for Prediction in E-Negotiation: An Approach, *CUBE 2013 International IT Conference, CUBE 2013 Proceedings*, Pune, India, IEEE-USA, November 15.

Mohammed Irfan Bala, Sheetal Vij, Debajyoti Mukhopadhyay (2013b) Negotiation Life Cycle: An Approach in E-negotiation with Prediction, *48th Annual Convention of the Computer Society of India, CSI 2013 Proceedings*, Visakhapatnam, India, Springer-Verlag Germany, December 13–15 2013, pp. 505–512, ISBN 978-3-319-03107-1

M. P. Bange, S. A. Deutscher, D. Larsen, D. Linsley, S. Whiteside (2008) "A hand-held decision support system to facilitate improved insect pest management in Australian cotton systems", *Computers and Electronics in Agriculture* 43; Elsevier journal; pp. 131–147.

N. Bansal, S. K. Malik (2011) A framework for agriculture ontology development in semantic Web; *International Conference on Communication Systems and Network Technologies*; IEEE Xplore; pp. 283–286.

J. G. A. Barbedo (2016, August) A novel algorithm for semi-automatic segmentation of plant leaf disease symptoms using digital image processing; *Tropical Plant Pathology*, vol. 41, no. 4; pp. 210–222.

N. Beaudry, G. Bourgeois, D. Choquette, G. Chouinard, D. Plouffe (2014) CIPRA - Computer Centre for Agricultural Pest Forecasting: Crop Guide; Agriculture and Agri-Food Canada.

R. Beheshti, N. Mozayani (2009) Predicting opponents offers in multi-agent negotiations using ARTMAP neural network, *Second International Conference on Future Information Technology and Management Engineering*, FITME '09, pp. 600–603.

Rokia Bendaoud, Mohamed Rouane Hacene, Yannick Toussaint, Bertrand Delecroix, Amedeo Napoli. (2007) Text-based ontology construction using relational concept analysis. In *Proceedings of International Workshop on Ontology Dynamics – IWOD 2007*. 1–14.

S. Benomrane, Z. Sellami, B. M. Ayed (2016) 'An ontologist feedback driven ontology evolution with an adaptive multi-agent system', *Advanced Engineering Informatics* vol. 30. pp. 337–353.

Chris Biemann, "Ontology Learning from Text: A Survey of Methods", LDV forum, 2005.

P. Boniecki, K. Koszela, H. Piekarska-Boniecka, J. Weres, M. Zaborowicz, S. Kujawa, A. Majewski and B. Rab (2015) 'Neural identification of selected apple pests', *Computers and Electronics in Agriculture*, vol. 110, pp.9–16.

A. Bouza, G. Reif, A. Bernstein, H. Gall (2007) 'SemTree: Ontology-Based Decision Tree Algorithm for Recommender Systems', *Proceedings of the 7th International Semantic Web Conference*, Germany.

M. Bowling, B. Browning, M. Veloso (2004) Plays as elective multi agent plans enabling opponent adaptive play selection, *Proceedings of International conference on automated planning and scheduling (ICAPS04).*

F. M. T. Brazier, Jonker C. M., Treur J. (2000) Compositional design and reuse of a generic agent model, *Applied Artificial Intelligence Journal*, vol. 14, pp. 491–538.

J. Brzostowski and R. Kowalczyk (2006) Predicting partner's behaviour in agent negotiation, *Proc. Int'l Joint Conf. Autonomous Agents and Multiagent Systems*, pp. 355–361.

P. Buitelaar, P. Cimiano, and B. Magnini, editors, (2005) "Ontology Learning from Text: Methods, Evaluation and Applications," Volume 123 of Frontiers in Artificial Intelligence and Applications, IOS Press, Nieuwe Hemweg 6B, 1013 BG Amsterdam, The Netherlands.

Paul Buitelaar, Daniel Olejnik and Michael Sintek. (2004) "A Protégé Plug-In for Ontology Extraction from Text Based on Linguistic Analysis," *The Semantic Web: Research and Applications*, LNCS Volume 3053, Springer Berlin Heidelberg. DOI 10.1007/978-3-540-25956-5_3. 31–44.

Ricardo Buttner (2006) A classification Structure for Automated Negotiations, *IEEE/WIC/ACM International Conference on Web Intelligence and Intelligent Technology*, Hong Kong, China, pp. 523–530.

M. Cao, X. Luo, X. Luo, X. Dai (2015) Automated negotiation for e-commerce decision making: A goal deliberated agent architecture for multi-strategy selection. *Decision Support Systems*, Elsevier Science Publishers, vol. 73, no. C, pp 1–14.

Mukun Cao (2010) Multi-agent automated negotiation as a service, *7th International Conference on Service Systems and Service Management (ICSSSM)*, pp 1–6.

Mukun Cao, Robert Chi, Ying Liu (2009) Developing a multi-agent automated negotiation service based on service oriented architecture, *Service Science Journal*, vol. 1, pp 31–42.

C. Caracciolo, A. Stellato, A. Morshed, G. Johannsen, S. Rajbahndari, Y. Jaques, J. Keizer (2013) 'The agrovoc linked dataset', *Semantic Web.* vol. 4, no. 3. 341–348.

Real Carbonneau, Gregory E. Kersten, Rustam Vahidov (2008) Predicting opponent's moves in electronic negotiations using neural networks, *Expert Systems with Applications: An International Journal*, vol. 34, no 2.

L. K. Chadha, D. S. Shikhamany (2002) *The Grape Improvement, Production and Post-harvest management*. New Dehi, India: Malhotra Publishing House.

R. Chen, Y. Huang, C. Bau, S. Chen (2012) 'A recommendation system based on domain ontology and SWRL for anti-diabetic drugs selection', *Expert Systems with Applications*; vol. 39. pp. 3995–4006.

A. Chougule, K. V. Jha, D. Mukhopadhyay (2016) 'AgroKanti: Location-Aware Decision Support System for Forecasting of Pests and Diseases in Grapes', Satapathy S., Mandal J., Udgata S., Bhateja V. (eds) *Information Systems Design and Intelligent Applications. Advances in Intelligent Systems and Computing*, vol. 433. Springer, New Delhi.

Limin Chuana (2013, January) Ping Hea; Establishing a scientific basis for fertilizer recommendations for wheat in China: Yield response and agronomic efficiency; *Field Crops Research*, vol. 140; pp. 1–8.

P. Cimiano, S. Staab (2005) "Learning concept hierarchies from text with a guided hierarchical clustering algorithm," C. Biemann and G. Paas, editors, *Proceedings of the ICML 2005 Workshop on Learning and Extending Lexical Ontologies with Machine Learning Methods*, Bonn, Germany.

P. Cimiano, J. Völker (2005) "Text2Onto," A. Montoyo, R. Muñoz, E. Métais (eds) *Natural Language Processing and Information Systems*. NLDB 2005. Lecture Notes in Computer Science, vol. 3513. Springer, Berlin, Heidelberg.

R. Ciprian-Radu, H. Olimpiu, T. Ioana-Alexandra, and O. Gheorghe (2015) 'Smart monitoring of potato crop: a cyber-physical system architecture model in the field of precision agriculture', *Agriculture and Agricultural Science Procedia*, vol. 6, pp.73–79, DOI: 10.1016/j.aaspro.2015.08.04.

M. Compton, P. Barnaghi, L. Bermudez, R. García-Castro, O. Corcho, S. Cox, J. Graybeal, M. Hauswirth, C. Henson, A. Herzog, V. Huang, K. Janowicz, W. D. Kelsey, D. L. Phuoc, L. Lefort, M. Leggieri, H. Neuhaus, A. Nikolov, K. Page, A. Passant, A. Sheth, and K. Taylor (2012) 'The SSN ontology of the W3C semantic sensor network incubator group', *Web Semantics: Science, Services and Agents on the World Wide Web*, vol. 17, pp.25–32.

C. Cornejo, H. W. Beck, D. Z. Haman and F. S. Zazueta, "Development and Application of an Irrigation Ontology," *2005 EFITA/WCCA Joint Congress on IT and Agriculture*, Vila Real, Portugal, 25–28 July 2005.

Elisabeth Crawford, Manuela Veloso (2005) Learning to Select Negotiation Strategies with Strategic Experts, 200X ACM.

Amir Vahid Dastjerdi, Rajkumar Buyya (2012) An Autonomous Reliability-aware Negotiation Strategy for Cloud Computing Environments, 12th IEEE/ACM International Symposium on Cluster, Cloud and Grid Computing, IEEE 2012, 978-0-7695-4691-9/12, DOI: 10.1109/CCGrid.2012.101, pp. 284–291.

DBPedia, http://dbpedia.org/ontology/Grape [Accessed on 2nd March 2017]

Fabiana Freire de Araújo, Fernanda Lígia R. Lopes, Bernadette Farias Lóscio (2010) MeMO: A Clustering-based Approach for Merging Multiple Ontologies. In: *IEEE 2010 Workshops on Database and Expert Systems Applications*. pp. 177–180.

Saurabh Deochake, Shashank Kanth, Subhadip Chakraborty, Debajyoti Mukhopadhyay (2012) *HENRI: High Efficiency Negotiation-based Robust*

*Interface for Multi-party Multi-issue Negotiation over the Internet*. CUBE 2012, 3–5 September, 2012, Pune, India. ACM 978-1-4503-1185-4/12/09. pp. 647–652.

T. Despina, A. Kapsalis, M. Papadopoulou, E. Karamanis, C. Patrikakis, I. Venieris, D. Kaklamani, (2015) 'An Ontology-Based Smart Production Management System', IT Pro November/December 2015, IEEE Computer Society, pp. 36–46.

R. Devraj Jain (2011) PulsExpert: An expert system for the diagnosis and control of diseases in pulse crops. *Expert Systems with Applications Journal*, vol. 38; 11463–11471.

Weiguang Ding, Graham W. Taylor (2016) "Automatic Moth Detection from Trap Images for Pest Management", *Computers and Electronics in Agriculture*. DOI: 10.1016/j.compag.2016.02.003.

K. Efstratios, M. Georgios, L. Despina, N. Bassiliades (2016) 'An ontology-based decision support tool for optimizing domestic solar hot water system selection', *Journal of Cleaner Production*, Volume 112, Part 5, 20 January 2016, pp. 4636–4646.

M. Eller (2008) Visual Tracing of Automatic Ontology Merging. In: *International Conference on Complex, Intelligent and Software Intensive Systems*; IEEEXplore; pp. 859–864.

Ulle Endriss (2006) Monotonic Concession Protocols for Multilateral Negotiation, *ACM Conference on Autonomous Agent and Multiagent System*, Hokkaido, Japan, ISBN:1-59593-303-4, pp. 392–399.

Muhammad Fahad, Nejib Moalla, Abdelaziz Bouras (2010) Disjoint-Knowledge Analysis and Preservation in Ontology Merging Process. In: *Fifth International Conference on Software Engineering Advances*. IEEEXplore. pp. 422–428.

Muhammad Fahad, Muhammad Abdul Qadir (2009) Similarity Computation by Ontology Merging System: DKP-OM. In: *2nd International Conference on Computer, Control and Communication, 2009. IC4 2009*. pp. 1–6.

P. Faratin (2000) Automated service negotiation between autonomous compositional agents, PhD thesis, Queen Mary and Westfield College, University of London, UK.

P. Faratin, C. Sierra, N. R. Jennings and P. Buckle (2000) "Designing Responsive and Deliberative Automated Negotiators, Proc. AAAI Workshop on Negotiation: Settling Conflicts and Identifying Opportunities, Orlando, pp. 12–18.

Farmer's Portal, http://farmer.gov.in [Accessed on 16th February 2017].

G. Flouris, D. Manakanatas, H. Kondylakis, D. Plexousakis, G. Antoniou (2008) Ontology change: Classification and survey; *Knowledge Engineering Review*, vol. 23; pp. 117–152.

Z. Fouad, S. Marta, D. Mathieu, M. Enrico (2009) 'Ontology Evolution with Evolva', L. Aroyo et al. (Eds.) ESWC 2009. LNCS 5554. pp. 908–912.

R. Francois, D. Olivier (2013) 'An agent-based modeling framework for integrated pest management dissemination programs', *Environmental Modeling and Software*, vol. 45., pp.141–149.

T. Gabel, Y. Sure (2004) Voelker J. Kaon – ontology management infrastructure. SEKT project. University of Karlsruhe.

B. Gajderowicz, S. Alireza (2009) 'Ontology granulation through inductive decision trees', *Proceedings of the Fifth International Conference on Uncertainty Reasoning for the Semantic Web*, Volume 527, CEUR-WS.org.

Y. Gal, A. Pfeffer (2008) Networks of influence diagrams: A formalization for representing agents' beliefs and decision making processes, *Journal of Artificial Intelligence Research*, vol. 33, pp. 109–147.

B. Ganter, R. Wille (1999) *Formal Concept Analysis, Mathematical Foundation*. Berlin: Springer Verlag.

Antonio-Javier Garcia-Sanchez, Felipe Garcia-Sanchez, and Joan Garcia-Haro (2011) 'Wireless sensor network deployment for integrating video-surveillance and data-monitoring in precision agriculture over distributed crops', *Computers and Electronics in Agriculture*, vol. 75, pp.288–303.

Toader Gherasim, Mounira Harzallah, Giuseppe Berio, Pascale Kuntz (2013) "Methods and Tools for Automatic Construction of Ontologies from Textual Resources: A Framework for Comparison and Its Application", *Advances in Knowledge Discovery & Management, SCI 471*, pp. 177–201, Springer-Verlag Berlin Heidelberg.

J. L. Gonzalez-Andujar (2009) "Expert system for pests, diseases and weeds identification in olive crops", *Expert Systems with Applications* 36; Elsevier journal; pp. 3278–3283.

Grape Profile (2016) National Research Centre for Grapes, Indian Council of Agricultural Research, Pune, India.

T. R. Gruber (1993) 'A Translation approach to portable ontologies', *Knowledge Acquisition*, vol. 5, no. 2, pp. 199–220.

M. Gunjan, R. Han, and M. B. Kweku (2007) 'CPEST: an expert system for the management of pests and diseases in the Jamaican coffee industry', *Expert Systems with Applications*, vol. 32, pp.184–192.

Rajesh Kumar Gupta, B. D. Chaudhary (2009) An Instance Based Methodology for Merging Domain Ontology. In: *Second International Conference on Emerging Trends in Engineering and Technology*, ICETET-09. pp. 848–855.

Galit Haim, Sarit Kraus and Yael Blumberg (2010) Learning Human Negotiation Behavior Across Cultures, *Second International Working Conference on Human Factors and Computational Models in Negotiation*.

W. F. Hans (2005) 'Using decision trees and text mining techniques for extending taxonomies', *Proceedings of Learning and Extending Lexical Ontologies by Using Machine Learning Methods, Workshop at ICML-05*. 1–8.

Pascal Hitzler, Markus Krötzsch, Bijan Parsia, Peter F. Patel-Schneider, Sebastian Rudolph, eds. (2012) OWL 2 Web Ontology Language: Primer (2nd Edition); W3C Recommendation, http://www.w3.org/TR/2012/REC-owl2-primer-20121211/

M. Holmes (1992) Phase structures in negotiation, Putnam L, Rolo, M (eds) *Communication and negotiation*, Sage, London, pp. 83–105.

C. Hou (2004) Predicting agent's tactics in automated negotiation, *Proc. IEEE/WIC/ACM International Conference in Intelligent Agent Technology (IAT'04)*, pp. 127–133, 2004.

J. Hou, D. Li, C. Qiu, and H. Han (2009) 'A semantic retrieval model based on domain ontology of orchard disease and pests', *Chinese Journal of Electronics*, vol. 25, no. 3, pp.460–466. DOI: 10.1049/cje.2016.05.011.

Chun-Che Huang, Wen-Yau Liang, Yu-Hsin Lai, Yin-Chen Lin (2010) The agent-based negotiation process for B2C e-commerce, *Expert Systems with Applications*, vol. 37, pp. 348–359.

Sebastian Hudert (2006) A Proposal for a Web Services Agreement Negotiation Protocol Framework, Diploma thesis, Otto-Friedrich-University Bamberg.

Takayuki Ito, Minijie Zhang, Valein Robu, Shaheen Fatima, Tokuro Matsuo, (2009) *Advances in Agent-Based Complex Automated Negotiations*, Springer-Verlag Berlin Heidelberg, Tokyo, ISBN 978-3-642-03189-2.

Takayuki Ito, Minjie Zhang, Valentin Robu, Shaheen Fatima, Tokuro Matsuo (2012) New Trends in Agent-based Complex Automated Negotiations, Series of Studies in Computational Intelligence Springer-Verlag, Berlin, Heidelberg, pp. 137–144.

Hamid Jazayeriy, Masrah Azmi-Murad, Md. Nasir Sulaiman and Nur Izura Udzir (2011) A review on soft computing techniques in automated negotiation, *Academic Journals for Scientific Research and Essays*, vol. 6, no. 24, pp. 5100–5106.

W. Jaziri (2009) A Methodology for Ontology Evolution and Versioning; *Third Proceedings of International Conference on Advances in Semantic Processing*, IEEE Xplore; pp. 15–21.

Jena Ontology API; http://jena.apache.org/documentation/ontology/ [Accessed on 1st January 2015]

N. R. Jennings, P. Faratin, A. R. Lomuscio, S. Parsons, C. Sierra, M. Wooldridge (2002) Automated negotiation: Prospects, methods and challenges, *International Journal of Group Decision and Negotiation*, vol. 10, no. 2, pp. 199–215.

T. Jing-Lei, C. Xiao-Qian, M. Rong-Hui, and W. Dong (2016) 'Weed detection using image processing under different illumination for site-specific areas spraying', *Computers and Electronics in Agriculture*, vol. 122, pp. 103–111.

X. Jinhui, Y. Yong, Y. Zhifeng, Wang Shuya (2010) An Online System for Agricultural Ontology Service; *Third International Conference on Intelligent Networks and Intelligent Systems*; IEEEXplore; pp. 479–481.

S. P. Juarez, H. E. Esquivel, M. C. Suarez-Fingueroa (2011) CreaDO – A Methodology to Create Domain Ontologies using Parameter-based Ontology Merging Techniques. In: *10th Mexican International Conference on Artificial Intelligence*; IEEEXplore; pp. 23–28.

L. Juhua, H. Wenjiang, W. Jihua, and W. Chaoling (2009) 'The crop disease and pest warning and prediction system', *FIP International Federation for Information Processing*, vol. 294, Computer and Computing Technologies in Agriculture II, vol. 2, Li, D. and Chunjiang, Z. (Eds.) pp. 937–945.

E. Karlos, D. L. Valera, J. A. Torres, L. Alejandro, and D. M. Francisco (2016) 'Combination of image processing and artificial neural networks as a novel approach for the identification of Bemisia tabaci and Frankliniell occidentalis on sticky traps in greenhouse agriculture', *Computers and Electronics in Agriculture*, vol. 127, pp. 495–505.

I. Karydis, P. Gratsanis, C. Semertzidis, M. Avlonitis (2013) WebGIS Design & Implementation for Pest Life-cycle & Control Simulation Management: The Case of Olive-fruit Fly; *6th International Conference on Information and Communication Technologies in Agriculture, Food and Environment (HAICTA 2013); Procedia Technology*, Elsevier; pp. 526–529.

Susanne Klaue, Karl Kurbel, Iouri Loutchko (2001) *Automated Negotiation on Agent-Based E-Marketplaces: An Overview, 14th Bled Electronic Commerce Conference*, Bled, Slovenia, pp. 25–26.

D. Klein, C. D. Manning (2003) Accurate unlexicalized parsing; *Proc. of the 41st Meeting of the Association for Computational Linguistics*, Sapporo, Japan; pp. 423–430.

P. Klinov, J. L. Maxlack (2006) 'Granulating Semantic Web Ontologies', *Proceedings of the 2006 IEEE International Conference on Granular Computing*, pp. 431–434.

Kostas Kolomvatsos, Dimitrios Trivizakis, Stathes Hadjiefthymiades (2015) An adaptive fuzzy logic system for automated negotiations, Elsevier BV, Fuzzy Sets and Systems, vol. 269, pp. 135–152, DOI: 10.1016/j.fss.2014.09.016.

Hyunjang Kong, Myunggwon Hwang, Pankoo Kim (2005) A New Methodology for Merging the Heterogeneous Domain Ontologies based on the WordNet. In: *Proceedings of the International Conference on Next Generation Web Services Practices (NWeSP'05).*

Sarit Kraus (2001) *Automated Negotiation and Decision Making in Multi agent Environments*, ACAI, Springer Verlag, Berlin, Heidelberg, pp. 150–172.

Petr Kremen, Marek Smid, Zdenek Kouba (2011) OWLDiff: A Practical Tool for Comparison and Merge of OWL ontologies. In: *22nd International workshop on Database and Expert Systems Applications, IEEEXplore*. pp. 229–233.

Karl Kurbel, Iouri Loutchko and Frank Teuteberg (2004) *Fuzzy MAN: An Agent-Based Electronic Marketplace with a Multilateral Negotiation Protocol*, Springer-Verlag Berlin Heidelberg, pp. 29–30.

K. Lah (2011) Effects of Pesticides on Human Health; http://www.toxipedia.org/

Raymond Y.K. Lau (2007) Towards a web services and intelligent agents-based negotiation system for B2B eCommerce, *Electronic Commerce Research and Applications.* Raymond Lau, Molin Tang, On Wong, Stephen W., Yi Ping (2006) An evolutionary learning approach for adaptive negotiation agents, *International Journal of Intelligent Systems*, vol. 21, Issue 1, pp. 41–72.

B. Lauser, M. Sini, A. Liang, J. Keizer, S. Katz (2006) 'From Agrovoc to the agricultural ontology service/concept server', Food and Agriculture Organization of the United Nations, pp. 1–10.

C. F. Lee, P. L. Chang (2008) Evaluations of tactics for automated negotiations, *Group Decision and Negotiation*, vol. 17, no. 6, pp. 515–539.

Shixiang Li, Hong Fan, Yuli Wang, Liang Hong (2009) A Model and Approach for Heterogeneous Ontology Automatic Merging. In: *International Joint Conference on Computational Sciences and Optimization*. pp. 214–217.

D. Li, L. Kang, X. Cheng, D. Li, L. Ji, K. Wang, Y. Chen (2011) *An ontology-based knowledge representation and implementation method for grape cultivation standard; Mathematical and Computer Modelling journal*, Elsevier Ltd.; pp. 1–8.

L. Li, T. Li (February 2014) An Empirical Study of Ontology-Based Multi-Document Summarization in Disaster Management', *IEEE Transactions on Systems, Man, and Cybernetics: Systems*, vol. 44, no. 2.

Guanyu Li, Zhenghai Luo, Jianshuang Shao (2010) Multi-Mapping Based Ontology Merging System Design. In: *2nd International Conference on Advanced Computer Control (ICACC)*, pp. 5–11.

Min Li, Pan Li, Liu Shijun, Wu Lei (2013) A win-win Multi-issue Service Negotiation Model Based on Bayesian Learning, *Conference of Cloud Computing and Big Data*, pp. 155–162, ISBN: 978-1-4799-2829-3.

Bangqing Li, Yulan Ma (2005) An auction-based negotiation model in intelligent multi-agent system, *International Conference on Neural Networks and Brain*, vol. 1, pp. 178–182.

A. C. Liang, B. Lauser, M. Sini, J. Keizer, S. Katz (2006) From AGROVOC to the Agricultural Ontology Service/ Concept Server An OWL model for managing ontologies in the agricultural domain.

Raz Lin, Sarit Kraus (2010) *Magazine communications of the ACM*, vol. 53, no. 1.

R. Lin, S. Kraus, T. Baarslag, D. Tykhonov, K. Hindriks et al. (2012) GENIUS: An integrated environment for supporting the design of generic automated negotiators, *Computational Intelligence*, Wiley Periodicals, vol. 30, no. 1, pp. 48–70.

Z. Liqiang, Y. Shouyi, L. Leibo, Z. Zhen, W. Shaojun (2011) A Crop Monitoring System Based on Wireless Sensor Network; *Procedia Environmental Sciences*, vol. 11; pp. 558–565.

X. Liu, X. Duan, H. Zhang (2012b) Application of Ontology in Classification of Agricultural Information; *IEEE Symposium on Robotics and Applications (ISRA)*, IEEE Xplore; pp. 451–454.

Zhimin Liu, Weidong Xiong, Xuewei Cao (2012a) Design of Precision Fertilization Management Information System on GPS and GIS Technologies; CCTA 2011, Part I, IFIP AICT 368, SpringerLink; pp. 268–277.

Ning Liu, Dong Xia Zheng, Yao Hua Xiong (2008) Multiagent negotiation model based on RBF neural network learning mechanism, *International Symposium on Intelligent Information Technology Application Workshops*, pp. 133–136.

F. Lopes, M. Wooldridge, A. Q. Novais (2008) Negotiation among autonomous computational agents: Principles, analysis and challenges, *Articial Intelligence Review*, vol. 29, no. 1, pp. 1–44, http://dx.doi.org/10.1007/s10462-009-9107-8

Miguel A. Lopez-Carmona, Ivan Marsa-Maestre, Mark Klein (2011) Consensus Policy Based Multi-Agent Negotiation. *The 4th International Workshop on Agent-based Complex Automated Negotiations Taipei, Taiwan*, May 3, 2011, ANAC 2011, pp. 1–8.

V. Lopez-Morales, O. Lopez-Ortega, J. Ramos-Fernandez, L. B. Munoz (2008) "JAPIEST: An integral intelligent system for the diagnosis and control of tomatoes diseases and pests in hydroponic greenhouses", *Expert Systems with Applications*, vol. 35; Elsevier journal; pp. 1506–1512.

Xudong Luo, Nicholas R. Jennings, Nigel Shadbolt (2003) Acquiring Tradeoff Preferences for Automated Negotiations: A Case Study, Workshop on Agent-Mediated Electronic Commerce V, Melbourne, Australia.

X. Luo, N. R. Jennings, N. Shadbolt (2006) Acquiring user tradeoff strategies and preferences for negotiating agents: A default-then-adjust method, *International Journal of Human-Computer Studies*, vol. 64, no. 4, pp. 304–321.

Y. Ma, L. Liu, K. Lu, B. Jin, X. Liu, (2014, May) 'A Graph Derivation Based Approach for Measuring and Comparing Structural Semantics of Ontologies', *IEEE Transactions On Knowledge And Data Engineering*, vol. 26, no. 5.

P. Maes, R. Guttman, A. Moukas (1999) Agents that buy and sell, *Communications of the ACM*, vol. 42, no. 3, pp. 81–91.

B. D. Mahman, P. Harizanis, I. Filis, E. Antonopoulou, C. P. Yialouris, A B Sideridis (2002) "A diagnostic expert system for honeybee pests", *Computer and Electronics in Agriculture*; Elsevier journal; pp. 17–31.

Sanjay Kumar Malik, Nupur Prakash, S. A. M. Rizvi (2010) Ontology Merging using Prompt plug-in of Protégé in Semantic Web. In: *2010 International Conference on Computational Intelligence and Communication Networks*. pp. 476–481.

R. J. Mangstl, F. L. H. Ward Judy (1997) The world agricultural information centre (waicent) faos information gateway; *First European Conference for Information Technology in Agriculture*, Citeseer.

M. Maree, M. Belkhatir (2015) Addressing semantic heterogeneity through multiple knowledge base assisted merging of domain-specific ontologies; Knowledge-Based System, 73; *Elsevier Journal*; pp. 199–211.

Ivan Marsa-Maestre, Miguel A. Lopez-Carmona and Mark Klein (2011) A Scenario Generation Framework for Consistent Comparison of Negotiation Approaches, The 4th International Workshop on Agent-based Complex Automated Negotiations Taipei, Taiwan, May 3, 2011, *ANAC 2011*, pp. 9–18.

J. O. Martin, T. Samson, N. Csongor, and A. M. Mark (2007) 'Querying the semantic web with SWRL', in *Proceedings of Advances in Rule Interchange and Applications, International Symposium, RuleML 2007*, Orlando, Florida. DOI: 10.1007/978-3-540-75975-1_13.

Viviana Mascardi, Angela Locoro, Paolo Rosso (2010) Automatic Ontology Matching via Upper Ontologies: A Systematic Evaluation. In: *IEEE Transactions on Knowledge and Data Engineering*, vol. 22, no. 5. pp. 609–623.

O. Medelyan, I. H. Witten (2005) Thesaurus-based index term extraction for agricultural documents. In: *Proc. of the 6th Agricultural Ontology Service (AOS) workshop at EFITA/WCCA 2005*, Vila Real, Portugal.

T. Mehta, T. Kshirsagar, A. Merchant, S. Nair (2015) 'Graduate prediction using ontology approach', *International Journal of Computer Science and Information Technologies*, vol. 6(5). pp. 4782–4784.

R. Mirambicka, A. S. Razia, G. Vadivu (2013) 'Decision tree applied to learning relations between ontologies', *Lecture Notes on Software Engineering*, vol. 1, no. 2. pp. 164–168.

Models Library. http://models.pps.wur.nl

Amruta More, Sheetal Vij, Debajyoti Mukhopadhyay (2013) Agent Based Negotiation using Cloud - An Approach in E-Commerce, *48th Annual Convention of the Computer Society of India, CSI 2013 Proceedings*, Visakhapatnam, India, Springer-Verlag Germany, December 13–15, 2013, pp. 489–496; ISBN 978-3-319-03107-1.

D. Mukhopadhyay, C. Chakrabarti, S. Chakravorty (2011) *A New Semantic Web Approach for Constructing, Searching and Modifying Ontology Dynamically*; The Computing Research Repository, Cornell University Library, USA; CoRR abs/1101.5763.

D. Mukhopadhyay, A. Chougule (2013) Petri Net based Approach for Merging Ontologies in Web Service Composition Scenario. In: *Fourth International Conference on Recent Trends in Information, Telecommunication and Computing, ITC 2013 Proceedings*, Chandigarh, India; pp. 155–160.

Debajyoti Mukhopadhyay, Aritra Banik, Sreemoyee Mukherjee, "A Technique for Automatic Construction of Ontology from Existing Database to Facilitate Semantic Web", *10th International Conference on Information Technology, ICIT 2007 Proceedings*; Rourkela, India; IEEE Computer Society Press, California, USA; December 17–20, 2007a; pp. 246–251, IEEE Xplore.

Debajyoti Mukhopadhyay, Archana Chougule; An Approach to Manage Ontology Dynamically based on Web Service Composition Requests; *CUBE 2012 International IT Conference, CUBE 2012 Proceedings*, Pune, India; ACM Digital Library, USA; September 3–5, 2012; pp. 653–658; ISBN 978-1-4503-1185-4.

Debajyoti Mukhopadhyay, Rituparna Kumar, Sourav R. Majumdar, Subhobroto Sinha, "A New Semantic Web Services to Translate HTML pages to RDF", *10th International Conference on Information Technology, ICIT 2007 Proceedings; Rourkela, India*; IEEE Computer Society Press, California, USA; December 17–20, 2007b; pp. 292–294, IEEE Xplore.

Debajyoti Mukhopadhyay, Suresh Sarode, Subhadip Chakraborty, Shashank Kanth, Saurabh Deochake (2012b) A negotiation model for alliances and multiple parties, *The Smart Computing Review Journal*, Korea, vol. 2, no. 5, pp. 308–317, ISSN 2234-4624.

Debajyoti Mukhopadhyay, Sheetal Vij, Amruta More (2015) An Efficient E-Negotiation Agent Using Rule Based and Case Based Approaches, *Advanced Research on Cloud Computing Design and Applications* - Book Chapter 16, IGI Global, USA, pp. 245–261; ISBN 978-1-466-68676-2; DOI:10.4018/978-1-4666-8676-2. (ACM Digital Library).

Debajyoti Mukhopadhyay, Sheetal Vij, Suyog Tasare (2012a) NAAS: Negotiation automation architecture with buyers behavior pattern prediction component, *The Fourth International Conference on Web & Semantic Technology, NeCoM 2012 Proceedings, Advances in Intelligent Systems and Computing*, vol. 176, pp. 425–434, Springer link Chennai, India; Springer-Verlag, Germany; July 13–15, 2012, ISSN 1867-5662, ISBN 978-3-642-31513-8.

Cao Mukun (2010) Multi-agent automated negotiation as a service, *7th International Conference on service System and Service Management (ICSSSM)*, Tokyo, IEEE, Print ISBN: 978-1-4244-6485-2. pp. 308–313.

Cao Mukun, Melody Y. Kiang (2012) BDI agent architecture for multi-strategy selection in automated negotiation, *Journal of Universal Computer Science*, vol. 18, no. 10, pp. 1379–1404.

Cao Mukun, Xudong Luo, Xin Luo, Xiaopei Dai (2015) Automated negotiation for ecommerce decision making: A goal deliberated agent architecture for multi-strategy selection, Decision Support Systems, Elsevier.

K. Y. Mundankar, S. D. Sawant, I. S. Sawant, J. Sharma, P. G. Adsule (2007) Knowledge Based Decision Support System for Management of Powdery Mildew Disease in Grapes; *3rd Indian International Conference on Artificial Intelligence (IICAI-07)*; pp. 1563–1571.

Pradnya Ravindra Narvekar, Mahesh Manik Kumbhar, S. N. Patil (2014, March) Grape Leaf Diseases Detection & Analysis using SGDM Matrix Method", *International Journal of Innovative Research in Computer and Communication Engineering*, vol. 2, no. 3.

Pradnya Narvekar, S. N. Patil (2015, January–February) Novel Algorithm For Grape Leaf Diseases Detection, *International Journal of Engineering Research and General Science*, vol. 3, no. 1.

N. F. Natalya, M. A. Mark (2002) 'PROMPTDIFF: A Fixed-Point Algorithm for Comparing Ontology Versions', *AAAI-02 Proceedings*, AAAI (www.aaai.org).

National Research Centre for Grapes. Good agricultural practices for production of quality grapes. pp. 1–63.

National Research Centre for Grapes, http://nrcgrapes.nic.in

National Research Centre for Grapes (2005) *Grape Profile*, Indian Council of Agricultural Research, Pune, India.

Thuc Duong Nguyen, Nicholas R. Jennings (2004) Coordinating multiple concurrent negotiations, *Proceeding of AAMAS'04*, pp. 1062–1069.

Marek Obitko, Vaclav Snasel and Jan Smid, "Ontology Design with Formal Concept Analysis," V. Snasel, R. Belohlavek (Eds.) *CLA 2004*, pp. 111–119, ISBN 80-248-0597-9. VSB – Technical University of Ostrava, Dept. of Computer Science, 2004.

C. Odile, B. Réjean, L. Jacques, and M. Wendy (2009) Identification Guide to the Major Diseases of Grapes, Agriculture and Agri-Food Canada, Publication.

T. Ojha, S. Misra, N. S. Raghuwanshi (2015) Wireless sensor networks for agriculture: The state-of-the-art in practice and future challenges; *Journal on Computers and Electronics in Agriculture*; Elsevier, pp. 66–84.

Mikoto Okumura, Katsuhide Fujita (2011) Implementation of Collective Collaboration Support System based on Automated Multi-Agent Negotiation, *The 4th International Workshop on Agent-based Complex Automated Negotiations Taipei*, Taiwan, May 3, 2011, ANAC 2011, pp. 71–76.

OpenNLP; https://opennlp.apache.org/ [Accessed on 2nd August 2015].

Li Pan (2011) Towards A Framework for Automated Service Negotiation in Cloud Computing, *Proceedings of IEEE CCIS 2011*, IEEE, ISBN 978-1-61284-204-2, pp. 364–367.

Sanghyun Park and Sung-Bong Yang (2006a) An efficient multilateral negotiation system for pervasive computing environments, *SICE-ICASE International Joint Conference in Bexco*, Busan, Korea, pp. 433–443.

Sanghyun Park and Sung-Bong Yang (2006b) An Automated System based on Incremental Learning with Applicability Toward Multilateral Negotiations, *SICE-ICASE International Joint Conference*, Bexco, Busan, Korea, DOI:10.1109/SICE.2006.315845, pp. 6001–6006.

Madhur Patrikar, Sheetal Vij, Debajyoti Mukhopadhyay (2015) An Approach on Multilateral Automated Negotiation, *4th International Conference on Advances in Computing, Communication & Control, ICAC3 2015 Proceedings*, Mumbai, India, Elsevier Computer Science, USA (Elsevier Digital Library).

Anna Perini, Angelo Susi (2003) Developing a decision support system for integrated production in agriculture, *Environmental Modeling and Software* 19; pp. 821–829.

D. Petros (2015) 'Modular structure of web-based decision support systems for integrated pest management: a review', *Agronomy for Sustainable Development*, vol. 35, pp. 1347–1372, DOI: 10.1007/s13593-015-0319-9.

L. D. Pieter, M. Tom (2008) 'Ontology Evolution State of the Art and Future Directions', Volume 7 of the series Computing for Human Experience. pp. 131–176.

C. Pontikakos, T. A. Tsiligiridis and M. Drougka (2010) 'Location-aware system for olive fruit fly spray control', *Computers and Electronics in Agriculture*, vol. 70, no. 2, pp. 355–368.

Costas M. Pontikakos, Theodore A. Tsiligiridis, Constantine P. Yialouris, Dimitris C. Kontodimas (2012) "Pest management control of olive fruit fly based on a location-aware agro-environmental system", *Computer and Electronics in Agriculture*; Elsevier journal; pp. 39–50.

Hoifung Poon, Pedro Domingos (2010) "Unsupervised Ontology Induction from Text", *ACL'10 proceedings of the 48th Annual Meeting of the Association for Computational Linguistics*, pp. 296–305, ACM Digital Library.

Porter (1980, July) "An algorithm for suffix stripping", *Program*, vol. 14, no. 3, pp. 130–137.

Rajkishore Prasad, Kumar Rajeev Ranjan, A K Sinha (2005) "AMRAPALIKA: An expert system for the diagnosis of pests, diseases, and disorders in Indian mango", *Knowledge-Based Systems* 19; Elsevier journal; pp. 9–21.

Pratibha G. P., T. G. Goutham, Rajas P. R., Kamalam Balasubramani (2014) Early pest detection in tomato plantations using Image Processing, *International Journal of Computer Applications by IJCA Journal*, vol. 96, no 12. DOI: 10.5120/16847-6707.

Protégé; http://protege.stanford.edu/ [Accessed on 21st March 2014].

Protege-OWL API Programmer's Guide, https://protegewiki.stanford.edu/wiki/ProtegeOWL_API_Programmers_Guide [Accessed on 17 May 2017].

X. Qiu, J. Yue (2010) Ontology Based Distributed Agricultural Knowledge Management; *Seventh International Conference on Fuzzy Systems and Knowledge Discovery*; IEEE Xplore; pp. 2858–2861.

C. Rad, O. Hancu, I. Takacs, G. Olteanu (2015) Smart Monitoring of Potato Crop: A Cyber-Physical System Architecture Model in the Field of Precision Agriculture; ST26733, *International Conference on Agriculture for Life, Life for Agriculture, Agriculture and Agricultural Science Procedia*; Elsevier; pp. 73–79.

Alma Delia Cuevas Rasgado, Adolfo Guzman Arenas (2006) A language and Algorithm for Automatic Merging of Ontologies. In: *15th International Conference on Computing, CIC'06*. pp. 180–185.

Hsin Rau, Chao-Wen Chen, and Wei-Jung Shiang (2009) Development of an Agent-Based Negotiation Model for Buyer-supplier Relationship with Multiple Deliveries. *Proceedings of the 2009 IEEE International Conference on Networking, sensing and Control*, Okayama, Japan, March 26–29, 2009, ISBN-978-1-4244-3492-3, pp. 308–312.

Hsin Rau, Chao-Wen Chen, Wei-Jung Shiang, Chiuhsiang Joe Lin (2008) Develop an adapted coordination strategy for negotiation in a buyer-driven E market-place, *Proceedings of the Seventh International Conference on Machine Learning and Cybernetics*, pp. 3224–3229.

Salvatore Raunich, Erhard Rahm (2011) ATOM: Automatic Target-driven Ontology Merging. In: *IEEE 27th International Conference on Data Engineering (ICDE)*, pp. 1276–1279.

Fenghui Ren, Minjie Zhang (2007) Prediction of partners behaviors in agent negotiation under open and dynamic environments, *Proceedings of International Conferences on Web Intelligence and Intelligent Agent Technology*, pp. 379–382.

Bartley Richardson, Lawrence J. Mazlack (2005) Approximate Metrics for Autonomous Semantic Web Ontology Merging. In: *The 2005 IEEE International Conference on Fuzzy Systems*. pp. 1014–1019.

D. Ritaban, M. Ahsan, A. Jagannath, D. Claire, D. Aruneema (2014) Development of an intelligent environmental knowledge system for sustainable agricultural decision support, *Environmental Modelling & Software*, vol. 52, pp. 264–272.

I. Roussak, I. Papaioannou, M. Anagnostou (2006) Employing neural networks to assist negotiating intelligent agents, *2nd IET International Conference on Intelligent Environments*, vol. 1, pp. 101–110.

Jitendra Roy (2015) *Soil Test Based Fertilizer Recommendation System (STFRS)*, Department of Agriculture, Government of West Bengal.

D. K. Sachin, A. B. Patil (2015) 'Plant disease detection using image processing', in *International Conference on Computing Communication Control and Automation*, pp. 768–771, DOI: 10.1109/ICCUBEA.2015.153.

S. Sanat, U. Jayalakshmi, K. Subrat (2016) 'Automation of agriculture support systems using Wisekar: case study of a crop-disease advisory service', *Computers and Electronics in Agriculture*, vol. 122, pp. 200–210.

S. S. Sannakki, V. S. Rajpurohit, V. B. Nargund, A. Kumar, P. S. Yallur (2011) 'Leaf disease grading by machine vision and fuzzy logic', *International Journal of Computer Technology and Application*, vol. 2, no. 5, pp. 1709–1716.

A. Schutz, P. Buitelaar (2005) RelExt: A Tool for Relation Extraction from Text in Ontology Extension. In: Y. Gil, E. Motta, V.R. Benjamins, M.A. Musen. (eds) *The Semantic Web – ISWC 2005*. Lecture Notes in Computer Science, vol. 3729. Springer, Berlin, Heidelberg.

Semantic Web Use Cases and Case Studies, Retrieved October 12, 2015, from https://www.w3.org/2001/sw/sweo/public/UseCases/FAO/

B. Sertkaya (2009) OntoComP: A Protégé Plugin for Completing OWL Ontologies, L. Aroyo et al. (eds) *The Semantic Web: Research and Applications. ESWC 2009*. Lecture Notes in Computer Science, vol. 5554. Springer, Berlin, Heidelberg.

Fatima Shaheen, Kraus Sarit, Wooldridge Michael (2014) *Principles of Automated Negotiation*, pp. 1–269. Cambridge University Press.

Jagdev Sharma, Ajay Kumar Upadhyay (2013) "Effect of Climate Change on Grape and Its Value-Added Products", *Climate-Resilient Horticulture: Adaptation and Mitigation Strategies*, Springer, India, pp. 67–73.

S. D. Shikhamany (2001) Grape Production in India; FAO Corporate Document Repository, produced by Regional Office for the Asia and the Pacific; pp. 1–101.

Kiran Shinde, Jerrin Andrei, Amey Oke (n.d.) Web Based Recommendation System for Farmers; *International Journal on Recent and Innovation Trends in Computing and Communication*; ISSN: 2321–8169, vol. 3, no 3, pp. 1444–1448.

Mansi Shinde, Kimaya Ekbote, Sonali Ghorpade, Sanket Pawar (2016a) Shubhada Mone; Crop Recommendation and Fertilizer Purchase System; *International Journal of Computer Science and Information Technologies*, vol. 7, no. 2, pp. 665–667.

Mansi Shinde, Kimaya Ekbote, Sonali Ghorpade, Sanket Pawar, Shubhada Mone (2016b) Crop Recommendation and Fertilizer Purchase System; *International Journal of Computer Science and Information Technologies*, vol. 7, no. 2, pp. 665–667.

Bahador Shojaiemehr and Marjan Kuchaki Rafsanjani (2014) A fuzzy system approach to multilateral automated negotiation in B2C e-commerce, *Journal Neural Computing and Applications*, Springer-Verlag London, UK, vol. 25, no. 2, pp. 367–377.

Jay Singh, Brajesh Kumar, Asha Khatn (2012) Securing Storage data in Cloud using RC5 Algorithm, *International Journal of Advance Computer Research*, vol. 2, no. 4, 6, pp. 94–98, ISSN (print: 2249-7277), ISSN (online: 2277-7970).

Sukanta Sinha, Rana Dattagupta, Debajyoti Mukhopadhyay; Designing an Ontology based Domain Specific Web Search Engine for Commonly used Products using RDF; *CUBE 2012 International IT Conference, CUBE 2012 Proceedings*, Pune, India; ACM Digital Library, USA; September 3–5, 2012; pp. 612–617; ISBN 978-1-4503-1185-4.

S. Sinha, R. Dattagupta, D. Mukhopadhyay (2014) Web-page Indexing based on the Prioritize Ontology Terms; *2nd International Conference on Advanced Computing, Networking, and Informatics; ICACNI 2014 Proceedings*, Calcutta, India, Springer International Publishing Switzerland; pp. 593–600.

P. Siricharoen, B. Scotney, P. Morrow, G. Parr (2016) *A Lightweight Mobile System for Crop Disease Diagnosis; Image Analysis and Recognition Chapter*, Volume 9730 of the series Lecture Notes in Computer Science; Springer International Publishing; pp. 783–791.

Smart Fertilizer. Retrieved July 1, 2015, from http://www.smart-fertilizer.com/

Leen-Kiat Soh, Costas Tsatsoulis (2001) Agent-Based Argumentative Negotiations with Case-Based Reasoning, AAAI Technical Report FS-01-03, Compilation copyright © 2001.

Sprectum Analytics Inc.; Fertilizing Grapes; www.spectrumanalytic.com [Accessed on 17th February 2017].

X. Su, H. Zhang, J. Riekki, A. Keranen, J. K. Nurminen, L. Du (2014) Connecting IoT Sensors to Knowledge-Based Systems by Transforming SenML to RDF; *Procedia Computer Science*, vol. 32, Elsevier; pp. 215–222.

Y. Sure, J. Angele and S. Staab (2002) 'OntoEdit: Guiding Ontology Development by Methodology and Inferencing', R. Meersman, Z. Tari (eds) *On the Move to Meaningful Internet Systems 2002: CoopIS, DOA, and ODBASE. OTM 2002.* Lecture Notes in Computer Science, vol. 2519. Springer, Berlin, Heidelberg.

S. Tang, Z. Cai (2010) Using the Formal Concept Analysis to Construct the Tourism Information Ontology; *2010 Seventh International Conference on Fuzzy Systems and Knowledge Discovery (FSDK 2010)*; IEEExplore; pp. 2941–2944.

Julia M. Taylor, Daniel Poliakov, Lawrence J. Mazlack (2005) Domain-Specific Ontology Merging for the Semantic Web. In: *NAFIPS 2005 – 2005 Annual Meeting of the North American Fuzzy Information Processing Society*. pp. 418–423.

TFIDF Algorithm, http://en.wikipedia.org/wiki/Tf-idf

Charles J. Thomas (2000) A Comparison of Auctions and Multilateral Negotiations, Federal Trade Commission, Harvard Law School and Bart J. Wilson, Bureau of Economics Federal Trade Commission Washington, Working, pp. 231.

V. Tilva, J. Patel, C. Bhatt (2012) Weather Based Plant Disease Forecasting Using Fuzzy Logic; *Nirma University International Conference on Engineering (NUICONE)*; IEEEXplore.

Vidita Tilva, Jignesh Patel, Chetan Bhatt (2013) "Weather Based Plant Disease Forecasting Using Fuzzy Logic", *Nirma University International Conference on Engineering (NUICONE)*; IEEEXplore.

Baarslag Tim, Fujita Katsuhide, Gerding Enrico H., Hindriks Koen, Ito Takayuki, Jennings, Nicholas R., Jonker Catholijn, Kraus Sarit, Lin Raz, Robu Valentin, Williams Colin R. (2013) Evaluating practical negotiating agents, results and analysis of the 2011 international competition, *Artificial Intelligence*, vol. 198, 73–103. DOI: 10.1016/j.artint.2012.09.004.

J. I. Toledo-Alvarado, A. Guzmán-Arenas, G. L. Martínez-Luna (2012) Automatic building of an ontology from a corpus of text documents using data mining tools, *Journal of Applied Research and Technology*, vol. 10, no.3, 398–404.

A. K. Tripathy, J. Adinarayana, K. Vijayalakshmi, S.N. Merchant, U.B. Desai, S. Ninomiya, M. Hirafuji, T. Kiura (2014) Knowledge Discovery and Leaf Spot Dynamics of Groundnut Crop through Wireless Sensor Network and Data Mining Techniques; *Computers and Electronics in Agriculture*, vol. 107; pp.104–114.

Paola Velardi, Stefano Faralli and Roberto Navigli (2013) "OntoLearn Reloaded: A Graph-Based Algorithm for Taxonomy Induction," *Computational Linguistics*, vol. 39, no. 3 665–707.

T. Vidita, P. Jignesh and B. Chetan (2012) 'Weather based plant disease forecasting using fuzzy logic', in *Proceedings of Nirma University International Conference on Engineering (NUICONE)*, IEEEXplore.

Sheetal Vij, Avinash J. Agrawal, Debajyoti Mukhopadhyay (2019b) Multi-strategy based e-negotiation using web services, *International Journal of Business*

*Information Systems*, vol. 32, no. 1, pp. 109–125, Inderscience publishers, Sept 2019, Scopus, DBLP indexed Journal.

Sheetal Vij, Amruta More, Debajyoti Mukhopadhyay, Avinash Agrawal (2015b) An E-Negotiation Agent using Rule Based and Case Based Approaches: A Comparative study with Bilateral E-Negotiation with Prediction, *Journal of Software Engineering and Applications, Scientific Research, USA*, vol. 8, no. 10, pp. 521–530; ISSN 1945-3124.

S. R. Vij, D. Mukhopadhyay, A. J. Agrawal (2019a) Automated negotiation in e commerce: Protocol relevance and improvement techniques, *Computers, Materials & Continua CMC*, Techscience press, vol. 61, no. 3, pp. 1009–1024, Nov 2019, SCIE, Scopus Journal, DOI: 10.32604/cmc.2019.08417; www.techscience.com/cmc

S. Vij, M. Patrikar, D. Mukhopadhyay, A. Agrawal (2015a) A smart and automated negotiation system based on linear programming in a multilateral environment, *Smart Computing Review*, vol. 5, no. 6, pp. 540–552.

Mira Vrbaski, Dorina Petriu, Amyot, D. (2012) Tool support for combined rule-based and goal-based reasoning in context-aware systems, *Requirement Engineering Conference, IEEE Xplore*, Chicago, Illinois, USA, ISBN 978-1-4673-2785-5, pp. 335–336.

T. Wang, Y. Li, K. Bontcheva, H. Cunningham, J. Wang (2006) Automatic Extraction of Hierarchical Relations from Text; The Semantic Web: Research and Applications vol. 4011 of the Series Lecture Notes in Computer Science, Springer-Link; pp. 215–229.

Z. Wang, X. Liu, M. Jiang, S. Cheng (2014) The application of image retrieval technology in the prevention of diseases and pests in fruit trees, CCTA 2013, *Part I, International Federation for Information Processing AICT* 419, pp.160–167.

Lijuan Wang, Jun Shen (2014) Multi-phase ant colony system for multi- party data-Intensive service provision, *IEEE Transactions on Services Computing*, DOI: 10.1109/TSC, pp 1–14.

F. Wang, G. Teng, L. Ren, M. JianBin; Research on Mechanism of Agricultural FAQ Retrieval Based on Ontology; *Ninth ACIS International Conference on Software Engineering, Artificial intelligence, Networking, and Parallel/Distributed Computing*; IEEE Xplore; pp. 955–958; 2008.

Y. Wang, Y. Wang, J. Wang, Y. Yuan, Z. Zhang (2015) 'An ontology-based approach to integration of hilly citrus production knowledge', *Computers and Electronics in Agriculture* 113. pp. 24–43.

Web Ontology Language (2016) [online] https://www.w3.org/OWL/ (accessed 21 September 2016).

D. Weiguang and T. Graham (2016) Automatic moth detection from trap images for pest management, *Computers and Electronics in Agriculture*, vol. 123, pp.17–28.

René Witte, Ninus Khamis, Juergen Rilling (2007) "Flexible Ontology Population from Text: The OwlExporter", *International workshop on Ontology Dynamics-IWOD2007*.

René Witte, Ninus Khamis, Juergen Rilling (2010) Flexible Ontology Population from Text: The OwlExporter. *The Seventh International Conference on Language Resources and Evaluation (LREC 2010)*. 3845–3850.

I. H. Witten, G. W. Paynter, E. Frank, C. Gutwin, C. G. Nevill-Manning (1999) KEA: Practical automatic keyphrase extraction; *Proc. DL '99*; pp. 254–256.

P. Wurman, M. Wellman, W. Walsh (1998) The Michigan internet AuctionBot: A configurable auction server for human and software agents. *Proceedings of the*

*Second International Conference on Autonomous Agents, (Agents'98), ACM Press*, pp. 301–308.

H. Xia, Z. Li, H. Wang (2007) A Lightweight Method of Web Service Ontology Merging based on Concept Lattice; *IEEE Asia-Pacific Services Computing Conference*; pp. 304–411.

H. Xiao, T. Qui, P. Zhou (2013) Integration of Heterogeneous Agriculture Information System Based on Interoperation of Domain Ontology; *Second International Conference on Agro-Geoinformatics*, IEEE Xplore; pp. 5476–5480.

Liu Xiaowen, Yu Jin (2012) Hybrid approach using RBR and CBR to design an automated negotiation model for tourism companies, *IEEE International Conference on Management of e-Commerce and e-Government*, pp. 197–201, ISBN-978-0-7695-4853-1, DOI: 10.1109/ICMeCG.2012.21.

Dong Xue-Jie, Chen Jian, Hu Ying-Lan, Jiang Guo Rui, Huang Ti-Yun (2013) *Multi-attribute Negotiation Model Based on Internal Factor Argumentation, IEEE Conference*, Harbin China, ISBN 978-1-4799-0473-0, pp. 20–27.

Feng Yang, Lei Liu (2009) A flexible Approach for Ontology Matching. In: *International Conference on Computational Intelligence and Software Engineering, 2009. CiSE 2009*. pp. 1–4.

Kai Yang, Robert Steele (2008) A system for service-oriented data aggregation. *International Journal of Services and Standards* 4(2) 119–140.

K. Yang, R. Steele (2009) Ontology Mapping based on Concept Classification; *3rd IEEE International Conference on Digital Ecosystems and Technologies*; pp. 659–661.

Y. Yong, X. Jinhui, W. Shuyan (2010) 'A Semantic Search Engine based on SKOS Model Ontology in Agriculture', *Proceedings of CCTA 2010, Part-I, IFIP AICT 344*. pp. 110–118. SpringerLink.

W. Yuanyuan, W. Rujing, W. Xue, H. Yimin (2010) 'Ontology-based knowledge representation for agricultural intelligent information systems', in *International Conference on Management and Service science (MASS)*, pp.1–4.

Q. Yu-Dong (2010) A Web based Framework for Developing Domain Ontology; *Proceedings of International Conference on Web Information Systems and Mining*; IEEE Xplore; pp. 305–308.

W. Yuhuang, L. Yusheng (2009) Design and Realization for Ontology Learning Model Based on Web; *International Conference on Information Technology and Computer Science*, IEE Xplore; pp. 485–488.

D. Zeng, K. Sycara (1998) Bayesian learning in negotiation, *International Journal of Human-Computer Studies*, vol. 48, pp. 125–141.

R. Zhang, G. Degui, G. Wenjuan, L. Lei (2016) 'Modeling ontology evolution via Pi-Calculus', *Information Sciences*, pp. 286–301.

J. Zhang, J. Yan, L. Fang, P. Wang (2009) Ontology Mapping Approach based on Concept Dimensions; *Sixth International Conference on Fuzzy Systems and Knowledge Discovery*; IEEXplore; pp. 436–440.

Sheng Zhang, Song Ye, Fillia Makedon, James Ford (2004) A hybrid negotiation mechanism in an automated negotiation system, EC 04, May 17, 2004, New York, New York, USA. ACM 1-58113-711-0/04/0005, DOI:10.1145/988772.988821.

Hao Zhang, Li Zhang, Yanna Ren, Juan Zhang, Xin Xu, Xinming Ma, Zhongmin Lu; Design and Implementation of Crop Recommendation Fertilization Decision System Based on WEBGIS at Village Scale. In: Li D., Liu Y., Chen Y. (eds) *Computer and*

*Computing Technologies in Agriculture IV*. CCTA 2010. IFIP Advances in Information and Communication Technology, vol. 345. Springer, Berlin, Heidelberg.

L. Zhimin, X. Weidong, C. Xuewei (2012) 'Design of Precision Fertilization Management Information System on GPS and GIS Technologies', *Proceedings of CCTA 2011, Part I, IFIP AICT 368*. SpringerLink. pp. 268–277.

## Web References/Internet Sources:

arxiv.org
chicagostateuniversity.edu
citeseerx.ist.psu.edu
csc.iiv.ac.uk
eprints.qut.edu
file.scirp.org
http://vikaspedia.in/agriculture/crop-production/integrated-pest-managment/ipm-for-fruit-crops/ipm-strategies-for-grapes/nutritional-deficiencies-of-grapes#section-1 [Accessed on 25th January 2017]
http://www.ipm.ucdavis.edu/PMG/selectnewpest.grapes.html [Accessed on 21st September 2016]
http://www.irrisoft.net/wr/insite.cfm
http://www.netafim.com/
http://www.smart-fertilizer.com/
http://www.smartvineyards.net/index.html
http://www.smartvineyards.net/index.html [Accessed on 13th November 2016]
https://cropx.com/
https://nrcgrapes.icar.gov.in/zipfiles/POP-Diseases_InsectPests-Grapes.pdf; http://ipm.ucanr.edu/PMG/selectnewpest.grapes.html
kmi.open.ac.uk
link.springer.com
manipal.edu
mcmba.blogspot.com
opus4.kobv.de
sdsu-dspace.calstate.edu
tracinsy.ewi.tudelft.nl
www.computingscience.nl
www.csulb.edu
www.grin.com, ijcsit.com
www.igi-global.com
www.ijert.org
www.inderscience.com
www.inderscienceonline.com
www.jucs.org
www.negotiationtactics.net
www.oppapers.com
www.sppu.edu.in
www.sunshineglobaleducation.net

# *Index*

Pages in *italics* refer to figures and pages in **bold** refer to tables.

G



H



I



J



K



L



M



N



O

For Product Safety Concerns and Information please contact our EU representative GPSR@taylorandfrancis.com Taylor & Francis Verlag GmbH, Kaufingerstraße 24, 80331 München, Germany